The NPR Curious Listener's Guide to

Blues

The NPR Curious Listener's Guide to

Blues

DAVID EVANS

Foreword by Taj Mahal

A Grand Central Press Book
A Perigee Book

A Perigee Book
Published by the Penguin Group
Penguin Group (USA) Inc.
375 Hudson Street, New York, New York 10014, USA
Penguin Group (Canada), 10 Alcorn Avenue, Toronto, Ontario M4V 3B2, Canada
(a division of Pearson Penguin Canada Inc.)
Penguin Books Ltd., 80 Strand, London WC2R 0RL, England
Penguin Group Ireland, 25 St. Stephen's Green, Dublin 2, Ireland (a division of Penguin Books Ltd.)
Penguin Group (Australia), 250 Camberwell Road, Camberwell, Victoria 3124, Australia
(a division of Pearson Australia Group Pty. Ltd.)
Penguin Books India Pvt. Ltd., 11 Community Centre, Panchsheel Park, New Delhi—110 017, India
Penguin Group (NZ), Cnr. Airborne and Rosedale Roads, Albany, Auckland 1310, New Zealand
(a division of Pearson New Zealand Ltd.)
Penguin Books (South Africa) (Pty.) Ltd., 24 Sturdee Avenue, Rosebank, Johannesburg 2196, South Africa
Penguin Books Ltd., Registered Offices: 80 Strand, London WC2R 0RL, England

PRODUCED BY GRAND CENTERAL PRESS
Judy Pray, Executive Editor

NATIONAL PUBLIC RADIO
Barbara A. Vierow
Andy Trudeau
With special thanks to Murray Horowitz
National Public Radio, NPR, and its logo are registered service marks of National Public Radio, Inc.

Copyright © 2005 by Stonesong Press and National Public Radio, Inc.
Text design by Tiffany Estreicher
Cover design by Jill Boltin
Cover art by Dan Baxter

PRINTING HISTORY
Perigee trade paperback edition / February 2005

PERIGEE is a registered trademark of Penguin Group (USA) Inc.
The "P" design is a trademark belonging to Penguin Group (USA) Inc.

Library of Congress Cataloging-in-Publication Information

Evans, David, 1944-
   The NPR curious listener's guide to blues / David Evans.—1st Perigee paperback ed.
      p. cm.
   Includes bibliographical references (p.) and index.
   Contents: What is blues?—The story of blues—Varieties of blues—Blues deconstructed—The
   performers—The music—Blues on CD—The language of blues.
   ISBN 0-399-53072-X
   1. Blues (Music)—History and criticism. I. National Public Radio (U.S.) II. Title.

ML3521.E92 2005
781.643—dc22

                                                                                    2004053486

PRINTED IN THE UNITED STATES OF AMERICA

10   9   8   7   6   5   4   3   2   1

Contents

Acknowledgments   vii

Foreword by Taj Mahal   ix

Introduction   xiii

1. What Is Blues?   1

2. The Story of Blues   9

3. Varieties of Blues   59

4. Blues Deconstructed   83

5. The Performers   99

6. The Music   165

7. Blues on CD   191

8. The Language of Blues   219

Resources for Curious Listeners   229

Index   247

Acknowledgments

Over the past forty years my understanding of blues and its place in the larger arenas of music and culture has been shaped by so many people that I am reluctant to try to list them for fear that I might leave someone out. I hope they will be content with the mention and citations of their names, writings, and musical accomplishments in this and my other publications and productions. They include teachers at Harvard and UCLA, researchers and scholars whom I have known personally and/or through their writings, and many musicians who I met and worked with in the course of field research, record production, performance, and sometimes only through their recordings. I have learned from all of you.

Specifically for my work on this book I have received good advice from fellow blues researchers Luigi Monge, Guido van Rijn, Chris Smith, and Scott Barretta. My minimal word processing skills were augmented by the timely and accurate work of Carolyn Logan, Lori Grissom, and Michael Fu. Thanks to all of you. I would also like to give special thanks to my daughter, Chloe O'Hearn, for the emergency use of her computer and to my wife, Marice Evans, for her patience and sacrifice of many days and evenings we could have spent together while I typed, read, and listened to music. Finally, I wish to thank my editor, Judy Pray, at Grand Central Press for her patience with my delays in meeting deadlines and her many helpful suggestions.

David Evans

Foreword
by Taj Mahal

Sometimes it helps to start with a song. Take any song by Little Richard or Sam Cooke. Any rock group of the last fifty years—including the Beatles and particularly the Rolling Stones—and you'll be able to find your way to the blues. Whether it's the shape of the chord structure—the sequence in which the chords are played—the way the melody's delivered, the rhythm, or even just the type of story that's placed in that sequence of chords and notes, you'll find the blues at work.

The blues is an American expression. The form had its humble beginnings in the rural South with the introduction of Africans into the labor force in the seventeenth century, and the musical styles they brought that collided with the poetic and melodic styles that came from Europe. In no other place has music been more successful at having a visceral effect on people around the world. It's a classic American style that's affected music all over the planet, and is doing so even at this very moment.

Recently, I met a guy in Slovenia who wanted to talk to me about Sleepy John Estes's "Floating Bridge." Why is the blues being learned in Slovenia or in Poland? Why is one of the best blues record labels in Austria? Why are some of the best compilations of the music—back to the original artists and field recordings—coming out of Europe, Asia, and Australia? Because it's a music that clearly resonates with the human condition anywhere and among any people.

The blues comes across in American English slang. You can't say, "I have been here in the morning, and, darling, I will be here at night for you." You have to say, "Baby, I been here in the mornin', an' you know I'll come roun' here late at night." In order to jump-start the rhythm—in order for the music to jump into your ears, somebody has to say, "I'm goin' get up in the morning, I BELIEVE I'll dust my broom." That's the poetry of the blues, delivered with a particular emphasis, often with double entendre, always delivering the news (in this case, "I'm outta here."). It's an African-American syntax and diction that has been popularized and resists standardization. You standardize it, and there goes the blues. In a sense, American civilization is the same.

Nowadays, people don't often experience the music in the high creative spirit that inspired it—and continues to inspire it. And when they do encounter it, their response is often surprising: I hear people at my performances say (a) they've never heard blues before, or (b) they've never liked it. Often, what they didn't like wasn't really blues. Technology has shaped people's listening through the replication of commercial hit music that often relies upon a formula. But, there's the cake you buy, and the cake that your grandma used to make.

The blues is not a formula, it's a form. (David Evans breaks it down in the following pages.) Little Brother Montgomery said the problem in the 1940s (when blues was a more commercially successful music) was that people were playing according to a pattern—like making dresses from a pattern—and that nobody was writing real blues songs. The whole point is that it *is* a *song*. And it tells a story. Each one is different. Even if it approaches the same form, it's personalized by the individual.

You know you're really experiencing the blues when you're not thinking about the form; when the music takes over and carries you along and you find yourself seeing pictures. And later on, the memory of the music comes back to you, resounding with all its excitement and energy. The spontaneity of the blues—celebrating the possibility of the moment—is what marks the difference between the real cake from the machine-made store-bought version. As you explore the blues, keep your eyes open for the cake made by loving hands.

I'm using the present tense here. The blues is a constant, on-going creative cultural force. Although many times not on the national radar screen, it is nonetheless vibrant and nourishing of whatever musical forms happen to be popular at a particular time—in our day, for instance, country, heavy metal, hip-hop, and other modern expressions—but it is also thriving, developing, and maintaining its vibrancy on its own. In my personal experience, not a week goes by without a new blues artist—or even a mid-career one—being discovered, rediscovered, or otherwise achieving prominence in the field.

The music business has changed. Its earlier incarnation was of music lovers who got involved in commerce. Just like everything else, that group of people has moved on, and what has taken over is a group of people less interested in the music than in the business. So, with marketing and the record companies and media consolidation, there's less art for art's sake.

It's safe to say that there's a bigger audience for the blues than we know—and this book is for that audience. You're part of it, and I hope you'll be part of it for a long time to come.

With over forty albums and countless collaborations to his credit, Taj Mahal is one of the recording industry's most celebrated contemporary blues artists. Now a legendary performer, songwriter, composer, and producer, Taj grew up in Springfield, Massachusetts, in a home that appreciated sounds from around the globe. Listening to various music forms—American Gospel, Caribbean, African, Latin, Cuban, and Jazz—he developed his own distinctive blend of blues and world music.

A self-taught musician, Taj plays over twenty different instruments, including the National Steel and Dobro guitars. Most notably, for more than forty years, he has enraptured audiences with an extraordinary voice that ranges from gruff and gritty to smooth and sultry. He has received eight Grammy Award nominations and won two Grammys for Best Contemporary Blues Album for his recordings with The Phantom Blues Band—the first in 1999 for Señor Blues *and the second in 2001 for* Shoutin' in Key.

Introduction

People all over the world have come to recognize blues as one of the great artistic and cultural expressions of modern life. Described by one singer as "the voice of the soul," blues seldom fails to move audiences with its heartfelt singing and its instrumental phrases that sound like further affirming voices. These voices seem to come from somewhere deep within the human sensibility. They speak of isolation and highly personal feelings but also of accumulated cultural experience, and they reach out to others, even beyond the culture that gave birth to this music. Blues has profoundly influenced, indeed is virtually the basis of, the two most important types of popular music of the past century, jazz and rock and roll. Blues has further helped shape country and western music, gospel, soul music, hip-hop, and a number of new international styles. None of these types of music would sound anything like they do if it hadn't been for the blues. Some would never even have come into existence without the blues. Yet only now, as so many of these musics blend with one another into modern "fusion" styles, has the blues begun to gain wide recognition as an important music in its own right. It did not simply go away after influencing and contributing to other styles, but instead it has survived with remarkable purity, with a timeless and universal message, and with a rich historical legacy.

Almost everyone today discovers blues through some related type of music, usually one or another type that has been influenced by blues or that incorporates the blues form. This is true not only for white American and international followers of the music, who are now the predominant sector of the blues audience, but also for many listeners in the black American community, which originally created this music. The latter typically discover the blues as part of the spectrum of black contemporary popular music that now mainly comprises rap, soul, jazz, disco, and gospel. They often recognize blues as a root form of these more current sounds, a connecting thread of stylistic influence as well as a nostalgic expression that variously conjures up images of community, ethnic solidarity, shared history, good times, and a "down-home" way of life. Black singers and musicians may be drawn to blues for these reasons as well, along with the appeal of the music as a powerful vehicle of personal expression, or simply because the blues scene offers more ready and lucrative opportunities for a long-term professional career in music than these other fields do. White American and international listeners may also discover blues as part of a spectrum of contemporary popular musical styles, but more often they come to it through some other genre, usually rock and roll but sometimes jazz, country and western, or even the range of styles grouped together as "folk music" or "world music." In whatever contemporary music they like, all types of listeners recognize songs employing a blues form, hear "cover" versions of tunes originally created by blues artists, or hear the pervasive stylistic influence of blues. These discoveries lead to a desire to hear more blues and to find the roots of the contemporary genres. As they become confirmed blues fans, they may even come to view blues as something more authentic and essential, and to view other types of blues-influenced music as superficial, derivative, watered-down expressions, or even outright rip-offs.

In all of these discoveries there is a search for "roots" and authenticity; a sense that blues lies behind or under the surface of more contemporary and popular forms of music, either in the historical background or in some sort of social or cultural "underground." It should not be forgotten, however, that for the black Americans who created and nurtured the blues, this music was an expression of everyday life. There was nothing historical, underground, or exotic about it. It only took on these qualities for others because black Americans remained socially marginalized for so long. Indeed, blues very likely came into being in the first place because of this marginalization.

There remains today a black audience for blues that is a direct extension of the audience of former times when blues was a major part of the spectrum of black music, or "race music" as it was often called then—music by and for the segregated Negro race. This audience today is found mainly in the rural and small-town South and in urban centers throughout America where a connection to "down-home" is still strongly felt. There are performers who play and sing to local black audiences or ply a "chittlin' circuit" of clubs, casinos, theaters, and showcase lounges, and there are a few record companies that cater especially to this market. These artists now are in the minority, and even many of them supplement their itineraries with appearances at blues festivals and overseas tours, performing for audiences outside their core constituency in the black community.

By far the majority of the audience for blues today consists of white American and international fans, along with black Americans who are sufficiently removed from a "down-home" outlook that they too can view blues as something to approach from a social, cultural, or generational distance. Many in this audience have only become acquainted with blues within the last ten or so years and have heard it mostly through derivative rock or jazz performances or from younger blues artists who have recently ascended to popularity. Many of these performers have gone through the same process of discovery described above and are trying either to recreate older songs and styles or to extend blues in some modern direction through new songs or connections to contemporary rock, jazz, rap, or international sounds.

This book is written primarily for this new blues audience, for those who have recently discovered blues or are in the process of doing so. It is also designed for the general music listener who wants a basic orientation toward one of the world's great and influential musical forms. It is assumed that readers are indeed "curious listeners" rather than merely "dummies" or "complete idiots." They are curious about the social and musical origins of this music and its history of stylistic development. They want to know who were the great and influential performers, what were the great performances and recordings, and how this music has evolved over the last century. It is hoped that this book will also appeal to those for whom blues is still part of an everyday lifestyle but who are curious enough to explore its history and background. For the longtime fan, the connoisseur, the purist, and the serious record collector, the contents of this book will likely be already familiar, and these listeners may already have formed variant understandings of the music's history, great figures, and great recorded moments. Nevertheless, this book may serve for them as a handy summary, a cause for rethinking their tastes and understandings, or as a reference that they can recommend to friends who are at an earlier stage of discovery and knowledge.

The historical development of blues is emphasized here and throughout this book. The recommended recordings will mostly be from several decades ago, usually from the 1960s or earlier. The recommended artists are mostly African American and flourished in this same time period. Indeed, most of them are now deceased. This is not meant to suggest that blues is dead music or merely a historical relic. Many of the blues artists of recent years are more versatile, more technically proficient, more professional, and better recorded than their predecessors of an earlier era. They have all the advantages of modern education and modern technology, and they appeal to a more affluent audience. Yet they will often be the first to tell anyone that their music is based on the work of earlier artists.

It is these older performers who created blues out of very raw musical material, who pioneered its major stylistic innovations, and who composed, performed, and recorded timeless songs. The music of the best of them has an extreme degree of individuality, yet it is also firmly based in a distinct culture and way of life. It is a way of life that relied on traditional wisdom handed down over generations but that was also shaped by racial discrimination and all of the handicaps it imposed. Early blues artists saw opportunities for themselves in personal expression, took elements from older traditions of African music and American folk music, and, despite technical and educational limitations, fashioned a music that remains utterly distinctive in its own right and has proved to be the most influential force in popular music in the past century. Once these artists made the decision to participate in secular as opposed to religious music (though some participated in both), they gravitated to blues as an almost inevitable consequence of their social status, their era, and their place of origin or residence. If they were of the generation that invented blues, they participated in the same processes of musical synthesis and creation as countless other musicians like themselves. If they were of a subsequent generation, blues was simply all around them. They performed almost exclusively for audiences of people from the same social background as themselves, who had experienced the sort of things they sang about.

The modern performers of blues who began their careers in the 1960s and later, usually came to the music by choice rather than inevitability. Blues was one of several musical alternatives available for them as they began their artistic development. Given its age, its origins in a class of people relegated to the lowest level of American society, its shaping in part by racial discrimination, and the esoteric quality of many of its references, it is perhaps surprising that blues should have such widespread appeal for so many musicians today. The only explanation can be a growing recognition of the extraordinary influence blues has had on almost every other type of recent and current popular music, and the basic humanity and universality of its themes. This essential humanity, expressed artfully and with great individuality, has bridged the widest of cultural and social chasms. Indeed, it has been a major force in breaking the very limitations that were imposed upon the creators of this music. It is these creators to whom blues musicians of today continue to pay homage, and it will be these early artists and their music that will be the chief focus of this book.

ONE

What Is Blues?

Blues is such a protean and flexible mode of expression that it almost defies any attempt to pin it down with a concise definition. One can't, for example, even state with any finality whether the word *blues* is singular or plural! It has been used both ways, whether in reference to a single piece of music, several pieces, or the genre as a whole. The word can also mean both a type of music and a psychological state. Sometimes in song lyrics, "Blues" or "Mister Blues" even occurs as some sort of spiritual being, usually one that menaces the singer.

For some people the blues can be defined by the example of a single song or a single personality. Such simplistic definitions don't get us very far, however, for, as we shall see, blues attracts many different personalities, has had many great and creative artistic figures over the years, expresses many moods and subjects, and occurs in many different styles.

A blues singer might be expected to offer a formal musical

definition, but most of them define blues as a feeling, generally one that corresponds to melancholy or depression. In this sense they use the term as it had been used in everyday speech going back several hundred years, long before the creation of the musical genre. One of the oldest such usages is the variant "blue devils," which suggests that blues is a feeling that attacks someone like a swarm of demons.

More specifically, singers associate the feeling of blues with uncertainty, ambiguity, loneliness, the nighttime and being "in the dark," worry, powerlessness, longing, poverty, hunger, wanderlust, evil thoughts, and, above all, dissatisfaction. "Got the blues and can't be satisfied" is one of the oldest and most frequently heard traditional verses. Feelings such as these can produce in some people a sense of paralysis and hopelessness, but they seldom do so in a setting where blues music is found. Although all of these themes are common enough in blues lyrics, the very expression of them seems to produce the opposite effect in singers and audience alike. Blues music thus can function as a form of personal and group psychotherapy. Singing or listening to the blues exorcises the feeling of the blues, at least for the time being.

Blues began about a century ago as an expression of African Americans who were familiar with southern rural life. Even after decades of urbanization, popularization, and international expansion of its audience, an African-American style and a "down-home" cultural sensibility pervade blues music. Thousands of performers around the world have tried to capture these qualities, and millions of fans have tried to relate to them. The masters of blues expression, for the most part, have been people who actually grew up with and lived with this sensibility. Now, as it becomes more and more a thing of the past and a subject for nostalgia, these masters, many of them deceased or retired from music, serve as models and inspirations for today's blues artists. They remain at the center of what defines the sound and meaning of the blues. The master artists of the future will join them in this sensibility and style, which will continue to provide the defining characteristics of blues music.

Blues is most readily understood through its subject matter and its manner of lyrical expression. It is intensely personal music. Whether or not the singer actually composed the song, and whether or not it is based on real events, he or she always purports to sing from personal experience, and the singer's life, feelings, needs, and wants assume primary importance. But blues seeks an audience, and it is most successful when that audience responds through dancing, applause, and shouts of approbation. While singers readily acknowledge the relief that their performance brings to their own troubled spirits, they are quick to point out that they are trying to "hit" members of their audience with their songs. Blues is thus "up close" as well as personal. It becomes a group celebration of life with all its ups and downs, expressed in a first-person manner to make it more dramatic. It covers a broad range of life's problems and daily activities, but concentrates especially on man-woman relationships. Almost all of its other prominent topics—travel, work, unemployment, poverty, sickness, death, luck, magic, gambling, alcohol, political issues, and current events—are somehow connected to the relationship between a man and a woman. Needless to say, this makes blues a highly secular type of song. Indeed, it is often quite erotic and frank in its treatment of sexual activity and feelings, causing it to be condemned from time to time by the more puritanical guardians of morality. Nevertheless, there is a deep, penetrating quality to the best of blues expression that causes many people to recognize profound truths and a spiritual quality in it and to compare it to religious experience.

Blues can also be recognized by some of its formal characteristics. It's one of the first types of popular song to include the instrumental accompaniment as an integral part of the song itself. In fact, many blues songs are best known by an instrumental figure rather than by their words or their melody. In the blues, the instruments are voices that respond to and comment on the singer's voice. Often an instrument is played by the singer, who thus creates a dialogue with his or her own voice.

The singing and its instrumental responses are usually framed in familiar formats, such as the twelve-bar, three-line (AAB) blues. This refers to the arrangement of verses in three-line stanzas, consisting of a line (A), followed by the same line repeated, and concluding with a different, rhyming line (B). Each of these three lines actually consists of a vocal verse and its instrumental response. Verse and response occupy four bars (measures), making a total of twelve bars for the three lines. Sometimes, however, these lines are extended by repetitions of a short instrumental figure known as a "riff." Riffs can even be incorporated into the twelve-bar AAB form, becoming signature figures for many songs. There are also two-line and four-line blues forms as well as a host of compound and exceptional forms.

Along with these familiar forms and the responsorial quality of the instrumental work, another distinguishing feature of the blues is the use of "blue notes." These are the bending and wavering tones and the neutral pitches, not quite major and not quite minor, that give the blues its fundamentally ambiguous quality, that make it seem always capable of change and surprise. Although these notes are quite normal within many types of African-American music and existed long before the blues genre came into being, they are especially associated with the blues and take their name from it. They seem like aberrations, however, within the normal major and minor scales of western music, and they have been challenging western music for years, working their way into it and at the same time drawing it away from its western sources. In their ambiguity, flexibility, and improvisational quality, they suggest mystery, freedom, and unlimited possibilities.

While blues has been central to American popular music for an entire century, it has been only recently that many music lovers have come to realize that blues is also a distinct musical genre with its own history. Some listeners still remain unaware of this. One frequently hears the questions: What is the difference between blues and jazz? Or rock and roll? Is blues folk music? Or, is such-and-such a (popular) song a blues? These are not foolish questions, nor should they be answered with pat statements such as "If you don't know what the blues is, don't mess with it."

Despite the rural isolation of some of the earliest creators of blues and the social isolation imposed by years of racial segregation, blues music itself has never been entirely isolated and has existed and developed in relationships with other types of American music. It arose as a new type of African-American folk music, fusing elements of older strains of nineteenth-century vocal and instrumental folk music as well as drawing upon stylistic qualities of traditional African music that had been transmitted through a succession of new genres created on American soil. A century after its initial creation, one can still encounter blues that are essentially folksongs, the products of oral transmission over generations.

But blues soon developed as a type of popular music, performed by professional entertainers and transmitted through the mass media of published sheet music, phonograph records, and eventually radio. It rose to popularity alongside other new types of music, such as ragtime and jazz. Popular blues at first were viewed as a novel type of ragtime music, but it quickly became apparent that the improvisational performer-centered quality of blues was different from the formal composer-centered quality of ragtime. Blues has had an even more intimate relationship with jazz, and one that has lasted until the present day. Many jazz pieces are simply instrumental blues, and virtually all jazz uses blue notes along with techniques and sound qualities shared with blues. The great master performers, from early New Orleans jazz to bebop and beyond, have almost all been blues masters as well. Indeed, many of them have played and recorded with blues singers. Many blues performances can thus be called jazz, just as many jazz pieces are blues in their musical structures. The main differences, when there are any, between a jazz and blues artist's approach to the blues genre, are that the blues artist tends to take a more "vocal" approach, treating the instrument as a complementary voice to the singing and concentrating on the melodic lines and variations on them, whereas the jazz musician tends to introduce more harmonic variations into the blues form and explore the harmonic implications of melodic lines. Jazz singers tend to treat the words and melodies of blues as vehicles for improvisation and often take a playful and "distanced" approach to the message of the song rather than getting "inside" it and presenting it as personal experience in the manner of blues singers.

Blues were embraced by the newly emerging genre of country music in the 1920s. Despite the walls of social segregation that separated southern whites and blacks, there had always been musical borrowing and interaction. The "blue yodel" quickly emerged as one of the distinctive new forms of country music, and over the years the blues form or blues style has pervaded new types of country music, such as western swing, honky-tonk, bluegrass, and country rock.

Although blues and gospel are often viewed as mutually exclusive musical fields, with blues sometimes referred to as "the devil's music," the two genres actually have much in common and have influenced one another over the years. Gospel songs seldom use the blues form, but they are full of blue notes, and several instrumental formats and styles are common to both genres. A good number of blues singers have gone on to become preachers or gospel singers and songwriters, including Thomas A. Dorsey, widely acknowledged as the "father of gospel music," who was known as Georgia Tom in his earlier blues career. On the other hand, many blues singers had their first musical experiences singing in church, and some began their careers as gospel singers. In the 1950s and 1960s a gospel-influenced "soul blues" style arose, and it has remained the most popular type of blues with black Americans.

"Blues had a baby, and they named it Rock and Roll," goes the line of a song. It's an apt description of what happened in the 1950s. For most of that decade the baby looked and sounded a lot like the parent. Early rock and roll was little more than blues and blues-based music that appealed to an adolescent sensibility. As the white audience for this type of music grew, the genre came to be called simply "rock" and expanded to encompass further styles and forms as well as anti-establishment themes. Blues, however, both as a form and a style, continued to be an important ingredient in many phases of rock and roll, including surf music, instrumental bands, British rock, folk rock, psychedelic rock, heavy metal, southern rock, and punk rock.

"Rhythm and blues" began as a music industry term in the late 1940s designed to cover a range of black secular vocal music larger than blues. Rhythm and blues inspired and contributed to early rock and roll, and over the years it has continued to interact and overlap with rock music. Types of rhythm and blues music that have often incorporated blues forms, styles, and instrumentations have been vocal harmony groups, soul music, and funk. In recent years many veteran soul and funk performers from the 1960s and 1970s have redefined themselves as blues artists in an effort to extend their careers through identification with this timeless genre. Modern rap music, in many of its characteristics, represents a break with the traditions of blues, rhythm and blues, and rock and roll. There is a link, however, in rap's sampling of "beats" from older rhythm and blues and funk music, many of which are simply bluesy riffs. Many of rap's lyric themes are also familiar to fans of older blues, although the rhetorical style of rappers is largely new.

For much of its history blues stood outside organized society and established institutions. It might be surprising, therefore, to note the degree to which blues has recently become part of the American cultural mainstream. This had long been accomplished in the world of music, although blues itself was often disguised behind the names of other genres such as jazz or rock and roll. But blues singers now appear on postage stamps, and blues music is used to advertise food, clothing, and automobiles. Earnest advocates of the music design programs for "blues in schools" and give awards to one another for "keeping the blues alive." In a culmination of these efforts the year 2003 was designated the "Year of the Blues" by an official proclamation of the United States Senate. Blues can't get much more mainstream than that!

TWO

The Story of Blues

Western civilization loves to ascribe every innovative cultural, scientific, and artistic development to some particular genius, some "father" (or, less often, "mother") figure who had the bright idea, created the first prototype, or opened the door for others to follow. It also likes to pin these developments down to a specific place and date. History books, Hollywood movies, and television specials are full of stories of such people as Thomas Edison, Alexander Graham Bell, the Wright Brothers, and Albert Einstein. Musical genres too have their father figures: Buddy Bolden for jazz, Jimmie Rodgers for country music, Bill Monroe for bluegrass, Elvis Presley for rock and roll, and so on. W. C. Handy was even long touted as the "Father of the Blues," a title that he appropriated for his autobiography. Most of these claims turn out to be less than solid as we learn that the breakthroughs made by these individuals were high points or turning points in movements that were already underway. This is especially true of the blues, a music whose remotest origins are actually far from western civilization. Ironically, however, blues has been the most potent force in western popular music for the past hundred years. Yet for much of that time it had to enter through the basement and remain hidden or viewed merely as a raw resource. It had its geniuses and innovators (including Handy), and we can identify significant dates, places, and events in its history. But if ever there has truly been a people's art, it is the blues. Many of its leading figures seem to have come out of nowhere, and unfortunately all too many of them returned to obscurity or met tragic fates after making their mark.

A few years after the beginning of the twentieth century, blues began to pop up in black communities all over the South, especially among individuals and groups that were on the move. They showed up in rural areas of Georgia, Mississippi, and Texas, where sharecroppers and cotton pickers were moving from one plantation to another on an almost yearly basis, looking for better land, a better bossman, a bigger crop. The earliest performers are often described as roustabouts, hoboes, street musicians, and small-time hustlers. Almost all of them are described as young, often as teenagers. Blues appeared in Memphis, New Orleans, St. Louis, Dallas, and Atlanta, and in numerous smaller towns. By the end of the first decade of the century blues were performed in black communities in the northern cities by professional theater entertainers and had started to appear in published sheet music. These songs were such a pervasive phenomenon that soon they were given a name: the blues.

Transitional songs bearing some of the characteristics of blues can be identified in reports stemming from the 1890s, and there can be little doubt that it was in this decade that the music began to take shape. Despite the claims of various places to be the "birthplace" or "home" of the music and various individuals to be its "father" or "mother," the origin of the music can not be pinpointed exactly. Blues simply was everywhere, all of a sudden. What is it, then, about the black American community in this time period that could give rise to such a revolutionary musical development?

Social Origins

The two decades on either side of the year 1900 were undoubtedly the lowest point since the slavery period for black social, political, and economic institutions and yet the highest point for artistic development. Virtually every hold that blacks had gotten on the American dream had been pried loose by a wave of racist reaction and systematic neglect. Lenders denied credit and foreclosed on little plots of land that were acquired during Reconstruction. Even the most menial of jobs that had been given to blacks now went to white-skinned immigrants from poverty-stricken parts of Europe. Floods, crop failures, the arrival of the boll weevil, and financial panics added to the woes of the mostly rural population. Political voices were stilled by disenfranchisement, poll taxes, literacy tests, and outright threats. Funding for black education was reduced to an absolute minimum, and Jim Crow laws dictated rigid social segregation. Many black businesses and churches were vandalized or destroyed. A large mobile force of unemployed or sporadically employed workers was created that whites used as a cheap source of labor when they needed them and viewed with suspicion when they didn't. The social tensions inherent in this situation led to a wave of terror and lynching that only gradually subsided over the twentieth century. Some blacks tried to resist; others made plans to resettle on the western frontier or even in Africa. Many headed for the cities or began a life of itinerant manual labor in levee, railroad, or lumber camps. Others wound up as sharecroppers and virtual peons on large plantations, living on credit for the entire year in hope of a positive cash balance from their crop at harvest time. Those who appeared to be without a job and without a white patron to vouch for them could be promptly arrested for vagrancy and shipped off to a prison farm to work for the state or to be leased out as virtual slaves to some plantation owner or contractor with political connections.

Those who bore the brunt of these hardships in the 1890s and the early years of the twentieth century were the young people, the first generation to grow up free from slavery but with their rights and opportunities severely curtailed. Their parents had gained freedom while trusting in a newly developed religious faith. This faith taught patience and forbearance, offering a reward in heaven. But heaven now seemed far off to the children and grandchildren of the ex-slaves. Some turned to the new pentecostal sects that promoted a more ecstatic style of worship and preached a doctrine of saintly living, Holy Ghost power, and success on earth. Others, however, turned to more secular forms of expression and lifestyle. In the border states and southern cities, where opportunities for economic advancement and formal education were a little better, ragtime music arose, combining elements of black improvisatory music with some of the formalism of western music. In New Orleans, black and creole musical elements merged in the first strains of what would come to be called jazz. In the rural and small-town South, the response was the blues. All of these new musics were worldly and featured a heightened sense of individualism. Blues and ragtime could be performed by a single player, and jazz gave prominence to the hot soloist. They all represented syntheses of the old and the new, of the African and European musical traditions.

Musical Origins

In a very general sense, one could state that the formal and static qualities of blues music stem from Europe, while the stylistic and dynamic qualities stem from Africa. Thus, the main musical instruments, the guitar, piano, and harmonica, are all European in origin, but the ways they are usually played by blues musicians owe much more to African performance practices. The grouping of verses into stanzas and the usual harmonic template of the standard AAB form are also typically European, but the repetition of the A line, the responsorial and "second voice" roles played by instruments, the frequent avoidance of full chords, the return to a fundamental tonal reference point at the end of each line, the use of heterophony and parallelism, the blues scale and the flexibility of blue notes, improvisation and the exploratory approach to sound quality, the use of riffs, and the complexity and dance orientation of blues rhythms all lead back to Africa. Some of the secondary instruments of the blues, such as the jug, kazoo, washboard, banjo, and one-string bass, also are derivatives and reinterpretations of African instruments. In America they came to be constructed out of new materials and given new roles in new types of music created by African Americans over the course of two or three centuries.

Besides stylistic features and musical instruments, it is even possible to detect African prototypes of the social role of the blues performer. Many traditional African societies supported wandering minstrels who traveled from village to village, playing an instrument and singing songs of personal

The Diddley Bow

One African-derived instrument especially associated with the blues came from a children's musical learning device, made in central Africa from the leaf stalk of the raffia palm. A stalk was laid horizontally over a hole in the ground or on an inverted pot or tub, with a sliver of its fiber raised slightly on two bridges while remaining attached to the stalk at each end. One player, usually an adolescent boy, would strike this fiber "string" rhythmically with two sticks, while another would slide a cup, a bowl, or some similar object along it to change the pitch and produce percussive effects. Some knowledge of this African instrument was retained in the United States and passed down, mostly among children, into the twentieth century. In America it became a single-player instrument known as a "diddley bow" and a variety of other names. The player was still usually an adolescent boy, who would take a strand of broom wire or baling wire and attach it along a board or on the wall of a house, stretching it over two bottles that served as bridges at each end. He would strike the string with a finger or stick and slide another bottle or some hard object along the string to create melodies and special effects. Some of these children graduated to the guitar and applied this sliding technique to that more complex instrument, using a pocketknife, bottleneck, or metal tube as the slider. It produced a crying sound that was perfectly suited to the new blues music.

experience and observation, gossip, and social commentary in return for small gifts. In the savanna region of West Africa, north of the tropical rain forest and below the Sahara Desert, this role often became institutionalized as a social caste, commonly known as griots. Members of this hereditary caste were entertainers who often attached themselves to wealthy and powerful patrons and sang songs of praise and flattery to them as well as historical epics and songs of social commentary. In their itinerant existence, low social standing, and preference for stringed instruments, these minstrels and griots resembled many of the early blues performers, and some concept of their role in society may have been perpetuated in the American black community even through the rigors of slavery. The sound of the music of the griots, with its wavy intonation, strident delivery, heterophony, and emphasis on a fundamental tonal reference point, also bears a number of striking resemblances to typical features of blues music.

The links between blues and African music constitute a fascinating topic, but when all is said and done, no specific African musical form can be identified as the single direct ancestor of the blues. Instead, many distinct African musical cultures contributed traits that filtered through eighteenth- and nineteenth-century African-American folk music in a series of recombinations as new styles were created in the New World. The young people who first began to sing the blues around the beginning of the twentieth century were removed from Africa by several generations. They viewed blues as something new, and they created it out of the elements in their immediate musical environment.

While the lyrics of blues were largely original, the vocal melodies were drawn especially from the singing of hollers. These were a type of worksong sung by farmers in fields and under other conditions of rural manual labor, such as building a levee or driving a wagon. They were performed solo and unaccompanied and served both for communication and self-expression. The words of these hollers were highly repetitious and usually concerned with the work itself or the singer's love life. The melodies were strident, free-form, melismatic, and full of blue notes. Some consisted partly or wholly of moaning, whooping, humming, whistling, and other wordless sounds. Similar types of vocal music were performed in Africa in work environments such as cattle herding and farming. Hollers sound much like primitive blues without any instrument answering to the singing. Other solo vocal forms occurred in the church in chanted prayers and sermons. If one allows for the different message that the words convey, the musical sound of these religious expressions is very similar to that of the hollers.

The earliest blues singers almost all came from a rural background and were exposed to hollers during the workweek and sermons and prayers on Sunday morning. The early creators of blues put this vocal raw material into verse and harmonic forms that came largely from folk ballads. Ballads were narrative songs that told stories of important people and events. They had been sung for centuries in Europe, and emigrants from the British Isles brought them to America and continued to sing them along with new ballads on American themes. Black singers began to learn some of these songs in the nineteenth century, and by the 1890s they were creating many new ballads about people and events of special interest to themselves. Most of these were about characters who were in some way "bad," who operated outside the restraints of the law and organized society. They included the gambler and murderer Stagolee, the train robber Railroad Bill, and Frankie who shot and killed her cheating man. These ballads explored the parameters of "badness," both the thrill of defiance and the endings suffered by many of the protagonists, all in an era when even the mildest expression of independent-mindedness by a black person could be a cause for severe retaliation by whites.

The black ballad tradition differed from that of the whites in its almost exclusive preoccupation with these outlaw themes, as well as its sacrificing of chronological storytelling in favor of dramatic depiction, the insertion often of the singer into the story as a participant or observer, the use of fast tempos and instrumental accompaniment in many performances, and the creation of a special verse form. The latter consisted of two rhyming lines that advanced the narrative theme of the song, followed by a one-line refrain that summarized the basic point of the story: "He was her man, but he done her wrong," or "That bad man, that cruel Stagolee." The three lines of this form, when accompanied by an instrument, such as a guitar, used exactly the same harmonic sequence as that found in the template of the twelve-bar AAB blues. It was these ballads, reaching their full development just as the blues were starting out, that contributed this form to the blues. The final ingredient in the new blues genre was the concept of the riff, a short, repeated, melodic-rhythmic figure. Riffs had been found in abundance in the nineteenth-century black instrumental dance music of banjos, fiddles, string bands, fife and drum bands, and in a variety of other formats. Blues, then, drew on most of the major forms of pre-existing black folk music—work songs, religious expression, story songs, instrumental dance music, and even children's music. They combined elements of songs created under the drudgery of manual labor that kept the workers poor and the bosses rich with elements of songs that celebrated the deeds of people who defied society as it was set up and who knew no restraints. They combined qualities of music associated with dance and physical pleasure with those of spiritual expressions addressed to God. They gave equal weight to the voice of the singer and the answering voice of the instrument. And most of all, they gave the thoughts and feelings of the performer center stage. The blues singer was the hard worker, the preacher, the dance instigator, the hero, and "bad" as he or she could be.

The Early Blues Environment

The earliest singers of blues were "songsters," who had varied repertoires of songs for all occasions and audiences: ragtime pieces, dance tunes, popular and minstrel songs, spirituals, ballads, and perhaps some tunes borrowed from white tradition. Over the years blues became an increasing part of their repertoires, until by the 1910s some perfomers had come to be known as blues specialists, or "bluesmen" and "blueswomen." The early singers came from a variety of backgrounds but were mostly attracted to blues for the freedom and self-expression it seemed to represent in its lyrics, its performance style, and its social environment and lifestyle. Henry Thomas, born in rural East Texas in 1874, hated the farming life and early on became a hobo, carrying his guitar and panpipes with him as he rode the rails. Huddie Ledbetter (Leadbelly) was the only child of parents who owned a farm in northwest Louisiana, but he left them to pursue the more exciting life of an itinerant musician in Shreveport and Dallas. Charley Patton's parents were also reasonably well-off renters on a Mississippi Delta plantation, but he too was attracted to the life of a traveling musician. Gertrude Pridgett grew up in Columbus, Georgia, and as a teenager left with a traveling show, eventually to marry entertainer "Pa" Rainey and become "Ma" Rainey, the "Mother of the Blues." For Lemon Jefferson, born blind to a poor family in East Texas, blues became a means to escape a dead-end life, and he went on to become Blind Lemon Jefferson, the first recording star of country blues. All of these early blues performers rejected the life of their parents, whether it was grinding rural poverty or a precarious security at the lower end of the white man's social order, and instead chose the life portrayed in the blues, where the times were always "better down the road."

Probably the main setting for early blues was the house party, either a "country supper" or "rent party" in an urban tenement. Both types of event had food and drink for sale, sometimes charged admission, and the latter used the proceeds to pay the monthly rent. The musician received a payment, tips, and refreshments, and was the center of attention. Some of these places became more or less permanent juke houses or "good-time flats." Blues singers also played on the streets and in parks for tips, serenaded in residential neighborhoods, and performed at stores, railroad stations, barbecue stands, livery stables, sporting events, picnics, cafés, saloons, gambling dens, moonshine stills, and anywhere else there was a crowd gathered or money to be made. Some caught on with travel-ing tent shows and medicine shows. Some made their entire earnings from music, but many were farmers, laborers, or domestic workers during the week and entertainers on the weekends.

Blues Become Popular Music

Blues was commercial music from the beginning, even if the payment was low or only supplemented another source of in-come. Soon, however, the music's evident popularity came to the attention of people in the world of professional enter-tainment and those with connections to the mass media. Blues melodies began to show up in ragtime sheet music published in the first decade of the twentieth century. W. C. Handy, leading a band of music readers in Clarksdale, Mississippi, encountered the blues around 1903 and began arranging these tunes for his musicians. "Ma" Rainey, on tour with a traveling show, heard the blues the year before and incorpo-rated them into her stage act. In 1909, a white New Orleans theater pianist published "I'm Alabama Bound," subtitled "The Alabama Blues." In the following year blues were mentioned in black newspapers as part of the repertoire of theater entertainers. Black vaudeville theaters in southern cities and towns became important venues for professional blues singers. Many of the earliest stars, like Baby Seals, Kid Love, and Butler "String Beans" May, did not survive the decade of the 1910s, and the sound of their music was never recorded. Others, like "Ma" Rainey, continued to perform and eventually made recordings in the 1920s, though not necessarily of the songs they were singing a decade or more earlier. Newspaper accounts and published sheet music, however, can give us some sense of what blues was like on the professional level in the 1910s, and later field and commercial recordings give at least some indication of the actual sound of this music.

W. C. Handy was one of the most successful of the early commercial popularizers of blues. He had already begun arranging this music for his band in the Mississippi Delta early in the century. He later moved to Memphis and in 1912 published "The Memphis Blues," a piece that went on to become a popular hit. Handy soon established his own music publishing company, which he advertised as "The Home of the Blues," and in 1914 he published "St. Louis Blues," a song that became one of the biggest hits of the twentieth century and one which brought some sense of this new music into almost every home in America and much of the rest of the world. Handy moved his songwriting and publishing operation to New York City in 1918 and consolidated his reputation as "Father of the Blues," although he was really only one of its many progenitors. His counterpart in New Orleans was Clarence Williams, who composed and published many blues during the 1910s and also later relocated to New York City to be closer to the center of the commercial music industry. Many other songwriters, both black and white, published blues songs during this decade, often taking ideas from street singers and vaudeville entertainers who did not know how to write their music down and get it published.

Blues As Sheet Music

Before the first phonograph records of blues were made in 1920, sheet music was the main mass media outlet for blues, and it remained an important supplement to records through the 1920s. It was closely tied to the vaudeville theater circuit, and blues sheet music pretty well came to an end when vaudeville collapsed under the twin onslaught of the Great Depression and talking pictures. The first items with the word *blues* in their titles were a couple of pieces published in New Orleans in 1909, both by white songwriters who obviously had their ears open to the sounds of the city's rich black musical tradition. In 1912 four new blues appeared: "The Dallas Blues" by Hart Wand, a white violinist and dance orchestra leader in Oklahoma City; "Baby Seals Blues" by Baby Seals, a black vaudeville singer and pianist who toured the southern circuit; "Memphis Blues" by black band leader W. C. Handy; and "The Negro Blues" by Leroy "Lasses" White, a white vaudeville singer and comedian based in Dallas, who usually appeared in blackface.

Band leaders and entertainers, both black and white, were the kinds of people who continued to write these songs and get them published. Some set up their own publishing companies, and those headed by Handy, Clarence Williams, Perry Bradford, Charles H. Booker, and George W. Thomas were early examples of successful black-owned musical enterprises. Handy Brothers Music Company, in fact, still exists in New York City and offers its founder's music for sale. Another white songwriter and publisher based in Memphis during the 1920s, Bob Miller, had the bright idea to package his blues compositions in an "African Opera Series."

The cover illustrations of blues sheet music add to their collectibility and interest. Some depicted popular vaudeville singers, both black and white. These singers would feature the song in their performances. If it was an instrumental arrangement, a photo of a band might appear on the cover. Other covers had original artwork related to the song's theme.

Recording the Blues

Before 1920 there were very few phonograph records of vocal blues, and they were only by white singers. Black and white dance and jazz bands began to record instrumental blues in 1917, but these were aimed mainly at a white audience. The kind of blues being performed in black vaudeville theatres was not recorded, simply because white-owned record companies didn't think there was sufficient buying power in the black community and assumed whites would be uninterested in this music unless it was performed by white vocalists. At the end of the decade, however, there was a wave of prosperity following World War I that affected even the black community. Many in this community also had served in the military overseas or had migrated to the cities to take jobs in defense industries. It was time to test the market for black popular music on records by black artists. All that was needed was to persuade the record companies, and that role fell to Perry Bradford, a pushy, aggressive songwriter and vaudeville performer from Alabama. Bradford finally made a breakthrough in 1920 with OKeh Records, a small upstart company that was looking to challenge the giants—Victor, Columbia, and Edison Records. Bradford put together the package. He rounded up the singer, Mamie Smith, a vaudeville and cabaret star, and gave her some of his songs. Smith's first record, "That Thing Called Love," was a modest success, but her next release, "Crazy Blues," another Bradford composition, was an instant hit. On the recording Bradford himself led the accompanying jazz band. There are claims that it sold a million copies, likely an exaggeration, but there's no doubt that it sold at least in the hundreds of thousands, and most of the purchasers were black. Columbia Records found another vaudeville singer, Mary Stafford, and quickly released a cover version of "Crazy Blues." When

Columbia's lawyer contacted Bradford asking him to waive his songwriter's royalty in return for Columbia promoting his composition through their record, Bradford replied that he didn't "waive" anything but the American flag!

The race was on among record companies to record blues by black singers. All they had to do was tap into the talent pool of established vaudeville singers and get in contact with a songwriter like Bradford, Handy, or Clarence Williams, all of whom were right there in New York City with a batch of potential hits. Most of them could round up accompanying musicians as well. In stepped Harry Pace, a black financier and former business partner of W. C. Handy. Pace established the Black Swan Record Company, the first significant black-owned label, and for a time in the early 1920s it had a string of hits with recordings by Trixie Smith, Alberta Hunter, and Ethel Waters. But by 1923 Black Swan was finished, having had difficulty getting distribution and seeing its stars enticed away by other companies with bigger budgets. It had shown what could be done, however, and its concentrated marketing to the black community probably helped inspire the concept of "race records." This concept was actually a two-edged sword. There was no doubt that records by black artists had special appeal to black buyers, and that this segment of the market needed to be addressed. Yet by isolating these records in special series advertised in the black press and promoted to stores that catered to black customers, the companies assured that most of this music would remain segregated and beyond the awareness of white listeners. It was not until the 1950s, when radio stations began broadcasting "rhythm and blues" (as race records were then called), that this pattern was broken and large numbers of American whites got to hear this music.

Vaudeville Blues in the 1920s

Whatever the merits of the race record marketing concept, it assured that black tastes would determine what sold, and to a great extent, what was recorded in the first place. Many of the top stars of the black vaudeville circuit got their chance in front of the recording horn in the early 1920s. Most of the blues singers at that time were women, a pattern perhaps established by the initial success of Mamie Smith. Male vocalists usually recorded in duos with a female partner, offering bluesy comic dialogues depicting the battle of the sexes. Not all of the first wave of black recording artists had been blues specialists in the vaudeville scene. Some were really pop singers trying to get on the bandwagon of blues, which was now all the rage. Others had been known more for their acting than their singing. Many of the songs now being called blues were really only bluesy pop songs. Some had intros and two or three different melodic strains, only one of which might be in a blues form. Some of the lyrics contained vestiges of sentimentality, southern nostalgia, and minstrel stereotypes typical of pop songs. But still, there was no doubt that blues had arrived in the record industry, and with it, black voices. The singers were, of course, accompanied by black musicians. In some cases it was only a pianist, who might also be the songwriter and manager of the singer. Their playing was usually simple and basic, just enough to give some structure and background to the singer. If the record company had confidence in the sales potential of the song or was recording a proven hitmaker, it might hire one or two sidemen, perhaps on banjo, clarinet, cornet, or trombone. Some blues recordings got the royal treatment, with backing by jazz bands of five or more pieces. Many of the finest jazz musicians of the 1920s, including Louis Armstrong, Duke Ellington, Fletcher Henderson, King Oliver, and Jelly Roll Morton, appeared on blues records as accompanists.

The first wave of vaudeville blues singers consisted mostly of artists based in and around New York City. By 1923, however, the record companies were searching for talent more widely, and they began to draw upon the artists based in Chicago and those that had been working a national theater circuit and southern tent shows. The circuit was known as T.O.B.A., standing for Theater Owners' Booking Association, but the performers knew it as "Tough on Black Artists" (or "Asses," as some put it less delicately). The working conditions were indeed tough, often Monday-through-Saturday engagements in a theater followed by a long ride in a Jim Crow train to the next engagement. Some theaters had inadequate dressing rooms; others had dishonest managers. Some of the show producers weren't so honest, either. But despite these problems, the circuit provided reasonably steady work for hundreds of entertainers, along with the adventure of life on the road. The singers who began recording blues in 1923 had been working these theaters for years, many of them mainly in the South. They included such stars as "Ma" Rainey and Ida Cox from Georgia, Clara Smith and Bertha "Chippie" Hill from South Carolina, Bessie Smith from Tennessee, Sara Martin from Kentucky, and Sippie Wallace and Victoria Spivey from Texas. These singers had more genuine feeling for the blues than many of those in the first wave of recording artists. They relied less on professional songwriters and composed a good portion of their songs. Some of them organized their own shows and handled the affairs of a dozen or more singers, dancers, actors, and musicians. When they recorded, it was usually in a simpler format with piano and sometimes one or two jazz sidemen. A few were even backed by guitarists or banjo players, and Sara Martin and "Ma" Rainey brought jug bands to the studio. On stage the singers appeared in silks and beaded gowns, wearing turbans and tiaras, with all the trappings and attitude of royalty or operatic divas. In fact, for a

number of years the black entertainment press had been referring to blues as "colored folks' opera."

Folk Blues on Records

With few exceptions, the type of blues recorded up to the mid
1920s was the music at its most professional and commercial
level. The sound of folk blues, self-accompanied singers, guitarists, barrelhouse pianists, and jug bands was still mostly
isolated in the southern countryside, in juke houses, and on
city streets. It took a combination of several factors to change
this situation. One was simply the growing migration of rural
black people to the cities, making their presence and their
musical tastes each year more apparent to the northern-based
record companies. Just as significant was a new technological
development, the invention of the microphone and introduction of the electrical recording process in 1925. The sound of
recorded music immediately improved. There was less surface noise on the records and a greater dynamic range. Certain instruments such as the guitar now sounded much better,
and regional accents could be understood more clearly by a
broader audience. Singers didn't have to shout into a horn
anymore and could use greater subtlety and softer voices on
their recordings. Another important factor that especially affected blues recordings was the growing competition of radio.
This new medium was providing nonstop entertainment that
was essentially free to those who could afford a receiver. Radio didn't broadcast much black music, however, especially
blues. The record companies, feeling the effect of this competition in the sales of their mainstream popular music, began
to look even more seriously at specialty markets, such as black
America and other ethnic and regional groups that had types
of music not well represented on radio. The new electrical
recording equipment was also more portable, and it now

became possible for the companies to make "field trips" and set up temporary recording studios in the cities where regional and local talent flourished. In the last half of the 1920s most of the major record companies made many such trips to Atlanta, Memphis, Dallas, St. Louis, New Orleans, Louisville, and other southern cities, recording blues as well as gospel, jazz, country music, and regional popular music. Some companies also maintained recording studios in Chicago, which was loaded with blues talent up from the South, joining other companies located in Indiana and Wisconsin that had begun recording blues artists. A southern blues singer no longer had to journey to New York City to make records.

Prior to these developments, very few male blues vocalists had recorded, especially solo performers accompanying themselves on guitar or piano. All that changed around the end of 1925 and beginning of 1926 with the debut recordings of Lonnie Johnson and Blind Lemon Jefferson. Although both artists composed their own songs and were excellent guitarists, in many other respects the two men represented opposite ends of the blues spectrum. Johnson grew up in New Orleans, a member of a family of professional musicians, and had resettled in St. Louis around 1920. He played violin and piano as well as guitar, and most of his work prior to recording had been in string bands and jazz bands on riverboats and in theaters. He entered a talent contest and won an opportunity to record for OKeh as a blues singer. His initial releases were successful, and he played this role on hundreds of records over a long career, occasionally stepping out to play jazz or sing pop material. As a singer-guitarist, he fit the image of a country blues performer, but his sound was urbane and sophisticated, his lyrics witty and philosophical, and his guitar playing delicate and jazzy. He was what many country blues artists aspired to be but couldn't, simply because they were just too "country." Jefferson, on the other hand, was country without a doubt, born on

Blues Record Collecting

Most of the first blues collectors were actually jazz collectors who picked up blues records that contained accompaniments by jazz musicians. By the 1950s more and more of them were picking up blues records for their own sake, finding them in junk shops, record store closeouts, old jukebox stocks, and sometimes actually canvassing door to door in black neighborhoods. As in any type of collecting, rarity, condition, and intrinsic appeal of the content determine an item's value. Collectors of 78 r.p.m. records, which was the main format for blues into the 1950s, especially prize country blues recordings issued in the late 1920s and early 1930s. These were often manufactured in very small quantities due to limited sales and the onset of the Depression. Country blues on the Paramount, Black Patti, and "Electrobeam" Gennett labels tend to be especially rare and valuable. A few records known to have been issued have never been found by collectors, and the original masters have been lost or destroyed. These items, like Son House's "Clarksdale Moan"/"Mississippi County Farm Blues," recorded for Paramount in 1930, remain the Holy Grail of blues record collectors. One such record, made for Paramount by King Solomon Hill in 1932, first came to light seventy years later!

Many blues records released on small independent labels in the 1940s and 1950s are also very rare. Today most of these items have been reissued on CDs, and collecting has become an activity for the very wealthy and for investors, although the amateur collector can still find the occasional treasure at a thrift store or flea market. In recent years a number of wealthy rock stars have purchased rare original records of the blues artists they admire, such as Robert Johnson and Muddy Waters, sometimes driving up the prices to astronomical levels. Others have used collecting as a springboard to performing blues. The three front artists of the blues band Canned Heat—Bob Hite, Henry Vestine, and Alan Wilson—were all serious collectors. B. B. King had a huge collection, which he donated to the Blues Archive of the University of Mississippi. Some collectors have started reissue record labels, and many others have cooperated with reissue programs of other companies, in some cases supplying missing items when the original masters were not preserved.

the outskirts of a small town in East Texas. He had brought his music to the city, but it was far from urbane. He was discovered by a black record store owner as he sang on the streets of Dallas and sent to Chicago to record, also meeting with great success with his first releases. Jefferson became a role model for other country blues artists simply because he had perfected the style to such a high degree. He seemed to play all over the neck of the guitar with dazzling new figures following every line of verse. His melodies had a wider range than those of most other singers, and his lyrics, while drawing on traditional blues themes and rhetoric, were more clever and seemed to strike deeper than those of other singers. He was a blind man with powerful musical and lyrical "insight," leading the way and opening the door for many other singers from poor and deprived backgrounds.

The record companies rushed to find more blues talent along the lines of Johnson and Jefferson. Over the next few years dozens of singer-guitarists got their chance to make records, coming from all over the South. Many of them were musicians who had left the countryside and settled in southern cities or in Chicago. Soon they were followed in the studios by string bands and jug bands, small urban combinations of stringed and wind instruments that served as alternatives to the more sophisticated jazz bands. By the end of 1928 barrelhouse and boogie-woogie pianists were being recorded, led by the success of Clarence "Pine Top" Smith, a Chicago musician up from Alabama. That same year saw the recording of guitar-piano duos. The most successful pairing was pianist Leroy Carr and guitarist "Scrapper" Blackwell from Indianapolis, who had a nonstop recording career up until Carr's death seven years later. Guitarist Tampa Red and pianist Georgia Tom launched the hokum style of raunchy double entendre blues with their big hit of "It's Tight Like That." Most of these new artists were a lot rougher in their sound and their lyrics than the women of the vaudeville stage. They were also used to playing for smaller audiences than could fit in a theater, but none of that mattered much on a phonograph record. It all sounded good to the black buyers, who now could purchase records by stars coming from their own communities. By the end of the 1920s, virtually every blues format in existence had been commercially recorded.

Blind Blues Singers

In 1916 W. C. Handy published a song that introduced the image of "the blind man on the corner who sings the 'Beale Street Blues'." This image has been part of the folklore and the reality of the blues ever since. The first recording star of country blues in the 1920s, Blind Lemon Jefferson, was soon followed on records by Blind Blake and Blind Willie McTell. In the 1930s one of the most popular country blues recording artists was Blind Boy Fuller with his blind harmonica partner Sonny Terry. Despite their handicap, or perhaps to some degree because of it, these artists were among the greatest instrumental virtuosos the blues has known. With little opportunity to make any other livelihood, they concentrated intensely on music and must have spent hours and days perfecting their senses of touch and hearing and their vocal skills. Jefferson and McTell in particular were remarkably independent and known to travel long distances by train on their own. McTell's cousin called him "ear-sighted" and described how he would make a clicking sound with his tongue and listen for the reverberations in order to avoid other people and objects while walking. He also carried a pistol to take care of marauding dogs. Fellow musician Buddy Moss even described how McTell once led him through the New York City subway system.

Some of these singers also presented remarkable visual images in their lyrics. McTell described a star falling in the sky and sang of his black, yellow, and brown-skinned women. Jefferson tried to give the impression that he was super-sighted, singing about driving a car, picking fruit from a tree, playing cards, reading the newspaper, and fighting against the Kaiser in World War I. Out of sympathy for their handicap, blind musicians were not criticized by black audiences for mixing blues and gospel material in their performances, as sighted musicians would have been. Ray Charles, perhaps the best known blind blues artist in the modern era, in fact, became a bridge between blues and gospel, altering the lyrics of a number of gospel songs to give them a secular meaning, but retaining the gospel vocal style to become one of the founders of "soul music" in the 1950s.

The 1930s: Depression and Consolidation

The first decade of blues recording was a golden age, but at its end the record industry went into serious decline because of the Great Depression. Actually much of black America was already in a Depression before the stock market crashed in October 1929. Most farmers and sharecroppers were living in poverty, and urban unemployment was high. Sales of race records declined significantly in 1929 and just got worse over the next few years. In 1932 the volume of new releases had slowed to a trickle. In fact, most of the record companies had either gone bankrupt or been sold. The Depression was particularly hard on vaudeville blues. Country blues had always been a low overhead kind of music of the poorest segment of society, but vaudeville blues depended on the maintenance of a touring circuit, and each singer had one or more accompanists who needed to be paid. It was designed to fill theaters accommodating several hundred people, not a house party where a hundred would be considered a large crowd. Essentially the Depression brought about the end of vaudeville blues and its circuit. From that point on, male artists would dominate the blues scene, and clubs would replace theaters as the main urban venues for the music. Many of the vaudeville singers retired. Others worked only local theaters and cabarets. Some, like Ida Cox, soldiered on, working tent shows and roadhouses in the South and Midwest. A few, like Ethel Waters and Hattie McDaniels, headed for Hollywood and picked up stereotyped roles in the movies playing maids and servants, a good survival option perhaps, but far different from the kind of glamour they had experienced on the vaudeville stage. Some, like Ida Cox, Bertha "Chippie" Hill, and Alberta Hunter, managed to catch on during the Dixieland jazz revival of the 1940s. Victoria Spivey and Sippie Wallace even lasted into the folk and blues revival of the 1960s.

The race record industry slowly began to recover in 1933, as Franklin D. Roosevelt began his first term as president and ushered in the New Deal. Things were not the same, however. For one thing, up until the early 1940s only three companies would produce almost all of the blues records: American Record Company (later to be absorbed by CBS), RCA-Victor (issuing blues under its Bluebird subsidiary label), and the new Decca company founded in 1934. Chicago became the main blues recording center, with New York City assuming a secondary role. Field sessions in the South were greatly reduced, and most blues artists had to get to Chicago if they had any hope of making records. A lot of recording sessions were aimed at getting the records placed on jukeboxes, which were becoming increasingly common in southern and urban clubs and cafés. Many people during the Depression couldn't afford the cost of buying a record but were willing to drop a nickel into a jukebox to hear their favorite blues played once while they enjoyed a drink. This led to something of an assembly line approach to recording, where artists would record in massive sessions, making enough original songs to have their records swapped out every few months on the jukeboxes. It meant that each new record by an artist tended to sound a lot like the last record, only with new lyrics. The companies also engaged the services of producers, who would scout the talent, conduct rehearsals, round up sidemen, and oversee the recording session. One of them, Lester Melrose, ran many of the sessions for Bluebird and CBS in Chicago in the late 1930s and 1940s, becoming a main conduit for blues artists who wanted to get on records. These producers operated music publishing companies on the side and usually obtained the copyrights to the original songs that their artists composed.

Most of the recording stars who sustained long careers during the 1930s and into the 1940s were based in Chicago or St. Louis, although virtually all had been born and raised farther south. The key to their success was the ability to compose new songs to feed the jukeboxes. A pleasant voice, sounding southern but with clear diction, was important, too, and most of the singers also had a distinctive sound on an instrument. Some, in fact, were virtuoso stylists. They included guitarists Big Bill Broonzy, Tampa Red, Lonnie Johnson, Bill Gaither, Johnnie Temple, Joe McCoy, Kokomo Arnold, Memphis Minnie, and Bumble Bee Slim, pianists Roosevelt Sykes, Peetie Wheatstraw, Walter Davis, Jimmie Gordon, Georgia White, and Memphis Slim, harmonica players Sonny Boy Williamson and Jazz Gillum, and one artist who made it big with an old-fashioned instrument, Washboard Sam. There were also a few sidemen who appeared frequently on records, such as Charlie McCoy on guitar, Robert Lee McCoy on guitar or harmonica, Black Bob

Folklorists and the Blues

Some of the earliest descriptions of country blues in print were made by academic folklorists, and in their field research they have continued to explore many of the music's hidden corners, traveling down country dirt roads, to prisons, rough juke houses, sharecropper shacks, and other environments where commercial record company scouts hardly ever went. As early as 1903 archaeologist and folklorist Charles Peabody published an article in the *Journal of American Folklore* describing the blueslike singing of his black workers who were excavating an Indian mound at Stovall, Mississippi, the same plantation where Muddy Waters would later start his musical career. In 1911 folklorist Howard Odum would publish the largest early collection and description of blues in the same journal, based on his fieldwork a few years earlier in Mississippi and Georgia. The greatest folklorist collectors were father and son John A. Lomax and Alan Lomax. Together and separately they made several thousand recordings of blues and other types of folksong for the Library of Congress between 1933 and 1942. On their first joint expedition they discovered Leadbelly (Huddie Ledbetter) in the Louisiana State Penitentiary at Angola, and upon his release the following year they promoted his professional career, helping him establish himself in New York City as one of the first participants in a new folk music revival movement. They also interviewed many artists who had already made commercial recordings, making some of the first investigations into the historical development of the blues. John A. Lomax, himself already past the age of seventy, conducted the first interview of Blind Willie McTell in Atlanta in 1940, getting him to talk about his career and the history of the blues. In 1941 and 1942 Alan Lomax participated in a remarkable field project in Mississippi's Coahoma County with scholars from Nashville's historically black Fisk University. On these trips they found such outstanding artists as Muddy Waters, Son House, Sid Hemphill, and David "Honeyboy" Edwards. In the late 1950s Alan Lomax returned to Mississippi and found slide guitar master Fred McDowell, while folklorist Harry Oster returned to Angola Penitentiary to discover the great Robert Pete Williams. In the 1960s and 1970s a new wave of younger folklorists, including William Ferris, George Mitchell, Jeff Titon, Bruce Bastin, Kip Lornell, and myself, made field recordings of some of the still vital remnants of the country blues tradition, many of which have been issued on LPs and CDs.

and Joshua Altheimer on piano, plus a few female vocalists who didn't play an instrument, such as Lil Johnson, Merline Johnson (The Yas Yas Girl), Lil Green, and Rosetta Howard. These musicians actually operated like a big club and backed one another on sessions and sometimes wrote songs for other artists. The favored format was a small group of two or three instruments. The piano-guitar combination remained popular throughout the 1930s. By mid-decade one could hear the harmonica with one or two guitars. Sometimes all three instruments were played on a recording, and toward the end of the decade the washboard and/or upright bass were often added to accentuate the beat.

Starting in 1936 a larger type of blues combo began to be heard on records. The seven-piece group that inaugurated the trend was the Harlem Hamfats, who despite their name were based in Chicago. The word *Harlem* suggested sophistication, but Hamfats suggested the opposite—a casual down-home approach to music. Led by singer-guitarist Joe McCoy, they were a combination of Mississippi blues and New Orleans–style jazz. McCoy's brother Charlie played mandolin or lead guitar to Joe's chords, and other musicians played piano, bass, drums, trumpet, and clarinet. Other similar combos began to record and act as backup bands for blues vocalists, and artists who had been working in the smaller formats, like Big Bill Broonzy and Tampa Red, also organized their "Memphis

Five" and "Chicago Five." Singing saxophone player Louis Jordan would form his Tympany Five and lead the evolution of this sound into the Jump Band format of the 1940s, giving the jazz elements greater prominence.

The 1930s also saw new developments in the solo styles of blues. Guitarists from Mississippi, like Big Joe Williams, Robert Johnson, and Tommy McClennan, introduced more frantic and swinging qualities in their rhythms, while Buddy Moss, Josh White, and Blind Boy Fuller from Georgia and the Carolinas developed the full-bodied ragtime-influenced picking style of their region to a degree of perfection. Guitarists Sleepy John Estes and Yank Rachel from Tennessee worked in duo formats with a harmonica player. A number of pianists from Texas recorded, thanks to some field sessions in Dallas, Houston, and San Antonio. Three artists in particular, all from the mid-south, were responsible for consolidating what had gone before on the guitar, piano, and harmonica in solo and duo formats and pointing these instruments toward their later roles in electric blues bands of the 1950s and subsequent decades. Robert Johnson from the Mississippi Delta played traditional blues in the slide guitar style but also adapted walking bass figures from pianists and translated the guitar-piano duo sound into a solo format. Unfortunately, he was tragically murdered in 1938, and it was left to disciples like Robert "Junior" Lockwood, Muddy Waters, Elmore James, and Jimmy Reed to place his innovations in a band setting some ten or fifteen years later. John Lee "Sonny Boy" Williamson was heir to the blues harmonica tradition of western Tennessee, where that instrument was used in jug bands or with one or two guitars. Williamson began adding piano, and by the 1940s bass and drums. He used his harmonica to answer and punctuate his vocal lines rather than just play full-chorus breaks, and he gave a lot of emphasis to blue notes in his playing, often working them into chords. He had started playing into a microphone and through an amp in Chicago clubs but never got a chance to record truly electric blues. He, too, was tragically murdered in 1948, and once again it was left to others to extend his innovations. The piano counterpart to these artists was Roosevelt Sykes, originally from Arkansas. He began his recording career somewhat earlier, in 1929, but reached his peak in the 1930s and 1940s. Equally adept at fast boogies and slower tunes, he developed a style featuring a deep muffled bass of insistent single notes and boogie riffs with a right hand that ranged freely over the keyboard, often playing an improvised melody in parallel lines, again emphasizing the blue notes. Although he lived into the 1980s, he was always something of a journeyman. He recorded with combos, but others like Memphis Slim and Otis Spann seemed to achieve greater fame and recognition in this style. Sykes spent his last years playing for tourists in New Orleans's French Quarter clubs.

From Spirituals to Swing

Just before Christmas in 1938 and 1939, a visionary producer named John Hammond staged concerts in New York City's Carnegie Hall dubbed "From Spirituals to Swing." They were sponsored by a far-left political organization and magazine called *The New Masses*. With advertisements by the Medical Bureau & North American Committee to Aid Spanish Democracy, Soviet Film Productions, and Workers Book Shop, but also by RCA Victor and Columbia Records and several New York City record stores, the program booklets announced "An Evening of American Negro Music." And what evenings they were! Hammond assembled an amazing array of talent in the jazz, gospel, and blues fields, bringing some of it in from Chicago and the South. The highlights of the 1938 concert were to have been the great Bessie Smith and Robert Johnson, representing the best in urban and country blues, respectively, but both had died in Mississippi a year or so before, Smith in an auto wreck and Johnson murdered by poisoning. Even so, the blues talent that did appear on the two concerts was most impressive and included vaudeville vocalists Ida Cox and Helen Humes, blues shouters Big Joe Turner and Jimmy Rushing, country blues artists Big Bill Broonzy, Sonny Terry, and Bull City Red on guitar, harmonica, and washboard respectively, and boogie-woogie pianists Pete Johnson, Albert Ammons, and Meade Lux Lewis. Add to these gospel music by such greats as Sister Rosetta Tharpe, the Golden Gate Quartet, and Mitchell's Christian Singers, stride piano by James P. Johnson, and jazz by Sidney Bechet's New Orleans Feetwarmers, the Count Basie Orchestra, and the Benny Goodman Sextet (one of the few racially integrated groups in jazz at the time), and you have some of the greatest musical events ever. Even more amazing is the fact that the music was recorded and is still available on CD. Almost every artist saw his or her career enhanced, as they reached a new type of audience for the first time. These concerts could be said to mark the beginning of the modern folk music revival, as well as its long running association with leftist ideology. Sonny Terry would move to New York City in the early 1940s and team successfully with blues guitarist Brownie McGhee to work the coffeehouse and college circuit for many years. Big Bill Broonzy would begin to play for predominantly white folk and jazz audiences in Chicago and by the 1950s would become an international ambassador for the music. Helen Humes and Ida Cox picked up gigs in the jazz scene of the 1940s, and the three boogie-woogie masters would ignite a popular craze for this style of blues music and perform in tuxedos at grand pianos in exclusive clubs through the next decade. John Hammond himself became an executive with Columbia Records and went on to work with the likes of Bob Dylan and Aretha Franklin and to see that his company recorded Son House, Robert Johnson's mentor.

Blues in the 1940s

The 1940s saw momentous changes in the blues and the beginnings of what could be called the modern blues sound. Several key factors influenced the music's development during this decade—World War II, some disruptions in the record industry, the rise of new independent record companies, and the use of the electric guitar. The war brought about a movement of people. Young male musicians were drafted, causing bands and combos to break up but also putting many draftees into new musical environments and exposing them to new sounds. Migration from the rural South to the cities was also hastened by the lure of jobs in the defense industry, the increasing mechanization of agriculture, and a growing desire to escape southern racism. All of this drew the blues to an increasingly urban sound, but one that was infused with elements of the rural music brought to the cities by recent migrants. During the last half of 1942 and all of 1943, a strike by the American Federation of Musicians against the record industry effectively shut down the recording studios. The union felt that recorded music was replacing live music in clubs and on the radio, and they were determined to save the livelihood of their members. Few blues musicians belonged to the union, but the strike had the effect of ending the recording careers of many of them. At the same time, a shortage of shellac, which was needed in the war effort, caused a rationing of its use in the making of phonograph records. This in turn resulted in a reduction in the number of blues recordings.

As the war ended and the rationing eased, many new record companies sprang up. They could be found in all parts of the country, and often they recorded local talent. Their founders came from a variety of backgrounds—record store owners, radio repairmen, broadcasters, club owners, jukebox suppliers, even musicians themselves. Blues was a growing field, and now there were plenty of companies to record the music in Chicago, New York, Los Angeles, San Francisco, Oakland, Nashville, Houston, Philadelphia, and other cities. A local artist had a chance to become a national star. The monopoly of the three major record companies was broken, and many new blues artists appeared on the new labels. Finally, the electric guitar ushered in new sounds in the blues. It had been around since the mid-1930s but was mostly used by a few jazz guitarists and a handful of the top blues recording stars in the late 1930s and early 1940s. But by the mid-1940s it was becoming a necessity for any guitarist who wanted to sustain a career in the blues.

The increasing urbanity of blues musicians and of the black American population in general caused one segment of the music to draw closer to pop music and jazz. Pop singers like Nat "King" Cole and Billie Holiday, both of whom actually sang few blues but had great crossover appeal to white audiences, became models of sophistication for many blues singers using a sentimental, intimate delivery. Blues crooners like Charles Brown and Cecil Gant were usually heard with a quiet "after hours" accompaniment of piano, string bass, and lightly amplified guitar, with perhaps a muted horn and light drums. Other singers like Big Joe Turner and Wynonie Harris opted for an aggressive, shouting delivery, usually with a hard-hitting "jump band" featuring a boogie-woogie–styled piano and a jazzy horn section. Both of these styles, crooning and shouting, symbolized a new worldliness and sense of confidence among blues singers. The music seemed classier and more urbane.

The electric guitar contributed to this trend, but it also gave new life to the country blues and solo performance. On the urbane side, it could now be heard as a lead instrument in a big band, holding its own with the piano, drums, and a brass section. A jazzy, hornlike sound was developed, featuring string bending and exploiting the longer sustain of notes on the electric instrument. The leader in this new trend was Aaron "T-Bone" Walker, who had begun his musical career as a lead boy for Blind Lemon Jefferson on the streets of Dallas in the 1920s. Walker took elements of Jefferson's solo and acoustic guitar style, plugged in, and applied them to the more standard structures and forms of blues in a big band setting. Singing in both the crooning and shouting styles, he extended Jefferson's string bending and his improvisational and harmonic approach to the guitar, creating a meeting of blues, jazz, and pop music. It helped that jazz bands from the Midwest and Texas had long been working with blues vocalists. All they needed was for the guitar to become another lead instrument. Who better to launch this trend than a blues singing guitarist like "T-Bone" Walker? Other guitarists from Texas and neighboring states, such as Lowell Fulson, Pee Wee Crayton, and Gatemouth Brown, some of them relocated to the West Coast, picked up the new style, often using it in smaller formats containing only one saxophone player. By the early 1950s electric lead guitar could be heard on recordings by B.B. King from Memphis and other guitarists coming out of the Deep South. It has remained as the most identifiable instrumental sound of the blues up to the present day.

Down-home solo performers also benefited from the greater volume and sustain of the electric guitar. One of these was Sam "Lightnin'" Hopkins, a Texan who began his recording career on a new independent label in 1946. A prolific composer of seemingly spontaneous lyrics, Hopkins too was a disciple of Blind Lemon Jefferson, but his approach was to simplify the elements of Jefferson's style, letting the greater volume make up for the loss of complexity in the playing. Hopkins's blues sometimes sounded like basic lead guitar without a band. His many recordings influenced countless other southern guitarists who didn't want to or couldn't afford to keep a band. Guitarists from

Mississippi and other parts of the Deep South used the greater volume of the electric instrument to give more power to the rhythmic, minimally harmonic, riff-based and dance-oriented sound that was characteristic of that region's country blues. A leader in this trend was Arthur "Big Boy" Crudup, who hoboed his way from Mississippi to Chicago to begin his recording career in 1941. By his second session he was using an electric guitar. Toward the end of the 1940s John Lee Hooker, another Mississippian who had worked his way up to Detroit, launched his recording career, incorporating piano boogie-woogie and big band swing rhythms into his solo guitar playing and rarely making chord changes. Like Hopkins, Hooker would record prolifically for a number of independent record companies and exert an enormous influence on other down-home blues guitarists. Some of these artists began to build small combos around their solo styles. Once again, Arthur "Big Boy" Crudup was a leader in this development. From his first session he worked with a bass player, and by 1944 he had added drums. Other guitarists sometimes added a harmonica or a second guitar or even hooked up with a pianist. By the beginning of the 1950s singer-guitarists like Muddy Waters would be working in combos of approximately five musicians. There was no doubt that by mid-century the guitar had become the emblematic instrument of the blues, and its sound was usually electric.

Blues in the 1950s

The 1950s saw an acceleration of many of the trends begun in the previous decade along with a couple of major new stylistic developments. By 1952 the three major record companies—RCA Victor, CBS, and Decca—had virtually abandoned the blues field to upstart independent labels. Meanwhile, black-format radio had entered the scene, starting with WDIA in Memphis in 1949. By the early 1950s, stations in every metropolitan area with a substantial black population were playing a steady diet of "rhythm and blues," as race records were now being called, and most of it was either live in the studio by local artists or from records on the new independent labels. The black community was experiencing some of America's postwar prosperity and could support its music on records and radio. A new pride was evident, along with a growing impatience at the hardened segregationist attitudes that had prevailed in much of America for so long. Blues and blues-derived music was flourishing, and many fans and historians view this decade as the music's second golden age after the 1920s.

During the first half of the 1950s, shouters with swinging jump bands and crooners with "after-hours" combos continued to be popular on the blues scene. There were female counterparts to the male singers in these styles, such as Ruth Brown, Big Mama Thornton, Big Maybelle, and Dinah Washington. Down-home performers like "Lightnin' " Hopkins and John Lee Hooker also enjoyed continued success, along with others like Li'l Son Jackson from Texas and the guitar-harmonica duo of Brownie McGhee and Sonny Terry, based in New York City but originally from North Carolina. More and more of the down-home artists, however, were forming small electric combos of up to five pieces or occasionally even more. This development was especially intense in Chicago, which had a huge and rapidly growing population of black migrants from Mississippi and elsewhere in the Deep South. The sound has come to be known simply as "Chicago Blues" wherever it occurs. To an electric guitar played in a solo style would be added a harmonica, now also "electric" and played through an amplifier, and any or all of a second guitar or upright bass, a piano, and drums. A few bands were able to keep a saxophone player as a symbol of urban sophistication, but in Chicago one was more likely to hear the "Mississippi saxophone," as the harmonica was sometimes called. Many of the

Chicago guitarists, like Muddy Waters, Elmore James, Johnny Shines, and Jimmy Reed, had been influenced by the older music of Robert Johnson and other fellow Mississippi artists recorded back in the 1930s with acoustic guitar. They put together the combo sound that Johnson's solo innovations had only portended. Other down-home elements were contributed by Howlin' Wolf's gravelly voice, falsetto cries, and raw riff-based music, and the harmonica mastery of Little Walter, who extended the innovations of Sonny Boy Williamson, recording them through an amp. The sound of Chicago Blues would be rediscovered a few years later and have a tremendous influence on white blues artists in the 1960s and after.

The jazz-influenced electric lead guitar style, with its long horn-like lines, was also gaining popularity in the 1950s, and by mid-decade many Chicago-style combos were adding a lead guitarist to their sound, usually a younger musician up from the South. Some singer-guitarists in this style, such as Otis Rush, Magic Sam, and Buddy Guy, formed combos of their own. These guitarists were especially influenced by the playing of B.B. King, who was based in Memphis and preferred to work with larger groups having three or four brass instruments. Those guitarists who couldn't afford to carry that many musicians simply grafted the lead guitar sound onto the smaller Chicago-style combo. But B.B. King was equally influential as a vocal stylist. When he lived in the Mississippi Delta, before his move to Memphis in the late 1940s, he had been a singer and guitarist in a gospel quartet. Lead gospel singers during this period favored a melismatic, passionate, pleading vocal style, singing as if their lives, or souls at any rate, depended on it. King brought this style to the blues, and its popularity grew throughout the decade. It spread to other types of songs that didn't strictly use a blues form and has come to be known as "soul music." Other gospel-influenced soul blues

Blues Nicknames

One of the most fascinating things about the blues is the colorful quality of the nicknames that many of the artists bear. Some, of course, are merely conventional names signifying family relationships, such as Little Brother Montgomery, Ma Rainey, and Papa Charlie Jackson. But since many blues artists were ramblers and had little conventional family life, these names collectively seem to evoke some kind of blues family that replaced the families many of the singers had become estranged from. Other nicknames have musical connections. Instruments and singing styles occur in such names as Piano Red, Guitar Slim, Washboard Sam, and Gatemouth Brown, popular song lyrics and titles in Bumble Bee Slim and Too Tight Henry, and a blues context in Barrel House Annie. Some tried to latch onto the fame of another artist. Sonny Boy Williamson inspired two more singers to take his name after his death in 1948, and there were several called Sonny Boy Williams. There was a Bessie Mae Smith and a Ruby Smith, the niece by marriage of the real Bessie Smith, whose actual name was Ruby Walker. Brownie McGhee began his recording career as Blind Boy Fuller No. 2, and Memphis Minnie's husband recorded as Mr. Memphis Minnie! Many nicknames described the physical appearance or personality of the artist, such as Fats Domino, Smiley Lewis, Little Buddy Doyle (a midget), Blind Lemon Jefferson, and The Black Ace. Others named a city or state, such as Memphis Slim, Chicago Bob, Tampa Red, or Mississippi John Hurt. Often these names were acquired after the artist had left that location, and they suggest a geographical network connecting various local blues scenes. Some of the most interesting names convey images of physical pleasures, powerful natural, mechanical, and social forces, and magic. Food and sex are especially common images and occur in such names as Jelly Roll Anderson, The Honey Dripper, Pork Chops, Butterbeans, Peppermint Harris, Smokey Hogg, and Steady Roll Johnson. Names like Muddy Waters, Howlin' Wolf, H-Bomb Ferguson, Bobbie Cadillac, and T-Model Ford suggest that these artists are forces of nature or unstoppable powerful machines. Other names suggest occupations or social statuses, such as Doctor Clayton or Black Ivory King. A few nicknames conjure up supernatural powers, such as Magic Sam, Mojo Buford, Peetie Wheatstraw (The Devil's Son-in-Law), and Papa Lord God! Over 40 percent of male blues singers have had nicknames and about one-sixth of the women. Taken together, they project many aspects of the reality as well as the fantasy of the blues world.

singers emerged from the South in the 1950s, such as Bobby "Blue" Bland, James Brown, Ray Charles, Albert King, Little Junior Parker, and Little Milton. This would remain the most popular blues vocal style with black audiences up to the present day.

The increasing presence of blues on the radio during the 1950s had the unexpected effect of attracting many young white listeners. They were especially drawn to the more realistic view of life and greater sexual freedom that the lyrics seemed to convey and to the lively rhythms of the fast pieces and the sensual dances that went with them. It wasn't long before whites in both the North and South were clamoring to see and hear black blues artists live, and by the middle of the decade young white singers and musicians would be performing and recording blues alongside their black counterparts. The result of it all, however, came to be called rock and roll rather than blues. Blues artists who had the big beat and sang lyrics that appealed to teenage sensibilities were drawn into the orbit of this new scene. They included New Orleans pianist Fats Domino, Georgia pianist Little Richard, St. Louis guitarist Chuck Berry, and Chicago bluesman Bo Diddley. Their white counterparts were generally from the South and included Elvis Presley, Carl Perkins, Jerry Lee Lewis, and

Gene Vincent. For a time in the mid-1950s, blues was becoming a truly integrated music, popular with both black and white audiences, where the race of the artist didn't seem to matter. But rock and roll was a youth music, and blues primarily expressed adult feelings and attitudes. Rock and roll pulled away from blues by the early 1960s or went off in very "white" directions like surf music that held little appeal for black listeners. In the mid-1960s, however, rock and roll would make a dramatic turn back toward the blues.

By the end of the 1950s the electric bass had replaced the upright bass, giving the blues a more clearly defined melodic line at the bottom end, and by the early 1960s the electric organ was sometimes heard in place of the piano. Now a blues band could be entirely electric with the exception of the drums. All of the ingredients were in place for what would be viewed as the "contemporary" blues sound of the next four decades. Blues had largely completed its stylistic evolution. From this point on, new artists, new songs, and new recordings would simply replicate and perfect the achievements of those who had gone before, but there would be few new stylistic developments. Instead, there would be change and growth in the social and demographic makeup of the blues audience and the ranks of blues artists, major growth of a blues industry, and a revival of various historical styles of the music.

The 1960s and the Blues Revival

With the arrival of the 1960s, blues began to experience a significant decline in popularity among black Americans. It was being replaced by one of its musical offshoots, soul music. The Civil Rights movement was reaching its full strength, and blues, with its emphasis on personal needs and the superficial image it presented of the singer lamenting his or her fate, just didn't seem congruent with the collective and militant spirit of the times. Some even viewed it as Uncle Tom music. Gospel music instead became the background sound of the Civil Rights movement, along with its secular counterpart, soul music. Significantly, the only style of blues to retain broad popularity in black America throughout the decade was soul blues, which was heavily influenced by gospel music. Artists performing in the style, such as B.B. King and Bobby "Blue" Bland, could still draw substantial numbers on the "chittlin' circuit" of black showcase lounges and auditoriums, and they regularly occupied the few slots on black radio playlists that were reserved for the blues. Most others saw their audiences and record sales diminished. Down-home blues seemed to make a last stand as a commercial force in the state of Louisiana. Jay Miller, a producer with a studio in the town of Crowley near Baton Rouge, recorded a number of local artists in simple formats such as electric guitar, harmonica, and drums. Artists he recorded, such as Lightnin' Slim, Slim Harpo, and Lazy Lester, had southern regional hits up to the mid-1960s in a style that came to be known as "swamp blues." Their records were advertised for mail-order sales through nighttime radio broadcasts on powerful stations that blanketed the South and reached rural listeners, and they made it onto jukeboxes in many little honky-tonks. Another company based in Shreveport, Jewel Records, managed to record or obtain masters of blues artists who had been popular in the 1950s, such as Lightnin' Hopkins and John Lee Hooker, and get these records onto radio and jukeboxes through aggressive promotion. And in the French-speaking area of southern Louisiana there was a growth in popularity of "zydeco" music, a type of Creole blues featuring lead accordion that had arisen in the 1950s in Houston and other southeast Texas cities among Louisiana Creole migrants.

As we look back on the rise of soul music in the 1960s, it is apparent that much of it was really close to blues in style and sentiment. It simply didn't employ a standard blues verse form all that much. But if one is willing to use other criteria to define the blues, then much of the soul music of the era would qualify. James Brown, Soul Brother No. 1, could easily be viewed as Blues Brother No. 1. In fact, a number of soul veterans of the period have recently begun redefining themselves as blues singers in order to extend their careers. At the time, however, blues and soul were viewed as two different things in the black community: One looked backward while the other was progressive.

Black Americans were not the only ones to define what was blues and determine its role during the 1960s. As the decade dawned, blues was finally ready to take on a distinct identity among whites, both in America and in the British Isles and Europe, just as it was beginning to lose some of its identity to soul music among black Americans. A milestone in this audience shift was the 1959 publication of Samuel Charters's book *The Country Blues* with an accompanying long-playing album that reissued old race records made by some of the outstanding performers of the 1920s and 1930s. This album and the history of this seemingly underground music that the book described were a revelation to the mostly white fans of the newly popular folk music as well as some rock and roll fans who had begun to enter their college years. Country blues seemed more meaningful, more personal, more intense, more real than rock and roll or the rest of folk music. Charters had located and re-recorded a few veteran performers in the course of his research. As more and more of the early race records came to be reissued on albums, there were attempts made to "rediscover" other great early country blues artists. By the mid-1960s Furry Lewis, Gus Cannon, Will Shade, Mississippi John Hurt, Scrapper Blackwell, Lonnie Johnson, Sleepy John Estes, Bukka White, Robert Wilkins, Son House, and Skip

James had all been found and recorded once again. Most enjoyed second careers performing at coffeehouses, college concerts and folk festivals, and sometimes touring overseas. The growing country blues movement also provoked field research by academic folklorists and fans that led to the discovery of fine new artists such as Robert Pete Williams, Fred McDowell, and Mance Lipscomb. These artists and the rediscoveries joined others like Big Joe Williams, Jesse Fuller, Josh White, and the team of Brownie McGhee and Sonny Terry, who were already performing on the folk circuit.

With so many country blues artists making recordings and appearing before the public, it wasn't long before some white musicians in the folk movement began specializing in blues. One of the most successful and long lasting was John Hammond, Jr., the son of the man who had produced Bessie Smith's last recording session and organized the groundbreaking "From Spirituals to Swing" concerts at Carnegie Hall in the late 1930s. The old jug band music proved particularly attractive to white musicians in the folk music scene, perhaps in part because it no longer appeared to be an extant style among black performers. Only a few younger black musicians participated in the blues end of the folk movement in the early 1960s, most notably Taj Mahal, who has continued to sustain a career. During this period there were also some young white musicians with residual rock and roll sensibilities who began exploring contemporary electric blues. This development took place especially in cities like Chicago and Memphis, which still had thriving ongoing blues scenes in ghetto clubs. White musicians began sitting in with their black counterparts, in some cases becoming regular members of the band or forming integrated blues bands. The Paul Butterfield Blues Band of Chicago, featuring guitarist Mike Bloomfield, was one of the most successful of such groups. In Memphis an integrated band, Booker T. and the

Rediscovering the Blues

In the early 1960s, the reissue of some of the great country blues records that were originally made some thirty or more years earlier prompted efforts to "rediscover" these artists. These efforts were often led by record collectors who had preserved or reissued the rare original recordings, but some were led by fans, folklorists, and writers. In a few cases all they had to do was to follow hints left by the artists in their old records. In 1928 Mississippi John Hurt sang "Avalon's my home town, always on my mind" in his "Avalon Blues," and sure enough, in 1963, he was located still living in the tiny town of Avalon, Mississippi. Buddy Moss precipitated his own rediscovery simply by showing up backstage at an Atlanta concert of one of his old partners, Josh White, whom he hadn't seen in about thirty years. Robert Wilkins wasn't hard to locate, as he was listed in the phone book in Memphis, the city where he had recorded in the late 1920s. The California sleuths who tried to track down Bukka White got lucky when they mailed a postcard to "Bukka White, Old Blues Singer, Aberdeen, Mississippi," on the basis of the hint in the title of White's early record of "Aberdeen, Mississippi Blues." The postmaster was intrigued, made some inquiries, and forwarded the card to White's address in Memphis. White got in touch with the folks in California, and the result was a renewed career over the last fourteen years of his life. Finding Skip James was the result of a hard search through many parts of Mississippi that finally led to a hospital in Tunica where he was being treated for cancer. He still managed to have a second career for a few years. The search for Son House was prompted by a false report by the newly rediscovered Bukka White that an acquaintance had recently seen House leaving a Memphis movie theater. On this slim lead a team of three northern blues fans launched an expedition that eventually led them into the Mississippi Delta and to a relative of House's who gave them his address and telephone number in New York, where he had moved many years earlier. He was found and also had a successful second career for about ten years. If these great artists had not been found, the blues scene of the 1960s and our knowledge of the early country blues would have been much poorer.

MG's, formed in the Stax Records studio and had many instrumental blues hits besides backing soul vocalists on their recordings.

In Great Britain and Europe the blues revival developed in a somewhat different way. During the 1950s American blues artists, such as Josh White, Big Bill Broonzy, and Muddy Waters, had begun to tour across the Atlantic. Broonzy even settled in Holland for a time. During the early 1960s a number of other American bluesmen would settle in Europe, including pianists Champion Jack Dupree, Curtis Jones, and Memphis Slim. They frequently cited American racism as their reason for moving but no doubt also sensed career opportunities in a new territory. Starting in 1962, two visionary German promoters launched the American Folk Blues Festival, which toured annually through major European cities, some even behind the Iron Curtain, with a lineup of outstanding black American blues talent in every style from vaudeville and country blues to contemporary electric formats. Thousands of British and European concertgoers became converts to the blues.

In Great Britain during the 1950s there were regular radio broadcasts of Leadbelly and other folk blues artists. The music precipitated a movement among young British musicians late in the decade that came to be known as "skiffle," a dialect form of the word *scuffle* that some black American musicians had applied to casual country blues and jug band music. Rock and roll had a major impact on Great Britain during the 1950s through the importation and radio play of recordings by American artists. Somehow, the range of recordings that crossed the Atlantic contained a stronger dose of electric blues than the rock and roll that was typically reaching the ears of white Americans during this period. The British particularly favored the artists recorded in Chicago, such as Muddy Waters, Howlin' Wolf, Little Walter, Chuck Berry, Jimmy Reed, and Bo Diddley. It wasn't long before performers in the skiffle scene would start plugging in and forming electric blues and rock bands, copying the recordings of their American idols. These bands played at small underground clubs in London, Liverpool, Manchester, and on the continent, and would soon make records of their own as the Yardbirds, the Rolling Stones, the Animals, Cream, and John Mayall and the Bluesbreakers. Even the world's first two blues magazines, *Blues Unlimited* and *Blues World*, were both founded in England during the 1960s!

The white American and British blues movements began to merge in 1964 with rock and roll's British Invasion. More and more American blues lovers, up to now involved in the folk music scene, started to go electric, many of them inspired by Bob Dylan's dramatic public plug-in at the 1965 Newport Folk Festival. White American blues artists like Johnny Winter and Canned Heat soon gained popularity alongside their British counterparts. The 1960s also saw a number of collaborative recording sessions between established black performers and younger white blues-rock musicians on both sides of the Atlantic. Harmonica wizard Sonny Boy Williamson (Aleck Miller) worked in England with both Eric Clapton and the Yardbirds and Eric Burdon and the Animals. Muddy Waters recorded with members of Paul Butterfield's Blues Band, Howlin' Wolf with an all-star line-up that included Eric Clapton, the Beatles's Ringo Starr, some members of the Rolling Stones, and John Lee Hooker with Canned Heat. These "fathers and sons" efforts (from the title of Muddy

Waters's best-known collaboration) had mixed results in an artistic sense, but they helped some aging but not yet over-the-hill black performers reach new audiences and they served to validate the blues credentials of the white performers. By the end of the 1960s soul blues singers who also played lead guitar, such as B.B. and Albert King, were reaching white audiences, supplementing their base of support in the black community. Electric blues especially had an influence upon the psychedelic movement in rock and roll of the late 1960s. One of the leaders of this movement, Jimi Hendrix, a young black American guitarist who first rose to fame in British rock circles, had an authentic blues background, having apprenticed for a time with Little Richard and a number of soul music stars. But psychedelic blues also produced some bummers, such as the attempts to graft it to classic Chicago Blues in products like *Electric Mud* and *Electric Wolf,* which Howlin' Wolf himself described as "dogshit."

The Modern Blues Scene

The period from the 1970s to the present has seen a consolidation of many of the trends established in the 1960s. Blues has continued to spread internationally, with strong scenes developing not only throughout most of Europe but also in Australia and New Zealand, Japan, and Latin America. The popularity of "The Twist" and soul artists like James Brown in the 1960s also brought elements of the blues to parts of Africa, the continent that had contributed so much to the origins of the music in the first place. The year 1970 saw the founding of the first American blues magazine, *Living Blues.* Since then there has been a growth of literature on the blues by American and European authors. There are hundreds of blues festivals in various parts of the world, and the music continues to be a part of folk, jazz, and rock festivals. Thousands of recordings have been made, not only of established and new artists but also reissues of early records made from the 1920s through the 1950s. Blues societies have been formed in many cities and regions, and in 1980 a national organization was inaugurated, the Blues Foundation, which stages the annual Handy awards for excellence in the field.

Much of this growing institutionalization of blues is impelled by a sense that the music is dying or is at least in danger of doing so. Indeed, by the end of the 1970s most of the great early country blues artists were gone, and before long many of the top tier of Chicago blues pioneers had perished. Today there are very few major black American stars of the blues still active who received their early validation from the black community. The majority of today's black artists and virtually all of the white artists came of age musically during the blues revival of the 1960s or later. Since the 1980s one has increasingly heard pleas to "keep the blues alive." These have been answered with the establishment of blues museums, the erecting of historical markers and gravestones at the burial sites of blues artists who died in neglect, educational blues programs in the schools, and the growth of a blues tourism industry that includes not only charter sea cruises with entertainment by blues stars but also guided tours of Mississippi blues gravesites and juke joints. There is a certain amount of hype and romanticism in all of this. Some "blues in the schools" programs purport to increase the reading and math skills of "at risk" students. A tourist can visit three competing gravesites of Robert Johnson, the artist who allegedly sold his soul to the devil in return for his musical talent, only to die under mysterious circumstances barking like a dog! One can even get the feeling of the blues by paying to spend the night in a restored sharecropper shack on a Mississippi plantation— with air conditioning and running water, of course. Nevertheless, much of this activity does preserve and shine a light on the remnants of blues history and introduce new generations to a great musical art that was truly ignored for a long time by a large segment of American society. Fortunately, a great amount of that art was recorded, and most of the best of these recordings remain available.

In the arena of performance and recording, white artists and audiences have continued to emphasize blues-rock, particularly the instrumental sounds of "guitar gods" like Eric Clapton and Stevie Ray Vaughan. This phenomenon has also benefitted the careers of outstanding black lead guitarists such as B.B. King, Albert King, Albert Collins, Luther Allison, and Buddy Guy. Black popular tastes in the blues have largely remained with soul blues, and a number of stars in the style from the 1950s and 1960s have had remarkably long careers. A few, such as Z. Z. Hill and neo-hokum singer Bobby Rush, have risen to the top in these later decades. Since the early 1980s Malaco Records, based in Jackson, Mississippi, has done much to consolidate the soul blues scene with the black audience. In the 1990s a number of electric country blues artists from Mississippi, such as R. L. Burnside and Junior Kimbrough, who had been performing for what was left of the traditional blues scene in their home communities, were promoted to the punk rock scene and successfully expanded their audience base. A number of younger black artists like Keb Mo, Corey Harris, and Guy Davis, also emerged in the 1990s as solo performers with acoustic guitar. And finally, there has been a black "fathers and sons" movement of sorts in recent years, as the sons and daughters of artists such as Muddy Waters, John Lee Hooker, Johnny Copeland, Luther Allison, Tabby Thomas, Curley Weaver, and others have launched recording and performing careers. These and the younger black acoustic artists have been heard mostly by white and international audiences.

The future of the blues is impossible to predict. Present trends, such as the music's international expansion and the popularity of soul blues with black listeners, are likely to continue for at least a little while. Whether the connection between blues and rock and roll will last as rock enters its geriatric years is hard to say. Blues itself, however, seems to be a music that stays fresh and young, constantly renewing itself. It doesn't look and doesn't act like it's a hundred years old!

THREE

Varieties of Blues

U nlike jazz, where the names of most of its varieties refer to recognizable styles, sounds, or instrumentations that came to fruition in a certain era (bebop, swing, cool, etc.), many of the terms for varieties of blues are derived from geographical regions or cities, which supposedly support a single style or sound. This approach to terminology does a disservice to the range of blues styles that actually exist in any one place and tends to exclude some artists from consideration because they don't fit the profile of their city or region. Many blues artists, in fact, have been itinerant and eclectic in their tastes and don't fall easily into any single category.

Several of the widely used terms are distortions of the historical record as we now know it and need to be abandoned or replaced. Others are overlapping with one another in meaning. Then there are whole styles that have no generally accepted descriptive term. In particular, these include the range of blues styles featuring lead electric guitar. To call this music "contemporary blues" is hardly adequate, as this sound has been around for the last half of the entire history of the blues. "Urban blues" is likewise inadequate on the grounds of being hopelessly vague.

Despite the need for an overhaul of blues terminology, the varieties of blues explained here are terms used commonly today. Explanations of what type of blues the terms usually refer to, and a critique when they seem to distort the historical reality will also be given, and some of the outstanding artists associated with each style will be mentioned. A few geographical terms sometimes encountered in the literature, e.g., Memphis Blues and Louisiana Blues, have been excluded because they are simply "catch-all" categories encompassing very diverse styles over the music's entire history. Other common terms, such as Piano Blues or Harmonica Blues, need no explanation.

Acoustic Blues: All blues were "acoustic" before the introduction of the electric guitar in the late 1930s. This term, however, is used mostly to refer to blues of the modern era, since the 1960s, played on acoustic instruments in contrast to those that feature heavily "electric" sounds. Many Acoustic Blues performances do, in fact, use a bit of amplification but without the distortion typical of electric blues. Acoustic Blues are also usually performed solo, especially with guitar, or in other small formats without drums, electric bass, or horns. Blues festivals in recent years sometimes have an "acoustic stage" where such acts can be heard apart from the louder, electric bands. Some players of Acoustic Blues try to recreate or simulate the sound of early blues from before the electric era, while others are modern blues singer-songwriters or perform a type of hybrid blues music with influences variously from New Age music, jazz, or other ethnic traditions. For a time in the 1990s there was a wave of "unplugged" blues artists—electric guitarists who reverted to acoustic instruments. Acoustic Blues artists are mostly white, but in the 1990s a number of black artists in the style emerged. John Hammond, Ry Cooder, and Taj Mahal are some of the more enduring veterans, while more recent figures include Keb Mo, Guy Davis, Rory Block, and the trio Saffire. Some artists, such as Bonnie Raitt and Doug MacLeod, have mined both the electric and acoustic veins of blues music. Veteran black Country Blues artists have often been placed in the Acoustic Blues category in recent years. *See also* Country Blues and Folk Blues.

Barrelhouse Blues: A barrelhouse is a rough juke house or honky-tonk, a place where a correspondingly rough type of rhythmic blues could be heard. Up to the 1950s most barrelhouses contained a piano, and the term *Barrelhouse Blues* has usually been used to designate rhythmic riff-based, dance-oriented piano blues, generally performed solo. This style flourished and was extensively recorded in the 1920s and 1930s. Boogie-woogie piano is a variety of barrelhouse style. Among the outstanding barrelhouse exponents were Roosevelt Sykes, Peetie Wheatstraw, Little Brother Montgomery, Walter Roland, Speckled Red, Piano Red, and other boogie-woogie artists. Many pianists who worked in duos and larger formats, such as Leroy Carr, Memphis Slim, Ivory Joe Hunter, and Otis Spann, began their careers as barrelhouse players. *See also* Boogie-Woogie.

Blue Yodel: This is a blues song with an added yodeling refrain. German and Swiss yodelers were popular on American vaudeville stages during the 1910s and 1920s. Some black vaudeville singers evidently heard them and incorporated yodeling refrains into songs in the new blues genre then sweeping through black popular entertainment. This style was in turn adopted by southern white performers, and its biggest popularizer by far was white singer-guitarist Jimmie Rodgers from Mississippi. Rodgers learned blues directly from black performers in his career as a railroad brakeman and hobo, and also participated in vaudeville entertainment. He was immensely popular on recordings and in personal appearances from 1927 until his death in 1933 and had many followers and imitators who continued to perform in the style up to the early 1950s. Since then blue yodels have mostly been heard in bluegrass music. The style has not been prominent in black music since the 1920s.

Blues-Rock: This term encompasses blues with a rock flavor from the 1960s onward; thus it excludes the sounds of 1950s rockabillies such as Elvis Presley and Carl Perkins and black rock-and-rollers such as Chuck Berry and Little Richard, even though most of their music was blues. It also excludes blues-based soul music artists of the 1960s and later, such as James Brown and Rufus Thomas. Thus, virtually all blues-rock artists are white (the most notable exception being Jimi Hendrix), and one sometimes encounters the term *white blues* as a synonym for blues-rock. The most prominent rock elements in the style are the electric guitar as the main lead instrument, heavy electronic distortion and other special effects, a pounding evenly-spaced beat, and an adolescent orientation and anti-establishment themes in the lyrics. The psychedelic and heavy metal styles of rock music often overlap with blues-rock. Some groups in this category prefer to view themselves as blues artists and perform mainly a blues repertoire, while others are more eclectic. Blues-rock arose in both the United States and Great Britain in the 1960s but is now an international style. Besides the artists listed under British Blues, prominent blues-rock figures have been the Paul Butterfield Blues Band, Canned Heat, Johnny Winter, Jimi Hendrix, Z Z Top, George Thorogood, and Stevie Ray Vaughan.

Others such as Bob Dylan have gone through blues-rock phases in their careers or recorded occasional songs or albums in the style. *See also* British Blues.

Blues Crooners: Crooners were the other side of the coin from Blues Shouters. They also generally came from a jazz or pop singing background and were especially influenced by stylists such as Nat "King" Cole and Billie Holiday. Their lighter voices typically had a softer accompaniment, often a "cocktail hour" or "after-hours" format of tinkly piano, lightly amplified jazzy guitar, an upright bass, and sometimes with light drums and a muted brass instrument. A number of the singers played an instrument, usually a piano or guitar. Some of the more prominent blues crooners were Cecil Gant, Johnny Ace, Charles Brown, Ivory Joe Hunter, Percy Mayfield, Lonnie Johnson, Hadda Brooks, and Julia Lee.

Blues Shouters: From the late 1930s to the mid-1950s, a number of blues vocalists achieved success singing in a strident, assertive, "shouting" style with a deep, chesty voice. The themes of their songs were often equally assertive and confident. Usually they were stand-up singers working with a jazzy swing band or jump band, but a few also played instruments, generally ones more associated with jazz, such as saxophone or drums. Centers of the style were Kansas City and Los Angeles, but shouters could be heard in most major cities that had a sizeable black community, including New Orleans, Memphis, Chicago, Atlanta, Cleveland, and New York City. Most shouters were male, including such stars as Big Joe Turner, Wynonie Harris, Jimmy Rushing, Roy Brown, Nappy Brown, Billy Wright, Bull Moose Jackson, H-Bomb Ferguson, Rufus Thomas, and Gatemouth Moore. (Notice that several of their nicknames suggest bigness, loudness, and power.)

There were also female shouters, such as Big Mama Thornton, Ruth Brown, and Etta James. Many shouters had backgrounds as vocalists in jazz bands, but a few started in gospel music.

Many singers, such as Jimmy Witherspoon, T-Bone Walker, Dinah Washington, and Big Maybelle, were actually adept at both shouting and crooning styles. In a symbolic sense, the rise of these vocal styles and their associated instrumental styles represented the growing urbanization, sophistication, and assertiveness of the American black community. These styles can be understood against the background of migration from the plantations to the cities, black participation in the war effort overseas, wartime and postwar prosperity, enhanced opportunities for formal education, and the first stirrings of the modern Civil Rights movement. These singers were taking steps toward "integrating" into jazz and pop music while holding onto the blues. *See also* Jump Blues.

Boogie-Woogie: The term *boogie-woogie* appears originally to have meant a dance occasion or a place where dancing took place, such as a juke house or honky-tonk. It soon came to designate the dancing itself ("boogie") and the type of music that occurred at these places. Boogie-Woogie is riff-based blues music, often set to the standard twelve-bar form. It is most often associated with the piano, but it can be played on the guitar or by a band. The riff figure is usually played in the lower register, most of the time with an overlay of an instrumental or vocal blues melody in a higher register. There are many different boogie-woogie riffs, including eight-to-the-bar (i.e., eight beats per measure) and "walking bass" patterns. The latter usually features alternating playing of the fifth and sixth degrees of the scale (*sol* and *la*). The riff is transposed as the blues pattern goes through its standard harmonic changes.

As a highly rhythmic piano style, Boogie-Woogie is part of the larger Barrelhouse Blues category. Although the style probably originated in the earliest days of blues among pianists with no formal training, it remained largely underground and unrecorded until Chicago pianist Clarence "Pine Top" Smith recorded "Pine Top's Boogie Woogie" at the end of 1928. The tune became a test piece for other pianists and has been adapted by guitarists and big bands. The success of Smith's record created opportunities for other Boogie-Woogie and Barrelhouse pianists to record over the next few years. Smith himself had the misfortune to die a few months after he made his record, the victim of a stray bullet in a saloon fight. A revival of piano Boogie-Woogie, spurred on by jazz fans and record collectors, began to take place in the late 1930s, leading to substantial careers for artists such as Albert Ammons, Meade Lux Lewis, and Pete Johnson, and documentary recordings of other artists such as Jimmy Yancey. By the 1940s Boogie-Woogie was a significant part of the world of jazz and pop music, as Ammons, Lewis, and Johnson, dressed in tuxedos, pounded on grand pianos in some of the finest clubs and auditoriums in America. Sometimes two or all three of them played together. Boogie-Woogie piano was viewed as a virtuoso art, somewhat as ragtime piano had been in an earlier era. Most beginning pianists in the 1940s tried to master a few boogies, and the style had a great influence on country music, pop music, and later on rock and roll. By the late 1940s blues electric guitarists like John Lee Hooker were adapting the boogie riff idea to their instrument. In the late 1960s the white blues band Canned Heat, inspired by Hooker's playing, introduced the idea of "boogie music" to the world of blues-rock. *See also* Barrelhouse Blues.

British Blues: This term usually describes the British electric blues bands of the 1960s and 1970s, some of whom continued to perform in subsequent years. It is also sometimes extended to cover British solo artists like Jo Ann Kelly. Inspired especially by the sound of American artists like Muddy Waters, Howlin' Wolf, Chuck Berry, and Jimmy Reed, along with some older country blues artists, a British blues scene coalesced in the early 1960s out of elements of the jazz revival, folk revival, rock and roll, and skiffle music scenes. (Skiffle was a British interpretation of the music of older acoustic black American artists such as Leadbelly and the early jug bands.) Alexis Korner, John Mayall, Eric Clapton, the Rolling Stones, the Yardbirds, the Animals, and Fleetwood Mac were some of the leading figures in this movement, although almost every rock band prominent in the "British Invasion" of 1964 and later years was considerably affected by it. American guitarist Jimi Hendrix also began his rise to fame in the British blues scene of the 1960s. The music of these artists was usually interpreted by Americans as being part of rock and roll, or rock as it soon came to be called, but British blues artists played an important role in making American rock fans more aware of the blues roots of rock music and some of the still-living creators of this music. Some British artists recorded collaborations with the black American artists they so admired. *See also* Blues-Rock.

Chicago Blues: Chicago has been a center of blues activity almost since the genre's beginning and a blues recording center since the 1920s. It was a main destination for black rural migrants from Mississippi, Louisiana, Arkansas, and western Tennessee, as well as other parts of the Deep South. These areas were traditionally blues country, and the migrants brought their music with them, building it into something bigger in the city. By the late 1940s, fueled by a huge wave of wartime and postwar migration from the South, Chicago blues artists had created a powerful electric small combo sound. Electric guitar and harmonica played through an amplifier were at the center of this sound as lead instruments, often joined or supported by a piano. Acoustic (and later electric), bass and drums would fill out the sound. A few bands had a saxophone, often in place of the harmonica. Some had a second guitar. Others had only three or four pieces. Whatever the instrumentation, the sound was loud, powerful, and full, sometimes distorted. The electric guitar was not played in the modern jazzy lead style but in a more rhythmic style showing strong traces of its Deep South country blues origin. Electric slide guitar was heard with many of the songs. This classic Chicago Blues sound flourished from the late 1940s through most of the 1950s. It was especially prominent on Chicago's South Side, where most of the recent Deep South migrants lived, and so it has sometimes come to be called South Side Blues. Leaders in this style were Muddy Waters, Howlin' Wolf, Little Walter, Jimmy Rogers, Elmore James, Jimmy Reed, Junior Wells, and Bo Diddley.

Around the mid-1950s blues artists based in another black neighborhood of Chicago, the West Side, began adding modern electric lead guitar to this small group format, with singing in a melismatic and dramatic soul blues style. Leaders in this trend were Buddy Guy, Otis Rush, and Magic Sam, and their style came to be known as West Side Blues. Bands on the South Side began adding lead guitarists, and an updated West Side sound has become the predominant trend in Chicago Blues from the 1960s onward. The homage paid to early Chicago Blues by British and American blues-rock groups, continued migration from the Deep South, the longevity of some of the style's early pioneers, blues tourism to Chicago, and a wealth of recording and touring opportunities for local musicians have kept a vibrant Chicago Blues scene alive through today. The term *Chicago Blues* is sometimes used to describe the sound of bands from other cities in this same format. Indeed, the social and historical factors that created the Chicago Blues scene occurred in many other cities at the same time and produced similar blues sounds there. This development was simply more intense in Chicago and better documented and promoted through phonograph records.

City Blues: City Blues should mean the same thing as Urban Blues, but the two terms have come to assume different meanings. City Blues refers to small combo blues sounds that developed from the late 1920s to the 1940s in midwestern cities such as Chicago, Detroit, and St. Louis. The combination of piano and guitar, pioneered by Leroy Carr and Scrapper Blackwell of Indianapolis and Hokum Blues duo Georgia Tom and Tampa Red of Chicago, remained very popular during this period. Guitar and harmonica, as in the combinations of Big Bill Broonzy and Jazz Gillum from Chicago or Sonny Boy Williamson and Yank Rachel from St. Louis, was also a popular sound from the mid1930s on. Often washboard and/or one-string bass were added to these combinations to strengthen the beat. In the last half of the 1930s larger combos began to form with piano, guitar, a percussion instrument, and one or more of clarinet, trumpet, or saxophone, played by musicians with a jazz background. The Harlem Hamfats, and later Louis Jordan's Tympany Five, were leaders in establishing this format, which would be a basis for later jump bands.

City Blues performers in the Midwest were extensively recorded, but similar developments, less well documented on records, took place in other urban centers during the same period. These small combo sounds, along with those of the jug bands, formed the basis of modern urban combos with the addition of electronic amplification in the 1940s.

Classic Blues: *See* Vaudeville Blues.

Contemporary Blues: This style is sometimes called modern blues, and it represents the sound of blues that is most prevalent and popular today. Actually it is a sound that has been popular since the 1960s and earlier. It features a jazz-influenced electric lead guitar, supported by electric bass and drums, usually with one or more other instruments such as second guitar, keyboard, amplified harmonica, a brass instrument, or a horn section. The singing is usually in a "soul" style. Some people use these terms to cover the entire range of blues heard today, as opposed to the sounds of earlier periods.

Country Blues: The term *Country Blues* came into common use following the 1959 publication of Samuel Charters's groundbreaking *The Country Blues*, the first attempt at a historical overview of the genre. It describes southern rural and small-town blues accompanied by guitar and/or harmonica and the blues in these styles that were brought to southern and northern cities. Some of the rougher solo piano blues styles are also included, especially those that occurred in southern barrelhouses. By extension, the term covers blues was performed by jug bands, string bands, juke bands, etc. Usually Country Blues are thought to be performed on acoustic instruments, but solo performances with electric guitar by southern artists like Lightnin' Hopkins are also often included. The term is problematic because many of the chief exponents of these styles used the music to escape country life and the drudgery of farming, either moving to cities, leading an itinerant existence, or becoming professional musicians within a regional circuit. The substitute term *Rural Blues* does nothing to solve this problem. In his book *Early Down-home Blues* (1977), Jeff Titon proposed to substitute the term *Downhome Blues*, suggesting the imagery the music conveyed rather than its specific geographical location. The efficacy of this term was undercut, however, in 1982 by Z. Z. Hill's hit recording of "Down Home Blues" in an urban contemporary style. *See also* Acoustic Blues, Deep South Blues, East Coast Blues, Folk Blues, Jug Bands, and Texas Blues.

Deep South Blues: This is a regional style of Country Blues heard in the sound of most performers in an area stretching from central Georgia westward to northern Louisiana and up the Mississippi River to encompass eastern Arkansas, southeastern Missouri, and the western parts of Tennessee and Kentucky. Much of this region consisted of cotton farms and plantations. The term is especially used to describe solo guitar–accompanied blues, but it is also applicable to most piano and harmonica blues of the region. The chief characteristics of the style could be summarized as intensity, harshness, minimalism, and traditionalism. The singing tends to be passionate and the rhythms insistent. Lyric themes sometimes become quite serious, dealing with deep issues of life and death and the state of the singer's soul. The voice gives the impression of coming from the back of the mouth, the throat, or the chest, and the singer's diction is often slurred. The guitar is played percussively, and the slide (bottleneck) style is found most commonly in this region. Many blues are based on a single riff or series of riffs and have minimal harmonic development. Scales of five or even fewer notes are common in both the vocal melodies and instrumental work. Lyrics are often part of a common stock of traditional verses. The musical elements of this style are particularly drawn from the African side of the blues tradition.

Despite the "roots" quality of this music, it can be quite innovative, and many of the new developments in blues over the years were pioneered by artists from this region. Deep South Blues forms the basis for many of the elements of Chicago Blues, which should not be surprising since many people from the Deep South region migrated to cities of the Upper Midwest. The Deep South style has been most recorded in the state of Mississippi, particularly in the northwest quarter of the state known as the Delta. Because of this the entire style is sometimes incorrectly referred to as Mississippi Blues or Delta Blues. The latter term has even been used by some writers to refer to all of Country Blues, creating even greater confusion. Among the many outstanding guitar playing artists in the Deep South style were Barbecue Bob and Peg Leg Howell from Georgia, Ed Bell from Alabama, Charley Patton, Son House, Robert Johnson, Fred McDowell, and Tommy Johnson from Mississippi, Robert Pete Williams from Louisiana, and Sleepy John Estes and Furry Lewis from Tennessee. More recent representatives among electric guitarists would be artists like John Lee Hooker, R. L. Burnside, and Jessie Mae Hemphill. Harmonica players like Jaybird Coleman and Sonny Boy Williamson and pianists like Walter Roland, Little Brother Montgomery, and Roosevelt Sykes also generally fall into this category.

Delta Blues: *See* Deep South Blues.

Downhome Blues: *See* Country Blues.

East Coast Blues: Like Deep South Blues, this term refers to the sound characteristic of another Country Blues stylistic region, especially its solo guitar–accompanied blues. The region encompasses the Atlantic Coast sections of Florida and Georgia, the Carolinas, Virginia, Maryland, and Delaware, stretching westward through the Appalachian Mountains to eastern and central portions of Kentucky and Tennessee. "East Coast" is thus a somewhat limiting term for this region, but nothing better has been proposed. The East Coast style is often referred to in print as Piedmont Blues. The Piedmont region of Virginia and the Carolinas (i.e., the eastern foothills of the Appalachian Mountains) was indeed an area of intense development of this blues style, but this is too limiting as a descriptive term to cover such a broad geographical area.

Many of the typical characteristics of East Coast Blues contrast with those of Deep South Blues. In general, the mood is lighter, both in the lyric themes and in the rhythms, which often have an even duple or a bouncy triplet quality. Guitar playing is less percussive, with more emphasis on the actual tonal quality of notes. Longer melodic lines are more prevalent than short riffs. A full seven-note scale is often used, and there is greater harmonic development, including frequent passing notes and chords. Most blues stick to the standard twelve-bar AAB form or some other standard pattern. The blues of this region are often mixed with ragtime and songster elements. The style has remained largely acoustic and solo, and has had relatively little influence on electric and band styles of blues. Among the notable East Coast blues stylists are Blind Blake from Florida, Buddy Moss from Georgia, Josh White from South Carolina, Blind Boy Fuller and Sonny Terry from North Carolina, Brownie McGhee from eastern Tennessee, and John Jackson and John Cephas from Virginia. Reverend Gary Davis, although primarily a gospel singer and guitarist, is often included in this category. Rather few blues pianists from the area were recorded, but Georgia's Piano Red could be considered a representative of the style. Many of the chief exponents of East Coast Blues were blind or otherwise physically handicapped, which often led them to pursue full-time careers in music and develop their skills to a high degree of virtuosity, setting the standard for other musicians in the region.

Folk Blues: This term is applied to those blues that contain many traditional lyrical and musical elements, i.e., blues that could be considered as folksongs. All blues contain some traditional elements, but this term is generally confined to Country Blues and is more or less synonymous with it, merely placing the emphasis on the traditional content rather than the geographical or social origin of the style. *See also* Acoustic Blues and Country Blues.

Gospel Blues: If ever there was a contradiction in terms for blues, this is it. Sometimes also called Holy Blues, this term refers to gospel songs performed with a typical blues instrumentation, particularly the solo performances of various "guitar evangelists" like Reverend Gary Davis and Blind Willie Johnson. The guitar styles are similar in a musical sense and have historical relationships to one another; a number of artists have performed both Country Blues and this type of gospel music, either at the same time or at different stages of their careers. Nevertheless, blues and gospel music play very different social roles and have separate repertoires and separate thematic emphases. There is no evidence that the musical elements that they share occurred in blues any earlier than they did in gospel music. Therefore, Gospel Blues is not blues at all, but merely a variety of gospel music. To add to the confusion, some writers have referred to gospel music in general as Gospel Blues, on the basis of the important pioneering role in gospel of ex-bluesman Thomas A. Dorsey (Georgia Tom).

Hill Country Blues: In the "hill country" of northeastern Mississippi, east of the better-known Delta region, a style of guitar blues developed that exhibits an extreme version of the characteristics of Deep South Blues. Almost none of the blues in this style use the standard twelve-bar form. Most are riff-based, and they have little harmonic development. Performances have a droning hypnotic quality and are highly rhythmic and percussive. Acoustic blues artists like Bukka White and Fred McDowell could be considered early exemplars of the style, but it has become best known since the 1960s through recordings by electric guitarists, often supplemented by drums or other percussion. Key representatives of the style are Junior Kimbrough, R. L. Burnside, Jessie Mae Hemphill, and Robert Belfour.

Hokum Blues: From the late 1920s through the 1930s, blues in the Hokum style were recorded extensively. These featured lyrics on humorous, mostly sexual themes, full of innuendo and double meaning. The instrumentation was usually piano and one or two guitars, but they were also performed by solo guitarists, banjoists, guitar duos, string bands, and other combinations. Virtuoso playing and fast tempos for dancing were often featured. The lively tone of the music seemed to offer an escape from the harsh realities of the Great Depression. Many artists participated in this style, and a few became more or less specialists in it. Among the latter were banjoist Papa Charlie Jackson, guitarist Bo Carter, the team of Tampa Red and Georgia Tom, vaudeville singer Frankie "Half Pint" Jaxon, and bands like the Hokum Boys, the Mississippi Sheiks, and the Harlem Hamfats. Singer Bobby Rush could be viewed as a modern representative of the Hokum Blues style.

Holy Blues: *See* Gospel Blues.

Jug Bands: A jug band is a combination of string, wind, and sometimes percussion instruments that includes a jug played as a bass instrument. A typical instrumentation might be one or two guitars, or guitar and mandolin, plus harmonica, kazoo, and jug, but some bands included violin, piano, banjo, or even a musical saw. A washboard or spoons could be used to provide percussion. This style coalesced in the early years of the twentieth century and reached its peak of popularity and development in the 1920s. By the mid-1930s some jug bands had added a simple drum set or even a saxophone, but most of them began to evolve into or be superceded by more modern blues combos. By the end of the 1930s the jug itself had largely been replaced by the one-string bass or a standard upright bass. Although most of the musicians had rural backgrounds, jug bands were heard especially in cities of the South and border states, and groups from Memphis, Louisville, Dallas, Birmingham, and Cincinnati made recordings. Among the outstanding bands were the Memphis Jug Band and Gus Cannon's Jug Stompers from Memphis and the Louisville groups led by Clifford Hayes and Earl McDonald. These bands performed mostly blues and bluesy rags, often mixed with humor and generally lighter in theme than other types of country blues. They were equally popular with black and white audiences, performing on city streets and serenading in residential neighborhoods as well as playing for minstrel and medicine shows, sporting events, private parties, excursions, and store sales.

String bands and washboard bands were variations on the same idea, simply featuring a different emblematic instrument. Other similar acoustic combinations were called juke bands (from the "juke houses" where they performed), skiffle bands, and spasm bands (from the informal, spasmodic, "pick-up" quality of their performances). Bands of this sort had virtually died out in African-American music by the early 1960s, and only a few were documented on recordings since that time. The predominantly white blues revival, however, at this time included an interest in jug bands, which led to the formation of new groups. Some of these evolved into rock bands such as the Lovin' Spoonful and the Grateful Dead. In Great Britain a similar skiffle band movement saw offshoots in the Beatles, Rolling Stones, and other groups.

Jump Blues: This was a small ensemble style that mixed jazz and blues elements and instrumentation. Five to seven pieces was a typical size, and guitar was not so prominent as a lead instrument, but instead piano and brass instruments were featured. The repertoire was mostly blues, but the musicians sometimes tried to simulate the section work of the larger big bands in the jazz field. Many of the musicians in jump bands

were, in fact, jazz players who simply could find more work in
this blues setting. These bands typically played for dancers in
urban clubs and lounges and featured a vocalist in the blues
shouter style.

Prototype groups began to form in the mid-1930s, such as
the Harlem Hamfats (rhythm guitar, second guitar or mandolin, trumpet, clarinet, upright bass, piano, and drums),
Tampa Red and the Chicago Five (one or two guitars, kazoo,
clarinet or trumpet, tenor saxophone, piano, and upright bass
or drums), and Big Bill and the Memphis Five (two guitars,
trumpet, alto saxophone, piano, and upright bass or drums).
Perhaps the first true jump band was Louis Jordan and His
Tympany Five (alto and tenor saxophones, trumpet, piano, upright bass, and drums—note the absence of a guitar), which
first recorded at the end of 1938. The style gained its greatest
popularity on the West Coast, especially the Los Angeles area,
in the 1940s and into the early 1950s, many of the players having migrated there from Texas and midwestern cities. A
boogie-woogie bass line played on the piano and a honking saxophone were important parts of the sound of these units. Besides Louis Jordan's group, other prominent jump bands
featured or were led by Jay McShann, Joe Liggins, Roy Milton,
Eddie "Cleanhead" Vinson, Big Jay McNeely, Tiny Bradshaw,
Bullmoose Jackson, and Johnny Otis. *See also* Blues Shouters,
Rhythm and Blues, and West Coast Blues.

Mississippi Blues: *See* Deep South Blues.

Modern Blues: *See* Contemporary Blues.

New Orleans Blues: New Orleans has always hosted many
varieties of blues and other types of music, most notably jazz.
The term *New Orleans Blues*, however, usually refers to a type
of rhythm and blues that reached its peak from the late 1940s

through the 1960s but has been kept alive through the present day by tourism and local musical pride. Jazz elements are an important part of the New Orleans blues sound, and the piano and brass instruments are especially prominent. Pianists Fats Domino, Professor Longhair, James Booker, and Doctor John, along with trumpet player and band leader Dave Bartholomew, have been some of the most important artists in this style, but guitarists like Smiley Lewis and Earl King have also achieved success. Afro-Caribbean rumba rhythms, Mardi Gras parade beats, and the two-line eight-bar form give many of the blues in this style a distinctive sound, as does the New Orleans accent of the singers. New Orleans blues was a major ingredient in rock and roll up to 1964, when the British Invasion, rooted more in Chicago blues, became the dominant element. *See also* Rhythm and Blues.

Piedmont Blues: *See* East Coast Blues.

Postwar Blues: Literally this term refers to all blues since World War Two, but acoustic country blues from this era are often excluded from the category. The presence of an electric guitar is thus often a determinant of this style, and it is the main thing that the various types of Postwar Blues have in common. The actual dividing line occurred during the war, from mid1942 to the end of 1944 when the Musician's Union instituted a ban on recording, thereby disrupting the flow of blues records. The war itself was another disrupting factor, creating movement of people through the military draft and the lure of jobs in the defense industry as well as stimulating new musical styles.

Prewar Blues: This term refers to all styles of blues that came into existence up to 1942 as well as their extensions into later years. Country blues is the main prewar style to have survived to recent times.

Rhythm and Blues: Rhythm and Blues was a music and record industry term that came into use at the end of the 1940s to designate all types of music popular among African Americans. Instrumental jazz and gospel, however, are usually excluded. The term has remained in use, although alternative terms such as soul music, urban music, or simply black music have been introduced. Rhythm and Blues suggests blues and something more, and that something has been blues-influenced music, whether it be ballads, pop tunes, soul anthems, funk, or disco. Many artists, such as Ray Charles, Fats Domino, James Brown, Bobby Bland, Johnnie Taylor, Little Milton, Dinah Washington, Etta James, and Ruth Brown, have straddled the line between blues and these other musical forms, often serving as influential role models for younger artists. Rhythm and Blues, and music derived from it that was played by white performers, became the main ingredients in early rock and roll. *See also* Jump Blues, New Orleans Blues, and West Coast Blues.

Rural Blues: *See* Country Blues.

Soul Blues: This term refers to a pleading, highly emotional, melismatic vocal style, influenced by gospel singing and sometimes featuring gospel mannerisms such as falsetto or a rough, gravelly quality. Although one could point to antecedents in singers like Son House and Doctor Clayton, the style really came into its own in the 1950s in the work of artists like B.B. King, Bobby "Blue" Bland, and Ray Charles. Soul Blues grew in popularity in the 1960s and the style was applied increasingly to songs outside the blues form. This range of songs came to be known as soul music. Soul Blues has continued to be the most popular style of blues with black American audiences to the present day. It is also popular with non-black audiences, especially when coupled with a prominent electric lead guitar.

South Side Blues: *See* Chicago Blues.

Swamp Blues: This is a style that arose in and around Baton Rouge, Louisiana, in the mid-1950s and remained popular through the 1960s. The term *swamp* comes both from the association of the state of Louisiana with swamps and the reverb-heavy, "swampy" sound of the music. It is best exemplified by the recordings of Lightnin' Slim, Slim Harpo, Lazy Lester, and Silas Hogan, and typically features a harmonica and electric guitar with some minimal percussion. Other instruments are sometimes added, but the sound is usually rather spare though made bigger through the use of reverb. In many respects it resembles early Chicago Blues, and indeed one of the great influences on this style was Chicago-area artist Jimmy Reed. Other influences came from the postwar Texas Blues of artists like Lightnin' Hopkins, postwar Deep South Blues, and New Orleans Rhythm and Blues.

Talking Blues: This term refers to two different phenomena. One is a set of humorous or ironic spoken verses set to rhythmic guitar strumming. This style was popularized by southern white country artists such as Chris Bouchillon in the 1920s and Woody Guthrie in the 1940s. The term is also associated with black artists delivering a monologue over a melodic guitar or piano accompaniment. It has especially been encountered among Country Blues artists from Louisiana such as Robert Pete Williams.

Texas Blues: This term is used to represent a country blues stylistic region that includes East Texas and adjacent sections of Louisiana and Oklahoma. As with Deep South blues and East Coast blues, it is most applicable to solo guitar–accompanied performances. There are actually two different styles found in the region. One features a steady rhythmic beat played on a single bass note or chord, often muffled, overlaid with melodic figures in a higher register. Henry Thomas, Leadbelly, Mance Lipscomb, and Li'l Son Jackson recorded many songs in this style. The other Texas style is more free-form and less rhythmic, featuring long hornlike lines and blue notes created by string bending. Blind Lemon Jefferson and Lightnin' Hopkins represent this style. It was an important precursor to modern electric lead guitar within an ensemble. The term *Texas Blues* is also sometimes used to describe the jazz-influenced lead electric guitar sound of artists from that state, both black and white, such as T-Bone Walker, Pee Wee Crayton, Gatemouth Brown, Lowell Fulson (actually from Oklahoma), Freddie King, Albert Collins, Johnny Copeland, Johnny Winter, Stevie Ray Vaughan, and Anson Funderburgh.

Urban Blues: "Urban" has become a code word for "black," and this term simply encompasses the postwar blues by black artists in the styles of contemporary blues, soul blues, jump blues, Chicago blues, New Orleans blues, and West Coast blues. Its equivalent prior to World War II would be City Blues.

Vaudeville Blues: Formerly called Classic Blues, this term refers to the style of blues performed on the vaudeville stage in black urban communities in the 1910s and 1920s and to a limited extent thereafter. The style only began to be recorded in 1920. Most of the singers were female, although a few men such as Frankie "Half Pint" Jaxon became stars. There were also male-female duos in the style, such as Butterbeans and Susie, who alternated verses in a dramatic "battles of the sexes" format. The songs of the female singers were often composed by male songwriters, who also sometimes served as managers and piano accompanists or band leaders. The accompaniment was provided by a piano, sometimes with one or two wind instruments played by jazz musicians, or by a jazz combo of five or more pieces. Many of the songs were introduced within dramatic skits or shows that were staged at theaters in black urban communities. Among the earliest recorded stars in this style were Mamie Smith, Lucille Hegamin, Trixie Smith, Ethel Waters, and Alberta Hunter. In 1923 a new wave of southern Vaudeville Blues singers began to make records, including Bessie Smith, Ma Rainey, Ida Cox, Sara Martin, Clara Smith, Sippie Wallace, and Victoria Spivey. The Great Depression, which began at the end of the 1920s, made it impossible to sustain the touring circuit that had supported this style of blues. Many of the stars retired in the 1930s or scaled down to tent shows, cabaret acts, and local theater appearances.

West Coast Blues: This term simply refers to the sound of African-American blues shouters (and crooners) and jump blues in California during the 1940s and 1950s. Many of these artists continued to perform up to recent times.

West Side Blues: *See* Chicago Blues.

White Blues: This term is inadequate to describe any particular blues style, although it is sometimes used to cover a range of styles by white artists since the 1960s including acoustic blues, blues-rock, and British blues.

Zydeco: This odd term is the result of a phonetic spelling of the French word for green beans: *les haricots*. It came to be applied to a type of music from the widely used song lyric, *'s haricots sont pas salés* (The beans are not salty). This phrase suggests a state of extreme poverty, and thus Zydeco can be viewed as poor people's music. It arose around 1950 in cities of southeast Texas, especially Houston, among Creole migrants from rural southern Louisiana, most of whom were bilingual in English and French. Some of the songs are sung in Creole French or a mixture of the two languages.

Zydeco has two main sources. One is the older Creole folk music of rural Louisiana consisting of French folksongs and dance tunes, such as reels and waltzes, performed on button accordion and/or fiddle with washboard accompaniment. This music was quite similar to that of the neighboring white Cajun population in the same region. The other major ingredient was the blues, introduced to the region from the music of English-speaking black Americans. In the 1920s and 1930s these two traditions began to mix, forming a hybrid prototype of Zydeco. As migrants from Louisiana left the region, especially in the 1940s, to settle in urban Texas communities, this blended music became modernized. The more versatile piano accordion, usually played with amplification, was substituted for the older button type, and the washboard became the *frottoir*, a corrugated aluminum vest worn over the player's neck or shoulders. Drums, electric guitar, and various other blues instruments were added, but the accordion remained the primary lead instrument and emblematic symbol of this distinctive music.

Clifton Chenier is largely responsible for developing and popularizing Zydeco in the early 1950s. From Texas cities the style quickly spread back to southern Louisiana and to cities on the West Coast where other Creoles had migrated. It has been carried on by artists such as Boozoo Chavis, Rockin' Dopsie, John Delafose, and Buckwheat Zydeco. Today Zydeco is one of the most thriving blues styles still strongly rooted in tradition. This is thanks to its infectious dance rhythms popular with both Creole and nonCreole audiences, tourism to Louisiana, local promotion of the music as a cultural asset, and a raised Creole consciousness that views this music as a cultural symbol.

FOUR

Blues Deconstructed

What does blues music sound like? What characteristics allow us to call a tune a blues and not something else? There are no simple answers, because blues overlaps with, influences, and is influenced by so many other forms of music. Perhaps the best approach is to identify the qualities that first captured the attention of Americans early in the twentieth century and served to distinguish blues from what had come before in popular music.

Blue Notes and the Blues Scale

Probably the most striking thing about the blues is its flexible treatment of pitch, melody, and scale. At certain points on the scale, especially the third and seventh degrees (*mi* and *ti*) but also sometimes at the fifth degree (*sol*) and elsewhere, singers and instrumentalists create so-called "blue notes." These occur variously as "neutral" pitches somewhere between the flat and natural pitches of those scale degrees, as flats where naturals might be expected, as waverings between flat and natural, or as upward slides from flat toward natural. Although these sorts of notes have long been found throughout African-American folk and popular music, it was through blues that they made a major impact on Western popular music, and it is appropriate that this genre has given them their name. They are now so commonplace in popular music as to be normal, but they were quite revolutionary early in the twentieth century. When a mainstream American audience first encountered blue notes, it often viewed them as deviations from normal notes and pitches. Blue notes were said to be "flattened," as if the singer or player deliberately distorted the normal or "correct" pitch. It is important not to think of blue notes in this way but instead to see them as typical expressions of the blues, a music whose scale contains certain flexible *pitch areas* rather than fixed pitches.

A full seven-note blues scale would thus consist of the tonic note (*do*), the second (*re*), the blue third (*mi*), the fourth (*fa*), the fifth (*sol*, sometimes a blue fifth), the sixth (*la*), and the blue seventh (*ti*). Many blues use fewer than seven notes, however, and five-note scales are particularly common. These are usually either tonic (*do*), blue third (*mi*), fourth (*fa*), fifth (*sol*, sometimes blue), and blue seventh (*ti*); or tonic (*do*), second (*re*), blue third (*mi*), fifth (*sol*), and sixth (*la*). In both types of five-note scale, the highest of these notes is frequently sung between the sixth (*la*) and flat seventh (*ti*). These blue pitches, as well as the quality of sliding or adjusting pitch (often to fit an implied harmony), stem from African concepts of pitch and scale, but blues musicians have found ways to play them on Western instruments and make them compatible with Western harmonic concepts, i.e., using them within "chords."

The Blues Form

Another striking thing about blues songs is the asymmetrical structure of their verse form. The majority of blues have a three-line structure, whereas most folk and popular songs had used a four-line structure or some other evenly balanced duple form (two, eight lines, etc.). The three lines of a typical blues stanza have an AAB arrangement. That is, the first line (A) is repeated, sometimes with a slight variation in the words (A'). The third and final line (B) is different yet rhymes or is assonant with the first two lines. For example:

A I'm going away to wear you off my mind.

A' I'm going away, baby, just to wear you off my mind.

B You keep me worried and bothered all the time.

Although some blues lines, such as the first and third above, have more or less an iambic pentameter metrical form when written out (five metrical feet, each short-long or unstressed-stressed, as in Shakespeare's plays and sonnets), they are almost never sung in such a mechanical way. The steady beat is kept by the instrumental accompaniment, while normally unstressed syllables are accented (or vice versa) by the singer, and words are rushed, held, or delayed to anticipate or follow the instrument's beat. Over the century or so of blues history, composers and singers have increasingly gotten away from the iambic pentameter model so that today it is scarcely recognizable. Most contemporary blues have more than this model's ten syllables per line.

A common variation on the AAB structure is to insert two rhymed lines into the space of the first A line. In such a case the last two lines become a refrain. Thus,

Got the hesitating stockings and the hesitating shoes.
I believe to my soul I got the hesitating blues.
Tell me how long do I have to wait?
Can I get you now, or must I hesitate?

The above lines, when written out, give the impression of a four-line structure, but when sung, the first two lines together occupy the same space and time as each of the last two.

There are also blues using two-line (AB) and four-line (AAAB) verse forms as well as some compound structures. Sometimes, especially when the verses are improvised on the spot, the A and B lines don't rhyme. The late John Lee Hooker, for example, made a specialty of this sort of free-verse composition. There are also examples of early folk blues where stanzas consist of only a single line repeated a number of times (e.g., AAA), and there are any number of blues that have exceptional, unique, or constantly varying verse structures.

The function of the repetition of the A line in blues stanzas is not, as has sometimes been asserted, to give the singer time to think up or remember a rhyming B line. Most A and B lines are sung from memory as single-stanza units. Instead, the repetition of the A line serves as a tension-creating buildup to the B line, which completes the thought of, answers, explains, justifies, expands, or offers a contrast to the A line. The A and B lines are thus a binary unit of thought. They do not usually present a narrative in a chronological sense. Nor is there usually a narrative thread from one stanza to the next. While many blues have a unity of mood or subject matter, many others contain contrasts of mood or opinion and juxtapose several seemingly disparate subjects. This sense of contrast and skipping around, whether between the A and B lines of a stanza, or from one stanza to the next in a song, or from one song to the next in a performance situation, is fundamental to a type of music rooted in dissatisfaction and dealing with life's temporary ups and downs. Rather than reflecting poor compositional technique, these lyric contrasts and juxtapositions reflect the essential meaning of the blues. Many blues, in fact, when analyzed as literary texts or poems, display a symmetrical structure, balancing opposite thoughts and alternative courses of action, rather than expressing one-way, linear thinking.

The Role of the Instrument(s)

A single line of blues normally occurs within four musical measures (or "bars"). Thus, the three-line AAB form would yield a twelve-bar blues. However, except in those cases like the previously mentioned "hesitating blues," where a rhymed pair of lines is forced into the space of a single line, the singing does not occupy the entire space of four bars. Instead, it ends a short way into the third bar, letting the instrumental accompaniment finish the four bars. This instrumental phrase completes or answers the preceding vocal portion of the line, acting as a second voice or commentary on the singing. Indeed, it maintains this role during the singing as well, punctuating the vocal line with single notes or short phrases, or playing a simultaneous variation of it (heterophony), or even offering a melodically contrasting line behind the singing. The instrumental portion of a blues is thus not merely a background to the singing. Although it keeps the beat and certainly offers rhythmic and some harmonic support to the vocal, it is essentially a second voice, or often several extra voices. It is, in fact, an integral part of the song itself and often provides the most memorable "signature" phrase of a blues. This elevation of the role of the instrumental part to something essential and to a status equal to that of the vocal part was something new in American popular song, something that the blues introduced. It stems from a widespread African understanding, preserved in African American tradition, of instruments as voices that "talk," as well as the typically African musical structural principle of call-and-response.

A blues song then, while appearing to be the vocal expression of one singer, actually has one or more additional voices, either generated by the singer on an instrument or by other players. A blues singer who plays an instrument will often state that he (or she) makes the instrument "say what I say." Both the human voice and the instrumental voice(s) are essential in a blues song. A purely vocal solo blues is usually either a field holler, and thus something functionally different from a real blues, or an amateur attempt by someone who can't play an instrument or doesn't have one handy. When an unaccompanied vocal group sings a blues, they usually imitate instrumental sounds with their voices. And when a purely instrumental blues is played, at least one instrument takes on the role of the singing voice.

Particularly among solo performers, where there is no need for several musicians to agree on a musical structure in advance, the instrumental portions of some four-bar lines may be shortened or extended, yielding such odd stanza lengths as eleven bars or thirteen and a half bars. It matters little for dancers or listeners as long as the performer keeps the beat and makes sense in the lyrics. By creating these variations the player often provides delightful surprises and breaks the monotony of an all-too-predictable form. One typical way of extending the standard four-bar line is to introduce a series of instrumental riffs following the vocal portion of the line. A riff is a short, repeated, melodic-rhythmic phrase, typically one measure or two measures in length. It can be repeated any number of times, creating an open-ended effect that breaks up the closed structure of the twelve-bar three-line blues or some other standard pattern. A riff can vary slightly melodically or rhythmically during its repetitions, and there can be two or more different riffs played in a song.

Riffs can also be played during the singing, and they can be incorporated into the standard twelve-bar structure and transposed according to its harmonic changes, as in the left-hand bass patterns of "boogie-woogie" piano blues. The riff is a fundamental concept of much African music and another contribution from that continent to the blues, as well as to much other American music.

Blues Harmony

The subject of blues harmony is a complex one and is plagued by many commonly held misunderstandings. In the first place, many blues really have no harmony, if by this one means chords and chord changes. Blues is usually sung by a single voice, and instruments often play single melodic lines, so that harmony is only suggested by the fact that vocal and instrumental lines happen to occur simultaneously. Chords become more noticeable when the instrumental texture is thickened, especially when the ensemble includes a keyboard instrument, a rhythm guitarist, and/or a horn section. Even then, these instruments often play a single melodic line in parallel. That is, they maintain a regular interval between two or more simultaneous renderings of an identical line. (Parallelism of this sort is a widely used African approach to harmony.)

There is, however, a harmonic pattern that is often sensed by listeners and musicians and that acts for them as a harmonic mental template. One "hears" this pattern in the mind even though it may be only suggested by a note here or there. Some blues conform to the pattern closely and really could be said to have "chord changes," while others conform barely or not at all. This pattern employs the tonic (I), subdominant (IV), and dominant (V) harmonies or chords and in its simplest form occurs as follows in the twelve-bar blues:

measure 1 (I) / measure 2 (I) / measure 3 (I) / measure 4 (I) /

measure 5 (IV) / measure 6 (IV) / measure 7 (I) / measure 8 (I) /

measure 9 (V) / measure 10 (V) / measure 11 (I) / measure 12 (I) /

There are many variations of this pattern, particularly due to jazz influence, as players modify these chords with added or substituted notes, or substitute other chords for them.

The harmonic pattern represented above contains a chord progression from tonic (measures 1–4) to subdominant (measures 5–6) to tonic (measures 7–8) to dominant (measures 9–10) to tonic (measures 11–12). This harmonic sequence (I–IV–I–V–I) has been in common use for several centuries in western music, and undoubtedly its presence in the blues harmonic template is to some degree part of this historical tradition of usage. It provides something familiar and satisfying to listeners and musicians steeped in the western musical tradition and no doubt is partly responsible for the acceptance and popularity of the blues in America and much of the world. This "western" quality of the blues is often deceiving, however. Blues musicians can be regularly heard subverting the pattern with additions, deletions, and substitutions of notes and chords. It will also be noted that each of the three lines of the pattern ends on the tonic chord for its instrumental response to the singing (measures 3–4, 7–8, 11–12). Indeed, two-thirds of the pattern's twelve measures are in the tonic chord. It is as if the musicians are constantly drawn back to this fundamental reference point. The dominant (V) chord that first appears in measure 9, at the beginning of the third line, is particularly problematical, and blues musicians use many devices to avoid expressing it fully. Often it is suggested only by a single note that fits within this chord, and its third degree is almost always sounded flat. More often than not, musicians substitute some expression of the subdominant (IV) chord in measure 10, making a quick escape from the dominant chord in the preceding measure.

Throughout the history of the blues there have been many pieces, including some that have three lines and twelve bars, whose harmony remains entirely within the tonic chord and others that use only the tonic and subdominant chords. Furthermore, when we examine the actual melodic and instrumental lines of the blues, we notice that many of them that are sounded during "changes" to the subdominant and dominant chords are simply transpositions of the same lines already heard with the tonic chord. Then again, sometimes the harmony offers the suggestion of a chord change, but the melodic or lead instrumental line stays the same. It is as if the musicians are constantly resisting the idea of "functional" harmony in the western sense and constantly trying to get back to a sound based simply in melodic progressions within a blues scale, progressions that can be transposed upward by a fourth to give the suggestion of a subdominant "chord," and with even greater reluctance upward by a fifth to give the suggestion of a dominant chord. This drawing back toward the basic blues scale and away from chord changes points blues toward the west African sources of its scale and of much of its style. Yet there is enough of a suggestion of western harmony in most blues to make the music distinctly African American and to allow for harmonic exploration to the degree that the musician desires. Anyone, however, who thinks that the blues has a simple structure that can be mastered merely by "playing the changes" is on the wrong track and is unlikely to produce any meaningful music.

Improvisation, Feeling, and Special Effects

Improvisation is another quality that has long impressed listeners of the blues. To a great extent, the improvisatory quality of jazz represents a blues influence, although jazz musicians have developed it to a much greater degree. It stems in part from the flexibility of blue notes and the need to find ways to express them on western instruments like the guitar and keyboard. The other great impetus for improvisation is blues' concentration on the present, the immediate moment of performance and the performer's feelings at the time. Seldom is a blues exactly the same from one performance to another. However, most of its improvisation is in the form of variation, and most blues have a more or less fixed set of lyrics and at least an outline of a distinct melody and instrumental part. Through the influence of jazz and rock music in recent decades, blues has become increasingly improvisatory, as musicians and singers try to distinguish themselves from the pack by emphasizing virtuosity and taking solos. Even in the early days of blues, however, there was some improvisation, particularly in the lyrics, as singers would draw from a large body of traditional verses and rhymed pairs of lines to put together songs on the spot. Some singers, such as John Lee Hooker, Lightnin' Hopkins, Robert Pete Williams, and Bukka White, were able to make up blues spontaneously with completely original lyrics, although they sometimes had to sacrifice rhyme in order to do so. By and large, the ability to improvise lyrics on the spot has been greatly diminished in the blues today, while improvisation has increased on the melodic and instrumental side.

Whatever the degree of planning, deliberate composition, and memorization that goes into a blues, the music is still essentially a performer's art. The greatest of compositions fall flat if they are not performed with real feeling. Blues explores a wide range of human emotions, drawing them out from the lyrics and musical lines. It is full of changes, surprises, ambiguities, and contrasts, some subtle and some quite dramatic, reflecting these qualities as they exist in daily life itself. It also explores a broad range of musical resources, techniques, and sound qualities. Rhythms may shift between a duple and triple feeling, or have an intermediate, ambivalent quality often described as "swing" or "shuffle." Voices range from a rough growl to a clear falsetto. Melodic instruments are played percussively and vice versa. There is no correct way to sound, and no type of sound is automatically forbidden. This openness and exploration of sound quality is typical of most African music and stands in contrast to the aesthetic of much of western music, particularly classical music, where certain ways of singing and certain qualities of sound on an instrument are idealized and others discouraged.

Among the most distinctive techniques in the blues are those used for making blue notes on instruments. Guitarists "bend" notes upward by pushing a string across the neck toward an adjacent string. They can also bend and vary pitches by using the technique of sliding a pocketknife held in the left hand over the strings, or a bottleneck, small bottle, or metal tube worn on a finger. This technique also adds a percussive quality to the sound. Other percussive effects are achieved by slapping or knocking on the body of the guitar, snapping the strings against the neck, or hammering or pulling off a string with a finger immediately after the string is played. Electric guitarists have added reverb, distortion, feedback, and wah-wah effects, creating many new sounds on the instrument. Most of the special effects of rock lead guitar were, in fact, pioneered by blues players. Harmonica players usually play the instrument in a key other than the one it is manufactured for, and they use special blowing techniques to bend notes, and cupping, tapping, and tonguing techniques to achieve percussive effects. Saxophone players use a similar range of techniques, and horn players often are masters at manipulating mutes. The piano is a less flexible instrument, because its strings are not touched directly by the player, and thus their pitch cannot be altered. Despite this limitation, blues pianists have developed a remarkable array of special percussive effects, and they suggest blue notes by playing the flat and natural pitches of a scale degree in quick sequence, rapid alternation, or simultaneously in different registers and within different musical lines.

Blues Ensembles

The guitar, harmonica, and piano are the premier instruments of the blues, and all have been played in solo performance. Other instruments are played only in ensembles. Traditionally, blues bands were highly egalitarian. Every instrument had a distinct role and was meant to be heard clearly. Often many or all members of a band shared the vocal duties, and many bands had a collective identity. With the growing emphasis on virtuoso display, influenced by jazz and rock aesthetics, blues bands have become more hierarchical, with the focus shifting to the star vocalist or player of a "lead" instrument, while the other members play supporting roles.

The Lyrics

Blues displays an intense concentration on the momentary feelings of the singer, or more accurately, the persona portrayed by the singer, i.e., the dramatized self. It incorporates and symbolizes a heightened sense of individualism, economic uncertainty, alienation from society, family, and community, and escape from problems through erotic activity, violence, gambling, drinking, and travel. Blues started as an "underground" and sometimes "underworld" or "outlaw" type of music, much despised by more respectable segments of society, who nevertheless often found it fascinating or titillating. It arose within an environment of massive racial oppression, which tended to intensify all these other qualities. Blues artists were not simply society's lower class but were part of a segregated low caste. Although blues has gained greatly in social respectability in recent years and racial oppression has eased, some of these qualities of alienation and escape still persist, and the stance of the singer is still highly individualistic.

No American popular song genre has displayed quite the degree of frankness and self-revelation as the blues does. Blues singers make themselves vulnerable as well as available to their audiences. Although themes of sadness, death, failure, drinking, and underworld activity had been addressed in earlier popular song, their treatment was always moralistic, sentimental, nostalgic, tragic, maudlin, or even comic. Blues has dispensed with all these interpretations and attitudes and addresses its subject matter head-on, offering deeper understanding but no permanent fixes. It gives American popular culture a much-needed dose of realism, tempered with irony, humor, and the ever-present possibility of change.

By far the main subject matter of blues songs is the relationship of man to woman: love, its pleasures and problems, rivalries, deceits, and conquests, sexual desire and sexual activity, boasting, praise, and verbal abuse of a partner. The songs are typically performed in settings that represent these themes, where men and women come with one another or singly in order to meet potential partners, where dancing can occur as an enactment of romantic relationships or as a display directed at others. The lyrics are aimed sometimes at the audience, at other times toward someone of the opposite sex who is not necessarily present, and they can be in the first, second, or third person. But even when they are directed toward someone else or toward the audience or when they describe the behavior of someone else, they deal with relationships of the singer toward these other parties and are delivered from the singer's point of view. Relationships are usually described as temporary, recently established, or under threat of breakup. Wives, husbands, and children are rarely mentioned, and mothers and fathers are usually described as deceased or somehow estranged from the singer. "Mama," "Papa," "Daddy," and "Baby" are, in fact, most often terms given to lovers, not family members of a different generation. By far the most frequent characters in blues are the singer and his or her lover, and an enormous amount of imagery and double meaning is used in the blues to describe romantic and sexual activity, much of it drawn from daily life and the world of nature and animals. Typical song titles like "Honey Bee," "Rootin' Ground Hog," "My Kitchen Mechanic," and "Something's Wrong with My Little Machine" give a sense of this imagery.

Other topics of blues songs include work or lack thereof, resulting in poverty; wanderlust and travel, often to escape from a bad relationship, poverty, or an unpleasant work situation; violence (often domestic), crime, the courtroom, and jail; luck, gambling, magic, and sorcery (hoodoo); drinking and drug use; sickness and death; and topical events as they affect the singer. The latter include natural disasters such as floods and tornados, wars, depressions, recessions, inflation, political programs and activities that affect the singer's daily life, and local events. These topical themes are typically related somehow to the man-woman relationship. For example, a flood separates a man and a woman, or a man goes to war to keep the enemy from slipping through his baby's back door! Religious topics are mostly left to spirituals or gospel songs, although occasionally blues singers express concern over the state of their souls. One might expect that African-American singers would compose a great number of blues about incidents of racial oppression or the system in general. There are such blues, but by and large the subject lies in the background of the other problems that are dealt with in the songs. Racial oppression, at least up to the 1960s when the Civil Rights movement achieved important victories, exerted overwhelming pressure on all the other problems described in the blues songs. One doesn't have to look far to encounter its effects in blues lyrics. It would have been dangerous for a singer to mention it directly, however, in the early years of the blues, especially in the South. A few singers, such as Josh White, Leadbelly, Big Bill Broonzy, and J. B. Lenoir, did discuss the subject in a number of songs, but usually only after they had achieved some success with sympathetic northern white audiences. Singers didn't really need to mention it overtly to black audiences, as they knew all about it.

For most of its history blues have reflected a working-class African-American secular lifestyle, rooted in southern rural experience, including racial oppression, but incorporating the transition to urban life. As blues has gained popularity with white American and international audiences, particularly since the 1960s, it has mostly continued to deal with the man-woman relationship, often to the exclusion of other themes, but some recent blues lyrics reflect the problems of middle-class existence and a more cosmopolitan outlook on the world. The themes of blues, and even its typical rhetoric, have had an enormous influence on other forms of popular music, particularly country and western music and rock and roll. One hears many reflections of them as well in more recent forms of music such as rap. This influence goes hand in hand with the formal and stylistic influence of the blues as musical sound.

FIVE

The Performers

M ost of the artists whose careers and music are described here would make anyone's list of the top two hundred or so figures in blues history. The problem lies in narrowing the list to a small number to highlight in this chapter. There are many artists who performed with equal brilliance to those mentioned here but who simply did not leave a large recorded legacy or who had little influence on the development of blues. Others were technically outstanding but not particularly innovative. Yet others were immensely popular in their day but achieved their popularity because they were well promoted or because their music represented a common denominator of taste.

In general, the artists listed in this chapter are widely regarded as great in their particular styles and influential on the blues tradition as a whole. They also left a substantial body of recordings, at least enough to fill a complete CD. All had a distinct sound and were innovators in their styles or as songwriters. Their music was also mostly consistent in quality over the course of their careers. The blues listener won't go wrong in purchasing any of their recordings.

Inevitably, a brief chapter such as this fails to include a number of artists of equal, if not greater, stature than the sixty who are profiled here. In the field of country blues one should definitely check out the music of Blind Blake, Tommy Johnson, Sleepy John Estes, Furry Lewis, Mance Lipscomb, Big Joe Williams, Josh White, the Memphis Jug Band, and the Mississippi Sheiks. Peetie Wheatstraw, Memphis Slim, Jimmy Yancey, and Albert Ammons were among the outstanding early blues pianists. Vaudeville blues singers especially worth investigating are Ethel Waters, Rosa Henderson, Victoria Spivey, Clara Smith, Mamie Smith, Butterbeans and Susie, and Frankie Jaxon. Important urban blues stylists of the 1930s include Lucille Bogan, Lil Green, Kokomo Arnold, Washboard Sam, Doctor Clayton, and the Harlem Hamfats. Among shouters, crooners, and performers with jump bands one would have to consider Jimmy McCracklin, Roy Brown, Cousin Joe, Cecil Gant, Wynonie Harris, Ivory Joe Hunter, Percy Mayfield, Bullmoose Jackson, Nellie Lutcher, Julia Lee, Big Jay McNeely, Amos Milburn, Roy Milton, Johnny Otis, Eddie "Cleanhead" Vinson, and Jimmy Witherspoon. Chicago blues artists include Otis Spann, Earl Hooker, J. B. Lenoir, Luther Allison, Johnny Shines, Magic Sam, Otis Rush, and Jimmy Rogers. Among electric down-home blues artists one should consider Doctor Ross, Li'l Son Jackson, R. L. Burnside, Junior Kimbrough, Jessie Mae Hemphill, and Willie King. Contemporary and soul blues artists would include Clarence "Gatemouth" Brown, Albert Collins, Guitar Slim, Freddy King, Little Milton, Junior Parker, Lowell Fulson, and Rufus Thomas. Important artists on the border of blues and rock and roll or soul music are Lavern Baker, Ruth Brown, Denise LaSalle, Little Richard, Fats Domino, James Brown, Ike Turner, Chuck Willis, and Elvis

Presley. Finally, in the blues revival field one should not over-look Johnny Winter, Paul Butterfield, Mike Bloomfield, John Mayall, Alexis Korner, Taj Mahal, Robert Cray, Bonnie Raitt, ZZ Top, Jo Ann Kelly, and Guy Davis.

Chuck Berry (b. 1926): Although he is widely viewed as one of the founding fathers of rock and roll, virtually all of the music that Chuck Berry has created is solidly based in the blues. Indeed, most of his best work occurred in the late 1950s and early 1960s, a time when rock and roll, especially as performed by African-American musicians, was little more than the latest phase of the blues. Berry was raised in St. Louis, learned guitar in the 1940s, and began playing locally. His playing was greatly influenced by the jazzy guitar style of the popular "T-Bone" Walker and the rhythms of boogie-woogie piano, especially as played by his longtime keyboard partner Johnny Johnson. Expanding his circuit to Chicago, he first recorded there in 1955 for Chess Records at the recommendation of their biggest blues star, Muddy Waters. His instrumentation was the classic Chicago lineup of electric guitar, piano, bass, and drums, lacking only the harmonica that would have given him a more down-home sound. He would keep this lineup for most of his career, establishing it as a model for many rock and roll bands. One side of his first record was a slow blues, "Wee Wee Hours," based on a 1937 record by bluesman Bill Gaither and featuring Johnson's spectacular piano. It was the other side, however, "Maybelline," that proved to be the hit. It too was based on a blues tune from the 1930s, the Harlem Ham-fats' "Oh! Red," with added musical material from the similarly titled country fiddle tune "Ida Red," all set to a fast, walking boogie beat. The recitative lyrics highlighting automobiles and male adolescent lust were sure to appeal to the newly developing rock and roll audience, and the record shot to number one on both the rhythm and blues and pop charts.

Over the remainder of the decade Berry produced one great song after another, painting a portrait that has never been bettered of the lifestyle of carefree teenagers and young adults of the era. During the 1950s Chuck Berry worked on many rock and roll package shows, playing for white and integrated audiences of young people, always impressing with his energy and stage showmanship. By 1965 Berry was recording collaborations with British and American blues-rock performers and falling into the role of godfather of rock. All of the adulation seemed to dry up most of his creativity, however, especially as a songwriter, and he continued to recreate his old hits. He did live shows of often mediocre quality, demanding his payment up front and working with unrehearsed pickup bands whom he expected to know all of his classic hits. Despite this long and disappointing decline, his place in blues and rock and roll history is secure through the great music he created in the first ten years of his recording career.

Big Maybelle (1924–1972): Mabel Smith wore the title of "Big" proudly and had a voice to match her size. She could belt and growl with the best of the male blues shouters of the 1940s and 1950s, but she could also sing sweetly on slow and sentimental numbers or move between the two styles in a song. Her voice was utterly distinctive and was shaped by her early background in gospel music in her hometown of Jackson, Tennessee. She had ambitions for popular success, however, and left home as a teenager to work as a vocalist with big bands, including the all-female Sweethearts of Rhythm. Her first recording was made in 1944 with Christine Chatman's jump band. Band vocalists often worked in obscurity and had a hard time establishing their own identity independent of the band or its leader. She didn't record again until 1947, this time with the band of trumpeter Hot Lips Page, featuring Lonnie Johnson on guitar. Mabel Smith became

Big Maybelle on the Okeh label in 1952, and she finally had major commercial success with "Gabbin' Blues" and "My Country Man." During the 1950s she toured on the rhythm and blues circuit and was especially popular with the notoriously critical audiences at New York City's Apollo Theater. During this time, or perhaps earlier, she developed a heroin addiction. In 1956 she switched to the Savoy label and recorded "Candy," a song widely interpreted as referring to the drug. In 1958 she appeared with a group of veteran musicians at the Newport Jazz Festival, gaining crossover success with white audiences, and in the following year she recorded a tribute album to the recently deceased W. C. Handy. In the 1960s she performed variously for jazz and rhythm and blues audiences but also made inroads in the rock and roll field. Switching to the Rojac label and billed as "America's Queen Mother of Soul," she had an unlikely hit in 1967 with a cover of "96 Tears" by ? and the Mysterians. Her drug habit and diabetes began to get the best of her in the late 1960s, but she continued making good recordings, finally recording an album of old spirituals in 1968, four years before her death.

Bobby "Blue" Bland (b. 1930): Although he has occasionally dropped the nickname "Blue," Bobby Bland has never dropped the blues in a career remarkable for its longevity and sustained level of success. This success has occurred almost entirely with black audiences, for as a non-instrumentalist he fails to match the image of the male blues singer held by most white fans of the music. If they don't pay attention to him, however, they are missing one of the great voices of the blues. Bland was born and raised in the country, north of Memphis, and moved to the big city at the age of seventeen. His ambition was to become a sophisticated pop singer like Perry Como or Nat "King" Cole, and he regularly participated in amateur contests at the Palace Theatre on Beale Street along with other future stars such as

B. B. King, Little Junior Parker, Rosco Gordon, and Johnny Ace. Here he had a chance to sing with a big band, and this became his preferred format for most of his career. He began recording in 1951 for local producer Sam Phillips, but his first releases had little commercial success. He sounded like a blues shouter but with elements of lead gospel singing and rural field hollers, along with falsetto cries. With Gordon and Ace, he joined the Duke label in 1952, but his career was interrupted by two years of military service. It was only after he returned to Duke in 1955 that his career began to take off, starting with a hit recording of "It's My Life, Baby." In 1957 he had a much bigger hit with "Farther up the Road," in which the gospel influence in his singing was more apparent. Along with B. B. King, Ray Charles, and James Brown, Bland was pioneering in what would eventually be called "soul" singing. He would start a song in a sincere, intimate tone of voice and build up to an explosive outburst that often could only be shut down by an extended fade-out. From this point on, through the end of the 1960s, Bland was unstoppable on the rhythm and blues charts, in what was otherwise a period of declining popularity for the blues genre among black listeners. Among his great hits were "I'll Take Care of You," "Who Will the Next Fool Be," and "Chains of Love," along with remakes of old blues standards, "Stormy Monday Blues" and "Driftin' Blues." After more than fifty years in show business, he is still able to draw loyal fans to the record stores and to his concerts, which are increasingly for audiences of retirees on the southern casino circuit.

Bo Diddley (b. 1928): As a child he was known as Otha Bates and Ellas McDaniel, but as a man he became Bo Diddley, a name that he has immortalized. He is one of the great rhythmic innovators of American popular music, the composer of many clever songs that have become blues and rock standards, and is one of the few blues artists to create a stage persona that is better known than the man behind it. He was born in Mississippi but raised in Chicago, where he played guitar and sang on the streets in the 1940s. His recording debut came in 1955 with a spectacular double-sided hit, "I'm a Man" and "Bo Diddley." The former track was straight Chicago electric blues with guitar, harmonica, piano, bass, and drums, featuring an insistent riff and lyrics announcing his prowess as a lover along with imagery of hoodoo and magic. The other side was a celebration of his own character, with lyrics drawn from a children's lullaby, a beat sounding like an African percussion time line, tremolo-laden guitar, and maracas to give it all a Latin flavor. Nothing like it had been recorded until then. He continued to work in both of these styles, drawing on a rich imagination and the deep well of African-American folklore to produce classics throughout the remainder of the 1950s and early 1960s, such as "Diddley Daddy," "Diddy Wah Diddy," "Who Do You Love," "Hey! Bo Diddley," and "You Can't Judge a Book By Its Cover." For a time he was a major star of early rock and roll, but by the late 1960s he was being relegated to an oldies circuit, undeservedly because he was still creating good original material. He tried to catch onto various musical fads and trends—surf music, soul, psychedelic rock, funk, and guest star collaborations—but never with the same degree of commercial success that he experienced in the 1950s. He has continued to work as an oldies act, write wonderful songs, and make recordings, some of them self-produced, and almost every Bo Diddley effort contains something worthwhile by this most original of American musical personalities. Although many artists have covered his greatest songs, no one has matched his musical vision with the same level of talent.

Big Bill Broonzy (1898–1958): This genial singer-guitarist became for a time the biggest star in recorded blues, then helped pave the way for the music's future development, before ending his career as a symbol of the old "down-home" folk blues. Broonzy was born in the Mississippi Delta and raised across the river in Arkansas. His first instrument was the violin, and in his youth he played around Arkansas at clubs, picnics, and country suppers. After military service during World War I, he found himself in Chicago and became attracted to blues guitar, influenced by recording stars Papa Charlie Jackson and Blind Blake. His recording career began in 1927, and popular success came slowly at first. A number of his early recordings were ragtime and hokum workouts featuring his deft guitar work, such as "House Rent Stomp" and "Skoodle Do Do." Through the 1930s Broonzy incorporated more elements of Deep South blues style into his guitar work, and his warm voice and songwriting skills made his records increasingly popular. His songs treated down-home topics, such as "Bull Cow Blues," "Mississippi River Blues," and "Black Mare Blues," but often from the standpoint of someone who was slightly distanced from them and happily settled in Chicago. On his records he collaborated with other Chicago-based stars, such as pianists Black Bob, Blind John Davis, Joshua Altheimer, and Memphis Slim, harmonica player jazz Gillum, and his alleged half-brother Washboard Sam. By the late 1930s he was using an electric guitar, forming small jazz-influenced combos, and developing a sound pointing toward a modern electric blues ensemble. An appearance at the 1938 "From Spirituals to Swing" concert at Carnegie Hall brought him to the attention of a jazz revival audience, and he would exploit this connection toward the end of the following decade, stepping into the role of the primitive southern bluesman and folk singer, performing solo, and adopting a repertoire of old blues standards and folksongs such as "John Henry" and "Blue Tail Fly." He also composed and recorded protest songs, such as "Black, Brown, and White" and "When Do I Get to Be Called a Man." In the

1950s Broonzy made several tours in Europe and played a great part in popularizing the blues there and helping to launch the British skiffle movement. Broonzy settled in Holland and married, but he returned to Chicago when he was diagnosed with lung cancer, and died there in 1958.

Charles Brown (1922–1999): Classically trained on the piano and probably the first blues artist to have a college degree, Charles Brown remained a model of sophistication throughout his long career. He was born in Texas City, Texas, and taught high school briefly before relocating to the west coast in 1943. He recorded the following year as pianist and vocalist with guitarist Johnny Moore's Three Blazers. He soon emerged as the group's star with "Drifting Blues," a huge hit in 1945. Brown sang in a lisping voice and played soft, tinkly piano, creating an "after-hours" mood, rather like a bluesier version of Nat "King" Cole. He continued to have hits as a member of Moore's group, including "Merry Christmas, Baby" in 1947, a song that continues to receive radio airplay every Christmas season to the present day. The following year he began to record under his own name and soon had hits with "Trouble Blues" and a remake of Leroy Carr's "In the Evening When the Sun Goes Down." In the early 1950s he scored again with "Black Night" and "Hard Times." Soon, however, a harder, guitar-centered blues sound began to overtake him, and the hits stopped. He continued recording and in 1960 revisited the Christmas theme to have a hit with "Please Come Home for Christmas." He soldiered on through the 1960s with only modest success, often emphasizing the Christmas theme and getting plenty of work every December. The 1970s and 1980s were lean years, but in the 1990s his career took a turn for the better, as Bonnie Raitt employed him as an opening act and he recorded a series of successful albums for Rounder Records. The blues revival audience had grown sophisticated enough to develop a taste for Brown's smooth sound. He had lost nothing over fifty years, and shortly before he passed away he was sounding as good as he had in the 1940s.

Canned Heat (founded 1966): One of the most successful white blues bands of the 1960s, this group popularized the concept of "boogie music," based on the older sounds of John Lee Hooker and other early Deep South stylists. Organized in Los Angeles, three of the group's founding members, Bob Hite, Alan Wilson, and Henry Vestine, were serious blues record collectors and historians. Their interest in and knowledge of prewar and acoustic blues made the group unusual among white electric bands of the era, most of whose influences began with Chicago Blues of the 1950s. Canned Heat not only drew upon early blues for song material, but they often placed its rhythms and other musical elements at the center of their band arrangements. Wilson, who had already recorded on Son House's rediscovery debut album on harmonica and guitar, was the member most responsible for keeping the band close to the roots of the blues. Their 1967 album, *Canned Heat*, drew about equally from prewar and postwar sources. "Catfish Blues," "The Road Song," and "Rich Woman" were portents of the extended one-chord workouts that would soon make the group famous. Their *Boogie with Canned Heat* album from 1968 revealed a fully mature sound and contained more singing by Wilson, who displayed a distinctive high reedy voice. His "On the Road Again" became a major pop hit. Along with the instrumental "Fried Hockey Boogie," it introduced a variation on a guitar boogie riff created by John Lee Hooker, played here by Wilson and bassist Larry Taylor. Their follow-up album the same year, *Living the Blues*, contained another hit vocal by Wilson, "Going up the Country," based on an early recording by Texas bluesman Henry Thomas, which became virtually the theme song of the famed Woodstock festival. In 1970 they released *Future Blues*, featuring the hit song "Let's Work Together." That year they also released *Hooker 'n' Heat*, a collaboration with their idol John Lee Hooker and one of the best efforts of this sort during the period. Unfortunately, Wilson died under somewhat mysterious circumstances later that year. Under Bob Hite's leadership the group carried on, but its popularity declined through the 1970s, and in 1981, Hite died. Drummer Fito de la Parra, who joined in 1968, has rebuilt the group and kept it faithful to its original sound and still on the road to the present day.

Gus Cannon (1883–1979): The only artist to successfully use the five-string banjo in a blues setting, Cannon led a jug band for many years and served as a bridge between the folk and popular music of the late nineteenth century and the newly developing blues. He lived nearly a century, long enough to participate in both the ragtime era and the folk and blues revival. Gus Cannon was born in Red Banks, Mississippi, and took up the banjo in his youth, just before the guitar began to replace it as the predominant stringed instrument for self-accompanied singers. His early repertoire consisted of traditional banjo tunes and rags, but he quickly adapted to the newly developing blues music. By the 1920s he had settled in Memphis, playing for tips on the streets and in parks, and was known as Banjo Joe. He recorded under this name for Paramount in Chicago in 1927, presenting a mixture of blues and rags, including the remarkable blues "Poor Boy Long Ways from Home" with the banjo played in the slide style like a guitar. In the following year he recorded for Victor Records in Memphis as the leader of Cannon's Jug Stompers. This group was, in the opinion of many, the greatest of the early jug bands. Cannon himself played the jug in his band, wearing it in a harness around his neck and alternating jug playing with singing, picking the banjo all the while. The band's recorded repertoire was predominantly blues but with a healthy dose of ragtime tunes. Among their most successful pieces were "Viola Lee Blues," "Last Chance Blues," and "Going to Germany." In 1956 Cannon was discovered by blues researcher Samuel Charters and recorded once again. His jug band's early recording of "Walk Right In" was reissued and later recorded by the Rooftop Singers. Their hit version led to renewed attention for Cannon, and in 1963, in his eightieth year, he recorded an album for the fledgling Stax label, containing mostly his earliest repertoire of banjo tunes. He lived another sixteen years, performing and recording sporadically.

Leroy Carr (1905–1935): Carr's intimate singing and lush, rolling piano established a model for blues singer-pianists in the late 1920s and for years to come. Along with guitar partner Scrapper Blackwell, Carr also established the guitar-piano duo format that remained popular for more than two decades and became the nucleus of modern blues bands. He was born in Nashville and raised in Kentucky and Indianapolis, Indiana, where he taught himself to play piano. After touring with a circus and serving in the army, he began to work at clubs and house parties between Indiana and St. Louis. Around 1928 he teamed with guitarist Francis "Scrapper" Blackwell. Blackwell's long guitar lines and string bending seemed to cut through Carr's full, rolling, rhythmic piano, adding a new texture and a second melodic line. Their first recording that year was a sensational hit, "How Long—How Long Blues." The two musicians were virtually inseparable in their many subsequent recordings and had a string of hits, including "Baby Don't You Love Me No More," "Prison-Bound Blues," and several follow-ups to "How Long." Many of Carr's songs used odd verse structures or melodies, and some had novelty themes, such as "Papa's on the Housetop" and "Carried Water for the Elephant." Carr's plaintive singing seemed to capture perfectly the mood of the Great Depression in tunes such as "Just Worryin' Blues" and "I Keep the Blues," but he could also lighten up with fast pieces like "Bobo Stomp." Carr and Blackwell recorded steadily through the worst years of the Depression in the early 1930s. In 1934 and 1935 they had another string of hits, including "Mean Mistreater Mama" and "When the Sun Goes Down." Carr's songs at this time became increasingly somber in theme, as in "Blue Night Blues," "Evil-Hearted Woman," and "Suicide Blues." Alcohol was getting the best of him, and in 1935 he died of nephritis of the liver. Many other artists adopted the blues sound of Carr and Blackwell, including Bumble Bee Slim (Amos Easton) and Little Bill Gaither, who billed himself as "Leroy's Buddy."

Ray Charles (1930–2004): With a solid foundation in the blues, Ray Charles added elements of gospel and jazz to his music and eventually conquered the fields of rock and roll and even country and western music, injecting everything he took on with a huge dose of soul. He was born Ray Charles Robinson in Georgia but raised in Florida, where he lost his sight from glaucoma at the age of seven. He learned to play the piano at a school for the blind, and it remained his main instrument, although he also mastered the alto saxophone and later occasionally used it on recordings. He moved to the west coast in 1948 and began recording the following year for the Swing Time label. This phase of his career, in which he performed in a trio format and sang as a crooner in the manner of Charles Brown or Nat "King" Cole, is often ignored or downplayed by critics, but he was actually quite successful and sang with a harder edge than the other crooners. His repertoire included blues standards like "Blues Before Sunrise" and "See See Rider," along with original pieces. Switching to Atlantic Records, he worked with top-notch jazz accompanists and developed his soulful, pleading singing style after a sojourn in New Orleans.

His "I've Got a Woman" became a hit in early 1955, a remarkable recasting of a gospel tune sung with a fervor that heretofore had been heard only in a church setting. It appeared at just the right time to be perceived as rock and roll, a field that he would re-enter four years later in a massive way with "What'd I Say." Throughout the latter half of the 1950s Ray Charles laid the foundations of soul music with secular adaptations of gospel tunes, aided on most by his female vocal trio, the Raelettes, and having one hit after another with "This Little Girl of Mine," "Hallelujah I Love Her So," and "Leave My Woman Alone." He established jazz credibility in collaborations with the likes of Milt Jackson, Oscar Pettiford, Kenny Burrell, Percy Heath, and Art Taylor, and came to be known as "The Genius" and "The High Priest." All of this work was interspersed with solid blues like "Blackjack," "Lonely Avenue," and "I'm Movin' On," the latter originally recorded by country music star Hank Snow. In 1960, at the height of his success with Atlantic, Charles switched to the ABC label, where he had more freedom to explore new fields. He had a hit with Percy Mayfield's "Hit the Road Jack" and distinguished himself as a producer of Mayfield, the Raelettes, and other artists on his own Tangerine label. The blues content on Charles's records of the 1960s dropped considerably. Instead, he chose to inject a blues quality into pop standards like "Georgia on My Mind," then into country and western hits like "I Can't Stop Loving You" and "Crying Time." In the 1970s he summed up his success and his overcoming of every adversity with an extraordinary soulful rendering of "America the Beautiful." He continued to give highly satisfying performances around the world up until his death in 2004 and became an icon of popular music.

Clifton Chenier (1925–1987): Definitely the founder and king of zydeco music, Chenier proclaimed himself "King of the South" and wore a crown and cape to prove it. He was born in the Creole community of Opelousas, Louisiana, the son of an accordion player. Clifton didn't take up music himself, however, until around 1947, after he had moved to Port Arthur, Texas, and then he chose the piano keyboard accordion rather than his father's old button model. He wanted a more modern sound and was attracted to the contemporary blues shouters and New Orleans rhythm and blues. Settling in Houston, by 1950 he put together a rhythm and blues band with electric guitar and drums and his piano accordion as the lead instrument. Essentially, this development represented the birth of zydeco music. Chenier sang mostly in French-accented English and performed mainly blues. In 1955 he had a hit for Specialty Records with "Ay-Tete-Fee," featuring a bilingual vocal and a fuller instrumentation of accordion, piano, guitar, bass, and drums. Switching to the Arhoolie label, in 1966 Chenier had another regional hit with "Black Gal," a version of a 1934 tune by Houston blues singer Joe Pullum but now featuring impassioned singing that seemed torn from Chenier's throat. Chenier launched a touring schedule that took him to many folk and blues festivals and recorded consistently fine albums for Arhoolie into the 1980s, with occasional excursions on other labels, and remained zydeco's greatest ambassador up to his death.

Eric Clapton (b. 1945): Rivaled only by Jimi Hendrix, Eric Clapton was the "guitar god" of blues-rock in the late 1960s. For millions of his fans, he proved that a white boy could play the blues. Later he proved that he could sing the blues as well. Clapton was born in Surrey, England. He took up guitar in the early 1960s and progressed quickly, caught up in the rapidly growing interest in American rhythm and blues music that was sweeping through Great Britain. He worked his way through several groups to become a member of the Yardbirds in 1963. His guitar playing with the group, including its backings of American blues artist Sonny Boy Williamson II, is still rather derivative, and he quit in 1965 when they went in more of a pop direction. At this point he joined John Mayall's Blues-breakers, where he became Mayall's co-star. His guitar work on *Bluesbreakers with Eric Clapton* showed that he could hold his own with the original American artists on covers of "Hide-away" (Freddie King) and "All Your Love" (Otis Rush), while adding original improvised solo choruses of his own. Clapton strove for overwhelming volume and distortion, helping to ini-tiate the psychedelic phase of blues-rock music. When he tackled prewar material, such as Robert Johnson's "Ramblin' on My Mind," he used the original recording merely as a song source, completely changing the guitar part, although he compensated by offering a fine vocal worthy of the original. He moved on to form Cream, one of the first blues-rock power trios, consisting of guitar, bass, and drums. On the al-bums *Fresh Cream, Disraeli Gears,* and *Wheels of Fire,* Clap-ton's playing is the very definition of "heavy," especially on tunes like Willie Dixon's "Spoonful" and Robert Johnson's "Crossroads," but he also distinguished himself as a singer and songwriter on "Sunshine of Your Love" and "Tales of Brave Ulysses." When Cream disbanded, Clapton joined Steve Win-wood's Blind Faith in 1969 before finally recording an album of his own the following year, simply titled *Eric Clapton.* This album holds Clapton's tendency toward extended solos some-what in check, making the songs more coherent and concise. In 1970 Clapton also had another musical project going, called Derek and the Dominos. "Layla," recorded with this group, is generally considered his masterpiece, especially for his fero-cious singing, although by this point he had gone well beyond the blues. In 1992 he returned to a mainly blues format, but in a rather odd way, with his *Unplugged* album, an entirely acoustic set designed to honor the roots of the music that launched him to fame. Although the album was highly acclaimed and extremely successful, his performances are rather ordinary within the realm of older country blues. In 2000 he recorded a successful collaboration with one of his blues idols, B. B. King, titled *Riding with the King*. Eric Clapton continues to perform and record, still turning out fine blues and extraordinary extended electric guitar solos.

Ida Cox (1896–1967): Ida Cox was a vaudeville blues singer of the first rank, who has rightly been called "The Uncrowned Queen of the Blues." She grew up in a religious household in small towns in Georgia but ran away from home at the age of fourteen, performing in vaudeville and minstrel shows through the 1910s. She remained a vaudeville star during the 1920s, usually as a headliner, and between 1923 and 1929 recorded nearly ninety titles for Paramount Records. Many of them were her own compositions, and quite a few became hits. She was especially popular with other singers and contributed several songs that continued to be covered over the years. Her voice was not powerful, but she sang with an exceptional depth of feeling that seemed to cut right to the heart of the matter. Most of her themes were serious, such as "Moanin' Groanin' Blues" and "Chicago Bound Blues (Famous Migration Blues)." The theme of death was especially prominent, as in "Death Letter Blues" and "Graveyard Bound Blues." Her accompaniments usually featured excellent piano by either Lovie Austin or Jesse Crump (her husband for a time) or a small jazz band such as Lovie Austin's Blues Serenaders that featured such outstanding artists as Tommy Ladnier, Jimmy O'Bryant, and Johnny Dodds. Although she made no recordings for another ten years, she remained very active and weathered the Depression better than most of her fellow vaudeville singers, working tent shows, cabarets, and theaters throughout the South. In 1939 she showed up at New York City's Café Society, recorded successfully once again with an all-star jazz lineup, and appeared in the "From Spirituals to Swing" concert at Carnegie Hall. Her career went well until she suffered a stroke in 1944. She was largely inactive in music thereafter but made occasional appearances and was coaxed back into the studio in 1961 to record a fine album for Riverside with a jazz band featuring veteran performers Coleman Hawkins, Roy Eldridge, Sam Price, Milt Hinton, and Jo Jones.

Arthur "Big Boy" Crudup (1905–1974): Although he will always be remembered as the blues artist that Elvis Presley covered on his first rock and roll record, Crudup was also important as an outstanding singer and songwriter who made an effective transition from prewar acoustic blues to postwar electric down-home blues. He was born in Forest, Mississippi, and took up guitar in the late 1930s after he moved to the Delta. His motivation was to make extra money to stay out of grinding rural poverty, and throughout his career he viewed music simply as one of several sources of income that would support his family. The year 1941 found Crudup in Chicago living in a packing crate and playing on the streets, where he was discovered by record producer Lester Melrose, who recorded him for Bluebird Records. His first session, with acoustic guitar and one-string bass, produced hits of "Black Pony Blues" and "If I Get Lucky." Crudup sang in a high, piercing voice, reminiscent of a field holler, and played simple, rhythmic guitar with few chord changes. By his second session in 1942 he was using an electric guitar, and more hits followed, including "My Mama Don't Allow Me" and "Mean Old Frisco Blues." By 1944 he had added drums, something seldom heard at the time with electric guitar, and throughout the rest of the 1940s and early 1950s he successfully used the combination of guitar, bass, and drums on his recordings. His guitar playing always remained simple but effective, and he had hits with "Rock Me Mama," "Ethel

Mae," "So Glad You're Mine," and many others that became standards performed later by countless blues singers. As other artists like Presley began to achieve success with his songs and his style, Crudup opted for the security of steady work, rather than music, and moved to Virginia. He re-emerged briefly in 1962 to record for the Fire label of New York City, sounding much like his old self. About four years later he emerged once again, finally to be recognized as a rock and roll ancestor.

Willie Dixon (1915–1992): Of only minor importance as a singer, Willie Dixon was nevertheless a giant in the blues field as a songwriter, producer, bass player, organizer, and benefactor. He was born in Vicksburg, Mississippi, and at an early age was writing and selling copies of his poetry. One of his initial efforts was "The Signifying Monkey," which later became a hit for his Big Three Trio and has endured as a toast recited at countless drinking sessions. He sang briefly in a gospel group and in the late 1930s moved to Chicago, where he sang bass in secular vocal groups and pursued a career in boxing. He learned to play upright bass and recorded with the Five Breezes in 1940, but his career was curtailed by a jail term as a conscientious objector during World War II. After the war he formed the Big Three Trio, which recorded a number of hits for the Bullet, Columbia, and Okeh labels from 1946 to 1952, many of them featuring Dixon's original songs. Toward the end of this period, Dixon was doing session bass playing for Chess Records and saw that a harder electric blues sound was the coming thing and that his vocal group's mellow "jive" style was on the way out. He quickly adapted and became a stalwart in the Chess studio through the mid-1950s, playing bass on great sessions by Chuck Berry, Muddy Waters, Little Walter, Bo Diddley, Howlin' Wolf, Koko Taylor, and a host of others. He produced many of the sessions and contributed great songs to most of these artists. Among his hits, many of which continued to be covered by blues-rock groups, are "My Babe," "Dead Presidents," "Violent Love," "Seventh Son," "(I'm Your) Hoochie Coochie Man," and "Wang Dang Doodle." In the early 1960s Dixon toured and recorded with pianist Memphis Slim and began organizing the American Folk Blues Festival tours that brought the cream of the Chicago blues scene to European concert halls. In the 1970s he began performing and touring more frequently with various groups of Chicago Blues All-Stars and worked to recover unpaid songwriter royalties and to gain control over the publishing of his songs. His work lives on in his many songs that have become standards and in the Blues Heaven Foundation that he established in 1982, which promotes blues in education and helps blues artists who have fallen on hard times.

Blind Boy Fuller (1907–1941): This artist perfected the East Coast style of blues guitar and was one of the most popular of all blues singer-guitarists during the last half of the 1930s. Born Fulton Allen in North Carolina, he learned to play as a youth before going blind in his early twenties. At this point he became a professional musician, working mostly in and around Durham, often with blind harmonica partner Sonny Terry. They performed at country suppers, on the streets, and at the entrances to tobacco factories. Fuller began his recording career in 1935 and maintained a steady popularity over more than 150 songs during a six-year period. He sometimes recorded alone but more often in duo or trio formats variously with guitarists Blind Gary Davis or Dipper Boy Council, Sonny Terry, and washboard player Bull City Red. Fuller had the ability to compose songs on a variety of topics, many of them conveying striking images or sexual double entendre ("Mama Let Me Lay It on You," "Trucking My Blues Away"). Many of his pieces used ragtime harmonic progressions ("Rag, Mama, Rag," "Piccolo Rag"). His playing was rhythmic and dance-oriented, with a dense texture and many passing notes and chords, all made more emphatic by his use of a steel-bodied guitar. He led a tempestuous lifestyle, and hard living eventually did him in. Fuller died from an untreated kidney ailment at age thirty-four. Many other blues artists covered his songs and imitated his style, including Brownie McGhee, who began his recording career as Blind Boy Fuller No. 2.

Buddy Guy (b. 1936): Arriving in Chicago in the late 1950s as its postwar blues scene was beginning to experience a commercial decline, this singer-guitarist achieved star status when the blues revival began to go electric and today has become the leading figure of Chicago Blues. George Guy was born near Baton Rouge, Louisiana, and as a youngster during the 1950s apprenticed in that city's rich blues culture. Like many young guitarists at this time, he was greatly influenced by B. B. King and developed an impassioned gospel-influenced singing style. In 1957 he relocated to Chicago in the hope of finding a place in the city's blues scene. His talent was quickly recognized by established artists like Muddy Waters, Willie Dixon, and Otis Rush, and the following year he cut two singles for the Artistic label that included such incendiary tracks as "Sit and Cry (The Blues)" and "This Is the End." By 1960 he had begun to record for Chess Records. With composer Little Brother Montgomery at the piano, Guy recorded an outstanding "First Time I Met the Blues." The following year he recorded "Stone Crazy," his only rhythm and blues chart hit. In 1965, he toured Europe with the American Folk Blues Festival, cut an album for Vanguard, and played guitar on harmonica player Junior Wells's highly acclaimed *Hoodoo Man Blues* for Delmark. His collaboration with Wells also established a partnership that would last off and on into the 1990s, to the benefit of both artists. In 1969 he did a State Department–sponsored tour of Africa and began recording collaborations with blues-rock stars, something he would continue up to the present. His guitar work, which had influenced Jimi Hendrix, became increasingly flamboyant, sometimes even overly histrionic, appealing especially to rock audiences. He continued to record successful albums in the 1970s and 1980s, often with Wells on harmonica and various guest stars. In 1991 his career received another boost with the album *Damn Right, I've Got the Blues,* containing guest appearances by Eric Clapton and Jeff Beck. With so many of the early giants of electric Chicago blues and even his disciple Jimi Hendrix long dead, Buddy Guy has been elevated to the status of reigning guitar god of the Chicago blues scene.

Jimi Hendrix (1942–1970): Although he was not perceived by most of his rock and roll fans as a bluesman during the last four years of his life, Jimi Hendrix nevertheless had a substantial blues background. After his death, the sonic innovations he introduced would affect many blues guitarists and help shape the future direction of the music. He was born in Seattle, Washington, and grew up in a home full of blues records by artists like Muddy Waters and Howlin' Wolf. In the mid-1950s, as he was beginning to learn bass and drums, he spent some time with relatives in Macon, Georgia, and began to take an interest in guitar. Toward the end of the decade he returned south to Kentucky for a brief stretch in the army, after which he worked as a journeyman guitarist on the "chittlin' circuit." Little Richard, the Isley Brothers, and King Curtis are some of the rhythm and blues artists he worked with, but he often crossed paths with other blues guitarists, such as Albert King and Albert Collins. Like King, Hendrix played left-handed, and he was influenced by the older artist's piercing electric sound and his smoky singing style. Hendrix moved to New York City in 1964 and got involved in the Greenwich Village folk music scene. Hendrix's band was

Jimmy James and the Blue Flames, an electric group that did mostly covers of Chicago Blues numbers. In 1965 he was persuaded by Chas Chandler, bass player of the British blues-rock group the Animals, to move to London and form a trio with drummer Mitch Mitchell and bassist Noel Redding, called the Jimi Hendrix Experience. Hendrix's time in Greenwich Village and London placed him in the center of the hippie and psychedelic cultural movement, for which folk song, protest songs, and blues served as the theme music. Hendrix effectively and creatively synthesized all of the musical and cultural forces to which he had been exposed in his 1967 debut album, *Are You Experienced*. For a young generation in Great Britain and America seeking a world of love, peace, freedom, and happiness, but also experiencing the conflicts and confusion of Vietnam, the Civil Rights movement, political assassinations, the sexual revolution, and experimentation with drugs, Hendrix encapsulated an era and a scene in tunes like "Manic Depression," "Love or Confusion," and "I Don't Live Today." His and the band's use of extreme volume, distortion, feedback, fuzztone, and one-chord riff patterns pounded these songs into the heads of listeners, who also had to pay careful attention to understand Hendrix's mumbled, conversational singing style and fragmented lyrics. While few of his fans at the time may have connected these qualities to the blues, the same interest in exploring tone color, use of riffs, harmonic minimalism, and spoken vocal asides characterized the music of primal Delta bluesman Charley Patton, who shared Hendrix's flamboyant image, sexiness, stage showmanship, and itinerant lifestyle. The Jimi Hendrix Experience recorded two follow-up albums, *Axis: Bold As Love* and *Electric Ladyland*. With many opportunities awaiting him but apparently also feeling pulled in many directions, Hendrix died in 1970 from the effects of a drug overdose. Although only a small percentage of his recordings, such as "Red

House," "Hey Joe," and "Voodoo Chile," are easily recognizable as blues tunes, blues musical qualities and a blues spirit pervade almost everything he created and performed.

Z. Z. Hill (1935–1984): No artist was more responsible for causing a resurgence of interest in blues among African-American audiences in the 1980s than Z. Z. Hill. He was born Arzell Hill in Naples, Texas, and spent his early years singing gospel, the typical background of younger blues singers who would emerge in the 1960s. He moved to Dallas in 1953 and began to take an interest in secular music, refashioning his name after B. B. King's and modeling his singing on that of Sam Cooke, who had himself recently switched from gospel. He moved to the Los Angeles area and began his recording career in 1964 for a small label owned by his brother, soon graduating to the Kent label, and from there to the Mankind and United Artists labels. He had success with songs that dealt with lovers' problems and themes of cheating, such as "I Need Someone (To Love Me)," "Don't Make Me Pay for His Mistakes," and "It Ain't No Use," but he remained somewhat of a journeyman soul blues singer, never quite making it to the top of the charts and always in the shadows of the more established artists that he emulated. In the late 1970s he recorded for Columbia Records and had a hit in 1977 with "Love Is So Good When You're Stealing It," but other tracks found him trying to catch hold of the disco bandwagon. Seemingly stalled in his career, Hill moved to the upstart Malaco label in Jackson, Mississippi, which brought him back to more of a blues sound. His "Down Home Blues," released in 1982, was a tremendous hit that stayed on the charts for nearly two years. Presenting an uncluttered arrangement with a simple and familiar riff and tapping into a residual blues nostalgia in the adult black audience, the song reversed the downward trajectory of blues on black radio and gave the genre a permanent and respected place in the spectrum of black popular music. Hill had follow-up hits with "Someone Else Is Steppin' In," "Shade Tree Mechanic," and "Get a Little, Give a Little." He was clearly the new star of soul blues with a bright future when he died of a sudden heart attack in his backyard in Dallas.

John Lee Hooker (1917–2001): For a Mississippi "country boy" with very little formal education and a musical style that many would characterize as simple and unrefined, this artist had an amazingly successful and prolific career in blues as well as the jazz, folk, and rock fields. He was born in the Mississippi Delta near Clarksdale, and absorbed the characteristics of the regional blues guitar style—a raw, percussive riff-based sound with little harmonic development combined with passionate singing. To this he added a remarkable ability to improvise spontaneously, both lyrically and musically, something that enabled him to create hundreds of songs over a recording career lasting more than fifty years. He left Mississippi in the early 1930s, eventually arriving in Detroit about a decade later via Memphis and Cincinnati with occasional visits back south. He played in clubs and sometimes worked with gospel groups, staying active in music but enjoying no great success. His idiosyncratic sound probably needed two things to succeed, both of which entered the picture in the 1940s. One was the rise of independent record labels that would take a chance on odd and unknown blues artists, and the other was the growing popularity of the electric guitar. These factors and the personality of John Lee Hooker came together in 1948, and with independent Detroit producer Bernie Besman acting as catalyst, Hooker had a huge hit with "Boogie Chillen." At the time the sound was something totally different, a raw blast of southern heat with nothing but Hooker talking and moaning over his insistent riffing guitar and foot patting, making no chord changes, and telling the world about his physical and musical coming-of-age. Over the next three years he followed this up with equally compelling hits, the brooding "Hobo Blues," "Crawling King Snake Blues," and "I'm in the Mood," along with further fine guitar boogies. In 1955 he began to record for Vee-Jay Records, usually with a band of guitar, bass, and drums, sometimes with added piano and saxophones. For the next nine years Hooker had hits with pieces like "Dimples," "No Shoes," "Tupelo," and "Boom Boom." During this period he took time out to record two albums with acoustic guitar for the growing "folk music" audience, present himself as the primitive "roots" of jazz in collaborations with stars in that field, and even make some records with the female vocal group the Vandellas. Hooker's successes and collaborations over the next three decades are almost too numerous to mention. His 1989 album, *The Healer*, on which major pop stars made guest appearances and paid homage, elevated Hooker to icon status, and he lived another dozen years to enjoy it, during which his greatest material from earlier years was reissued and reached new generations of fans.

Lightnin' Hopkins (1911–1982): One of the greatest poets of the blues, this artist managed to inject the essence of Texas country blues into an urban musical setting and then become a star in the folk and blues revival scenes. Sam Hopkins was born in Centerville, Texas, and grew up playing guitar along with his two brothers. In the 1920s and 1930s he came in contact with blues recording stars Blind Lemon Jefferson and Texas Alexander and absorbed stylistic and repertoire elements from them. These included a melismatic singing style not far removed from the field holler, mixing long held notes with loose, almost conversational phrasing, and guitar playing featuring held notes, pauses, string bending, and shortened and lengthened measures. On slower numbers his playing exhibited a series of bursts of energy, but he also excelled on fast boogies. He was almost impossible for other musicians to follow and was at his best when performing solo or with one or two Texas musical buddies. He was discovered by a talent scout and sent to Los Angeles in 1946 to record with pianist Thunder Smith. At this point Sam Hopkins became Lightnin' Hopkins, and the following year he had a big hit with "Short-Haired Woman." Through 1954 Hopkins recorded about two hundred songs for many independent record labels and was commonly heard on southern jukeboxes and radio stations. Along with John Lee Hooker, he introduced a more distorted, raw electric sound to solo guitar—accompanied blues and influenced many other aspiring guitarists all over the South. His recording career petered out in the mid-1950s, but in 1959 he was contacted by local blues researcher Mack McCormick and recorded again, this time with acoustic guitar for an album designed for the folk revival audience. Hopkins was perceived as a major new folk blues talent and soon began a series of concert tours. Many of his early recordings were reissued and sold alongside his more recent efforts. In 1969 he even managed to get back on southern jukeboxes and airwaves with the half-sung, half-spoken "Mister Charlie." Before his death in 1982 he had appeared at major folk festivals and even in Carnegie Hall.

Son House (1902–1988): A mentor of two of the greatest blues artists of all time and a great artist in his own right, Eddie James House, Jr., was born in the Mississippi Delta near Clarksdale and spent his youth there and in Tallulah, Louisiana. As a young man, he became a preacher and disliked secular music and all that it seemed to represent, but in the mid-1920s, he was increasingly attracted to the guitar and to alcohol. He was especially drawn to the slide style of blues guitar playing and by 1928 had taken up the instrument himself, inspired by local Delta musicians. He developed a percussive, riff-based style with minimal harmonic changes, singing with a rich, melismatic, gospel-influenced voice. In this regard, he might be viewed as a prototype "soul blues" singer. In 1930 House met bluesman Charley Patton, who recommended him to Paramount Records. The two-part masterpieces that House recorded that year, "My Black Mama," "Preachin' the Blues," and "Dry Spell Blues," were stark and moving testaments to the greatness of Delta blues. At the Paramount session House became acquainted with Patton's longtime second guitarist, Willie Brown. House moved to Robinsonville in the northern Delta to be near Brown, and the two became partners for the next twelve years. There a young Robert Johnson came under House's influence and another young local guitarist, Muddy Waters, also admired House's music. In 1941 and 1942 House recorded for folklorist Alan Lomax and a team of researchers from Fisk University. Soon after the 1942 session he moved to Rochester, New York, and took up railroad work, letting his music career languish. On the strength of his early recordings, a team of three blues researchers located House in 1964 and persuaded him to take up music again. He recorded for Columbia Records and had a successful career performing for folk and blues revival audiences in North America and Europe, inspiring many younger performers in the revival scene. Son House retired from music in 1975 and spent his final thirteen years in declining health.

Howlin' Wolf (1910–1976): Bridging the gap between rural Mississippi folk blues and urban electric combos, and later becoming a symbolic figure and mentor to rock musicians, Howlin' Wolf embodied all the raw power and sense of menace that blues is capable of. He was born Chester Burnett near West Point in northeastern Mississippi. He relocated to the Delta when he was a youngster and he soon adopted Charley Patton's gruff singing style and riff-based percussive guitar technique, although his large fingers prevented him from achieving the subtlety of Patton's playing. In the 1930s he learned to play harmonica from Aleck Miller, who later became known as Sonny Boy Williamson II. Sometime in this period Chester Burnett became known as Howlin' Wolf, a name that seemed to fit his rough falsetto cry as well as the fearsome image he projected. He moved around Mississippi and Arkansas, farming and playing music, and after serving in the military during World War II, he approached Memphis studio owner Sam Phillips about making recordings. Phillips sold masters, sometimes alternate versions of the same songs, simultaneously to Modern Records of Los Angeles and Chess Records of Chicago. Wolf's records were popular on jukeboxes, and he had hits with "Moanin' at Midnight," "How Many More Years," and an updated version of the Charley Patton song "Saddle My Pony." After some wrangling between the two record companies and Phillips, Wolf relocated to Chicago at the end of 1953 and remained with Chess for the remainder of his career. In the mid 1950s he made a remarkable series of records of consistent power and quality, perfectly balancing elements of country and city, South and North, and expressing a broad range of moods. These included classics such as "No Place to Go," "Forty-Four," and "Poor Boy." In 1960 Howlin' Wolf began to work with producer and songwriter Willie Dixon and had another series of powerful and enduring hits, such as "Wang-Dang Doodle," "Back Door Man," and "Killing Floor." Toward the end of the 1960s he increasingly reworked his older repertoire and recorded collaborations with rock musicians. Wolf remained active for several more years, playing in prestigious venues in the United States and Europe, until cancer brought about his retirement and eventually his death.

Mississippi John Hurt (1893–1966): A gentle soul and a hard worker in a musical tradition that often glorified hard hearts and the fast life, John Hurt was perfectly suited for his success-ful but brief career in the folk music revival scene of the 1960s. Except for part of this latter period, he lived his entire life in or near the small community of Avalon, Mississippi, where he farmed or herded cattle and sang and played guitar on week-ends for small gatherings of his neighbors. He acquired a vast repertoire of blues ("Got the Blues Can't Be Satisfied"), rag-time tunes ("Nobody's Dirty Business"), ballads ("Frankie"), and spirituals ("Praying on the Old Camp Ground"), accom-panying all of them in a guitar style that featured alternating bass notes and delicate, syncopated treble work. His friendship with two local white musicians, who were country music recording artists for Okeh Records, led to two sessions by Hurt in Memphis and New York City in 1928. The records were only moderately successful commercially, and Hurt returned to his life of farming and making music on the side. On the basis of the reissue of some of his early recordings and the clue he left in the title of his "Avalon Blues," Hurt was rediscov-ered in Avalon in 1963 by a fan from Washington, D.C. His skills as a singer and guitarist had not deteriorated a bit, and he displayed a far greater repertoire than could have been imagined from the few tracks he had recorded thirty-five years earlier. He was probably the most successful of the blues "rediscoveries" of the 1960s in respect to popularity with the folk and blues revival audience, income from music making, and closeness to the sound of his early recordings.

Elmore James (1918–1963): This artist's raw, impassioned vo-cals and distorted slide guitar brought Robert Johnson's Missis-sippi country blues to a Chicago electric combo setting. By the mid-1930s Elmore James was playing guitar around the Delta, learning from Johnson as well as from records by artists like Tampa Red. He was probably one of the first slide guitarists in Mississippi to go electric, and his distorted sound was enhanced by his knowledge as a radio repairman. James recorded "Dust My Broom," an old Robert Johnson number, at a Sonny Boy Williamson session for Trumpet Records in Jackson in 1951, and it proved to be a big hit. He left Trumpet, however, and headed for Chicago, eventually recording through 1956 for the Los Angeles–based Flair label. He dropped the harmonica and substituted one or two saxophones in his band, often adding a second guitar as well. Thus he maintained the power of electric small-combo Chicago Blues but sometimes approached the massive sound of a big band. The fact that many of his recordings used variations of the slide guitar idea of his first record didn't seem to matter, as the sincerity and immediacy of his singing and the ferocity of his playing made every song sound fresh. He had hits with "Hawaiian Boogie," "Sunnyland," and "Standing at the Crossroads," the latter based on another Robert Johnson original. In 1959 he began to record for the Fire label, based in New York City, and had another hit with "The Sky Is Crying." Over the next four years he updated blues standards and composed original songs, never losing the cutting edge of his performance style. He was on the verge of major crossover success, and a European tour was in the works, when a heart condition, probably worsened by years of heavy drinking, led to his sudden death in 1963.

Etta James (b. 1938): Starting her recording career as a teenager sounding much older than her years, Etta James has become the grand dame of soulful blues and has achieved iconic status. She was born Jamesetta Hawkins and grew up in Los Angeles and San Francisco, distinguishing herself early as a gospel singer. In 1954 she auditioned for band leader Johnny Otis and had a big hit with her first record, the dance-oriented "The Wallflower," also known as "Roll with Me, Henry." She soon partnered with manager and boyfriend Harvey Fuqua and followed up her success with "Good Rockin' Daddy" and

"W-O-M-A-N." All of these records used a big band format with horns and backup singers. When the hits stopped, Fuqua brought her to Chess Records in Chicago in 1960, and she recorded for that company's Argo and Cadet labels for the next fifteen years. Throughout the 1960s she sustained commercial success in a soul blues style, sounding somewhat like a female Ray Charles but with lusher orchestrations. Among her great hits during this period were "All I Could Do Was Cry" and "Tell Mama." Most of the 1970s and 1980s were lean years for her career, as she battled drug problems, but when she did record, the incendiary voice was still there. She began to make a comeback at the end of the 1980s, recording for a series of labels and demonstrating that her ordeals had taken nothing from her singing while providing her with an added depth of experience. In recent years she has emphasized jazz and pop material, always giving it a bluesy treatment, but she frequently intersperses her performances with blues standards or outstanding versions of her older blues hits.

Skip James (1902–1969): Although he was deeply rooted in the Mississippi folk blues tradition, Nehemiah "Skip" James developed one of the most unusual blues sounds, both on guitar and piano and in his singing. He grew up near the small town of Bentonia in central Mississippi and learned guitar and some songs from local musicians, later developing blues piano skills in the 1920s in lumber camps and urban barrelhouses. While residing in Jackson, Mississippi, he made a successful audition for a blues talent scout and was sent to Wisconsin to record for Paramount Records in 1931. The eighteen surviving songs from that session include several masterpieces. Most of the guitar blues are played in a D minor tuning in a style that seems to vacillate between a major and minor feeling, never quite resolving itself. His playing was very precise and delicate, sometimes very fast, and unlike anything else that had been recorded up to that time. His lyric themes were almost universally bleak, as indicated in such titles as "Devil Got My Woman," "Hard Time Killin' Floor Blues," and "Drunken Spree." Despite some influence on other Mississippi blues artists, Skip James's records were commercially unsuccessful, and he became discouraged about his musical career. Intense interest in his music developed among blues aficionados following the reissue of some of his early recordings, and in 1964 he was rediscovered in Mississippi by a team of three researchers. Although he had a moderately successful career for the next five years, he was suffering from cancer and never quite regained the power of his early recordings.

Blind Lemon Jefferson (1893–1929): The first recording star of country blues, Jefferson opened the door for many other blues singer-guitarists to make records. He was born blind to a poor family in the tiny rural settlement of Couchman, Texas, but quickly showed an interest in music and an independent streak that helped him to overcome his handicaps. By 1912 he was traveling by train to Dallas to play on the streets for tips, and it was at this time that he partnered with twelve-string guitarist Huddie Ledbetter (Leadbelly). He returned to Wortham and Mexia, near his birthplace, in the early 1920s during an oil boom. All during these years he was increasingly developing a blues repertoire and perfecting his guitar skills. Jefferson returned to Dallas and was sent to Chicago to record for Paramount Records around the end of 1925 or beginning of 1926. He sang comfortably in a two-octave range and seemed to have limitless guitar ideas. His playing featured long improvised hornlike lines, punctuated by held notes and pauses, an acoustic and solo prototype of the style of electric lead guitar in a modern blues band. Jefferson had many enduring hits, including "Long Lonesome Blues," "Got the Blues," and "See That My Grave's Kept

Clean." He had a remarkable poetic gift and often depicted himself in situations that would be difficult or impossible for a blind man, such as driving a car, reading the newspaper, and serving in the military. In the late 1920s, he traveled around the South with a car and a driver, having no trouble drawing an audience due to the success of his records. He died in Chicago under mysterious circumstances at the end of 1929, apparently suffering a heart attack and/or freezing to death after leaving a party during a blizzard.

Lonnie Johnson (1899–1970): As a singer and lyricist, Johnson was a model of smooth sophistication, cool and philosophical. As a guitarist, he was known for long single lines, string bending, use of passing chords, excellent technique, and a beautiful, shimmering tone that influenced countless other guitarists, including in later years lead electric guitar players like B.B. King. Johnson was born in New Orleans into a large family of musicians, and his singing always retained a soft New Orleans accent. In 1918 he and his family resettled in St. Louis. He was not especially known as a singer or a guitarist, but in 1925 he entered a blues talent contest in St. Louis and won a recording contract with Okeh Records. His first release, "Falling Rain Blues," on which he played violin, was a hit, and he continued to record steadily for Okeh until 1932. On most records he played guitar, sometimes accompanied by a pianist, but he also took time out to record with the jazz bands of Louis Armstrong and Duke Ellington and to make records of dazzling guitar solos and duets with jazz guitarist Eddie Lang. Instrumental masterpieces like "Playing with the Strings" and "Hot Fingers" still remain challenging to guitarists today. He became one of the first blues guitarists to adopt the electric instrument, and in 1947 he had a huge hit with "Tomorrow Night." He performed and recorded with jazz musicians in the 1950s and caught on with the blues revival in the 1960s, where audiences admired his guitar skills but were sometimes dismayed when he sang pop songs and failed to fit the image of the "country" blues singer-guitarist. Despite this, he recorded steadily and appeared in clubs and festivals, touring Europe successfully in 1963. In 1965 he settled in Toronto and worked steadily there for the last five years of his life.

Robert Johnson (1911–1938): Robert Johnson was early in life attracted to the guitar, blues music, and a career as a traveling musician. He grew up in Robinsonville, Mississippi, in the Delta, and, after making a start on harmonica, was attracted to the guitar blues of local celebrities Son House and Willie Brown. Among the other artists who influenced him, either in person or through records, were Charley Patton, Leroy Carr, Kokomo Arnold, Peetie Wheatstraw, Little Brother Montgomery, Johnnie Temple, Lonnie Johnson, and Skip James. In 1936 and 1937 he recorded twenty-nine blues, all accompanied only by his own guitar, for American Record Company in San Antonio and Dallas. Many of these songs are widely regarded as among the greatest blues ever recorded. Johnson's musical ideas were capable of standing as a solo style, being part of an ensemble, and making a successful transition to the electric guitar. Lyrically, his songs explored the extremes in such themes as rambling ("Rambling on My Mind"), lovemaking ("Phonograph Blues"), drinking ("Drunken Hearted Man"), sorcery and victimization ("Stones in My Passway"), and direct dealing with God ("Cross Road Blues"), Satan ("Me and the Devil Blues"), and the blues personified ("Preaching Blues"). Robert Johnson died mysteriously ten months after his final recording session, allegedly poisoned by the jealous husband of a woman he was courting.

Louis Jordan (1908–1975): Working with swing bands in the 1930s, then with smaller blues combos in the following decade, this artist used a combination of humor and musicianship to become one of the greatest pop stars of the 1940s and one of the few blues singers of that era to achieve crossover appeal with white audiences. More than any other artist of the period, he paved the way for rock and roll. Ironically, this new music caused Louis Jordan to go into a commercial slump from which he never recovered. He was born in Brinkley, Arkansas, the son of a music teacher, and by the 1930s he was playing alto saxophone with big bands and doing occasional vocals. He joined Chick Webb's band and got to sing opposite Ella Fitzgerald, but by the end of 1938 he had formed his own band in the small blues combo style, which became known as the Tympany Five. He had hits with "A Chicken Ain't Nothin' But a Bird," "Mama Mama Blues," and a cover of Casey Bill Weldon's "I'm Gonna Move to the Outskirts of Town." During World War II he had a hit with "G.I. Jive" and scored again after the war with "Reconversion Blues." The hits from the late 1940s are almost too numerous to mention, but they include "Barnyard Boogie," the Calypso-themed "Run Joe," "Saturday Night Fish Fry," and "School Days." In 1952 he entered the presidential race against Eisenhower and Stevenson in "Jordan for President," but the hits had stopped coming as harder guitar-based blues styles began to prevail. Louis Jordan continued making fine records for another twenty years. His sound was increasingly dated, however, and he passed away too soon to be reevaluated and rediscovered in the blues revival scene.

Albert King (1923–1992): One of the stalwarts of soul blues from the 1960s through the 1980s, Albert King created a distinct left-handed guitar style featuring extreme string bending and became an important influence on blues-rock. He was born Albert Nelson, and his early years are shrouded in mystery and myth. He claimed to have been born in Indianola, Mississippi, and to be related to B.B. King, whose surname he later adopted. What is more certain is that he was raised in Osceola, Arkansas, where he played guitar with gospel groups and drums with local rhythm and blues artists in the 1940s. In the early 1950s he worked his way up to the Chicago area and cut one record for the Parrot label in 1953 with no great success. He settled in St. Louis and began his recording career in earnest in 1959 for the local Bobbin label, having a hit two years later with "Don't Throw Your Love on Me So Strong." It revealed a distinct smoky voice and a crackling electric guitar style in which every note seemed to be found through the effort of bending a string to the breaking point. King's early records were fine, but he didn't make a major and sustained impact until 1966 when he began recording for the Stax label of Memphis. Working with their house band of Booker T. and the MG's, supplemented by the Memphis Horns, King had a hit with "Laundromat Blues," followed by "Oh Pretty Woman," and "As the Years Go Passing By." King influenced fellow left-handed guitarist Jimi Hendrix as well as Eric Clapton, and later Stevie Ray Vaughan, making his approach to the guitar one of the most recognizable in blues-rock circles. When Stax folded, he continued to have hits in the late 1970s with tunes like "Cadillac Assembly Line" and "Call My Job" for the Utopia and Tomato labels before winding up in the 1980s with Fantasy, the company that had acquired his Stax material. He recorded rather little in the last ten years of his life but continued to perform at prestigious venues throughout America and abroad, as well as showcase clubs on the "chittlin' circuit" in African-American communities. He died alone in a cheap Memphis motel room of a sudden heart attack.

B.B. King (b. 1925): There can be little doubt that B.B. King has been the most influential blues singer and guitarist of the last half of the twentieth century. He is also the most respected and honored figure in the blues and the most recognized within the broader spectrum of American music. Constantly seeking to improve his condition and his music, he moved from Mississippi to Memphis in the late 1940s and incorporated ideas from every musical style he encountered. He had worked in a gospel quartet in Mississippi and absorbed that genre's melismatic, emotional singing style with its falsetto leaps. His guitar playing was a remarkable synthesis of the work of early blues greats Blind Lemon Jefferson, Lonnie Johnson, and Bukka White (his cousin), jazz masters Charlie Christian, Django Reinhardt, and Calvin Newborn, and pioneering electric bluesman T-Bone Walker. In Memphis he polished his lead guitar playing with frequent appearances at amateur talent shows in Beale Street's Palace Theater, where he could front a big house band of professional musicians. When he got a program on radio station WDIA, Riley B. King became B.B. King, the Beale Street Blues Boy. His first two records in 1949 for the Bullet label show him still struggling to achieve his style, but by 1951, when he began recording for the RPM label, it was fully formed. He had a hit the following year with "3 O'Clock Blues," in which all of the elements were in place that would sustain him for the next fifty years—the soulful vocals and ringing, hornlike guitar responses floating over the harmonic and rhythmic bed laid down by the band. He had a string of hits over the next fifteen years, such as "Woke Up This Morning," "You Upset Me Baby," and "Blue Shadows." In 1962 King switched to the ABC label and two years later recorded the acclaimed *Live at the Regal* album in Chicago. He scored further hits with "Don't Answer the Door," "Why I Sing the Blues," and "The Thrill Is Gone." The latter title was in a minor key and used a string section. It was his biggest pop success. Rock guitarists began expressing their admiration and clamored to record collaborations with him. From the 1970s onward he has continued to have hit recordings and hold his core black audience while expanding his base to become an international star and ambassador for the blues. He has performed and recorded with many pop, jazz, and blues greats, received presidential honors and honorary degrees, performed in every conceivable setting from prisons to royal concert halls, been the subject of several books, and lent his name to blues clubs. He has never let any of this go to his head and remains one of the most gracious figures the blues has ever known.

Leadbelly (1888–1949): The unpromising career of an itinerant musician and jailbird in Texas and Louisiana eventually put Huddie Ledbetter on the road to success and fame in New York City and an enduring international reputation. He was born near Mooringsport in northwest Louisiana, and learned accordion, guitar, and a bit of piano in his youth. He drifted around East Texas, farming and playing music, working with Blind Lemon Jefferson in Dallas around 1912. During this period he adopted the twelve-string guitar as his main instrument and later called himself "the king of the twelve-string guitar players of the world." In 1917 he began serving a sentence in the Texas State Penitentiary for murder and was not released until 1925. By 1930 he was back in prison, this time in Louisiana's notorious Angola Penitentiary. There he was recorded in 1933 and 1934 by folklorist John A. Lomax and his son Alan Lomax. Leadbelly's repertoire at this time was a mix of early blues, ballads, ragtime and dance tunes, and old sentimental songs. When he was paroled in 1934, John A. Lomax employed him as a driver on his folksong hunting expeditions. Leadbelly soon began supplementing his repertoire with material he encountered from the singers Lomax recorded. Leadbelly made commercial recordings for the first time in 1935, featuring mainly his blues repertoire, but he also made a more representative selection of documentary recordings for the Library of Congress. In the late 1930s and the 1940s he performed increasingly for mostly white audiences in New York City and on many tours, presenting himself as a representative African-American folk singer. In the 1940s he made many recordings for Folkways Records, but he also sought more mainstream success with recordings for RCA Victor and Capitol, the latter on a trip to California seeking roles in Hollywood films. His RCA session included some remarkable collaborations with the popular Golden Gate Quartet, recreating prison songs. By the time of his death in 1949 he had played a major role in establishing the folk and blues revival movements, contributing many songs that became standards.

Meade Lux Lewis (1905–1964): This artist was one of the early creators of boogie-woogie piano and one of its main popularizers in the late 1930s and 1940s. He was born in Chicago and grew up there in the 1920s playing at house rent parties, learning from and interacting with other pianists such as Pine Top Smith, Albert Ammons, and Jimmy Yancey. In late 1927 he recorded a piano solo titled "Honky Tonk Train Blues." Many train imitations were recorded by blues guitarists and harmonica players, but this piano recording was perhaps the most inventive of all. His performance so impressed the young recording executive John Hammond that he made a deliberate attempt to locate Lewis for the purpose of bringing him back into a studio. He was found in 1935, working as a car washer, and soon he re-recorded his earlier masterpiece, along with "Yancey Special" and "Celeste Blues." In 1938 and 1939 he appeared at Hammond's "From Spirituals to Swing" concerts at Carnegie Hall, performing solo and in a piano trio format with his old buddy Albert Ammons and Kansas City boogie-woogie pianist Pete Johnson. The three men created a sensation, and from that point on and through most of the 1940s they appeared separately and in duo and trio formats in the finest jazz clubs around the country, dressed in tuxedos and seated at grand pianos. The boogie-woogie style that they performed had an enormous influence on popular music, jazz, country music, and eventually on rock and roll. Lewis remained active in the late 1940s and 1950s, even as the boogie craze died down. In 1961 he made a final album of favorite boogies, blues, and pop standards with a five-piece jazz band. Three years later he died in an auto wreck.

Little Walter (1930–1968): In the early 1950s Marion Walter Jacobs defined the sound of amplified blues harmonica that would influence virtually every other player for the next fifty years. Little Walter was born in rural Louisiana and was on his own at the age of twelve, headed for Chicago by way of New Orleans, Memphis, and other places in between. He arrived in the Windy City in the mid 1940s and began playing with other blues musicians up from the South for tips in the Maxwell Street market area. In 1947 he made an obscure record for a local label with two guitarists, showing the influence of John Lee "Sonny Boy" Williamson. Little Walter had also been influenced by the other Sonny Boy Williamson (Aleck Miller) and Big Walter Horton on his way to Chicago, as well as by jazz saxophone players. Muddy Waters took in Little Walter in 1950 and added him to his band, where he contributed to some of Muddy's greatest records. His big solo break came in 1952 when he recorded an instrumental piece, "Juke," during a Muddy Waters session for Chess Records and it became a number one hit record. Little Walter took over another band and began touring throughout the South as well as working the Chicago clubs. He continued with a series of hit recordings, many of them now featuring his sensitive and vulnerable-sounding singing voice. These include such classics of electric Chicago blues as "Mean Old World," "Sad Hours," and "My Babe." He had a hit as late as 1963 with "Dead Presidents," and by this time he had made his first of several tours of Europe. He recorded little during the decade, however, becoming increasingly unreliable due to heavy drinking and fighting. His appearance on a 1967 *Super Blues* album with Bo Diddley, Muddy Waters, Otis Spann, and Buddy Guy was disappointing. A year later he was dead, the victim of one too many beatings.

Fred McDowell (1904–1972): This artist was one of the greatest traditional blues singers and slide guitar players, but he languished in obscurity until 1959, long after his style had fallen out of the mainstream of blues tastes with black American audiences. McDowell grew up in Rossville, Tennessee, just east of Memphis. He farmed and played music there and across the state line in northern Mississippi, with occasional sojourns into the Delta where he encountered artists such as Charley Patton. McDowell developed a percussive, riff-based style on the guitar, featuring few chord changes. He often used open-chord tunings and employed the slide style on a good half of his pieces. His style was characteristic of western Tennessee and the northern Mississippi hill country, but it was little represented on early recordings. Not too many years after he settled in Como, Mississippi, McDowell was recorded by folklorist Alan Lomax. The few tracks that were released on albums on the Atlantic and Prestige labels caused a sensation in the folk and blues revival scene of the early 1960s. In 1964 he began an association with Arhoolie Records, but he also recorded during the decade for Testament and other companies catering to the folk and blues revival audiences. In 1969 he recorded for Arhoolie and Capitol with bass and drums in an attempt to build a band sound around his solo style. His repertoire consisted of traditional blues such as "Write Me a Few Lines" and "61 Highway" along with distinctive adaptations of older hits such as "Shake 'Em On Down," "Kokomo Blues," and "Louise." In all of his concerts and tours he was very generous in sharing his music with other players. He left many disciples, including Bonnie Raitt, although no one ever matched the intensity and perfection of his music.

Blind Willie McTell (1898–1959): While he never had a hit record, Blind Willie McTell maintained a recording career over the span of three decades and left us with around 150 wonderful recordings. He was born blind in Thomson, Georgia, and raised in Statesboro. He learned guitar at an early age and showed a strong ability to get around on his own, traveling to several parts of the country. He attended schools for the blind and learned to read Braille, all the while developing his guitar skills and a repertoire of blues, ragtime, folk ballads, spirituals, and popular songs suited for both black and white audiences. In the mid-1920s he settled in Atlanta, and in 1927 he made his first recordings for Victor Records. By this time he had adopted the twelve-string guitar, which he would use on all of his recordings. McTell sang with a very expressive voice and precise diction, displaying considerable poetic skills. Among his best early recordings were "Mama, Tain't Long Fo' Day," "Statesboro Blues," and "Georgia Rag." In 1940 he recorded a session for folklorist John A. Lomax, representing the Library of Congress. This included a number of folk ballads as well as monologues about his life and the history of the blues. In 1949 and 1950 he made his last commercial sessions for Atlantic and Regal Records, presenting cross sections of his repertoire and still sounding as strong as ever. In 1956 he made a final session for the owner of a record store in Atlanta and contributed further interview material. Thousands of people, both black and white, heard him in Atlanta and on his travels, and he never failed to make an impression with the high quality of his music, the breadth of his repertoire, and his intelligence, dignity, and independence. His recordings were extensively reissued from the

1960s onward and have influenced many in the folk and blues revivals, including Taj Mahal and Bob Dylan, who composed a song about McTell.

Memphis Minnie (1897–1973): Few women blues singers accompanied themselves on an instrument in the early days, and even fewer had their playing ranked as highly as their singing. Memphis Minnie excelled at both. She was born Lizzie Douglas across the river from New Orleans, the oldest child in a large farming family that moved gradually up the Mississippi River through the Delta to the outskirts of Memphis. Along the way she learned to play guitar and was performing in the country and on the streets of Memphis when she was still a teenager. In 1929 she teamed with Joe McCoy, a guitarist from Mississippi who had settled in Memphis, and later that year they made their first recordings together. McCoy was fond of using nicknames and pseudonyms, and on their records he became Kansas Joe. Perhaps to provide geographical balance, his female partner, up to then known as Kid Douglas, chose her home city of Memphis and probably became Minnie simply for the sake of alliteration. The success of her first records caused her to keep the name for the rest of her career. After 1930 she and Joe relocated to Chicago, the main center of blues recording, although throughout her career Minnie made frequent trips back to Memphis and the Delta. Outside of a few solo efforts and appearances with jug bands, she recorded in a two-guitar format with McCoy. She and Joe often traded verses in the manner of vaudeville man-woman teams, and many of their songs were in the hokum style with sexual double entendre. Minnie and Joe broke up around the end of 1934, and she began working with pianists, sometimes with added instruments such as second guitar, trumpet, clarinet, bass, or drums. A number of her songs from this period used food imagery, such as "Selling My Pork Chops," "Wants Cake When I'm

Hungry," and "Good Biscuits," but she also dealt with the supernatural in "Hoodoo Lady" and "Haunted Blues." In 1939 she married guitarist Ernest Lawlars, who became known as Little Son Joe. He was also sometimes known as Mister Memphis Minnie, suggesting who was the boss in their relationship. Minnie and her new Joe had a number of hits during the 1940s, including "Me and My Chauffeur Blues" and "Please Set a Date." By 1947 she brought the piano back into her recording ensemble, but her sound soon gave way to that of younger and louder Chicago blues artists like Muddy Waters and Howlin' Wolf. Minnie and her husband settled back in Memphis in the mid-1950s, where they kept a five-piece electric band going until the end of the decade. Little Son Joe died in 1961, and Minnie suffered a stroke soon after and spent her remaining years in a rest home.

Charlie Musselwhite (b. 1944): A southern white boy who immersed himself in blues in the early 1960s, Musselwhite has gained a well-deserved reputation as one of the music's finest harmonica players and a master of tone on the instrument. He is also a fine songwriter and blues guitarist in down-home and early Chicago styles. He very much fit the demographic pattern of somewhat older rockabilly pioneers, being born in a small town in Mississippi and brought to Memphis in the late 1940s. Indeed, some of his formative musical experiences came listening to Elvis Presley and Jerry Lee Lewis as well as to recordings of blues by black artists played over WDIA radio station and by crazed white deejay Dewey "Daddy-O" Phillips. He spent hours hanging out with senior blues and jug band musicians like Furry Lewis, Gus Cannon, Will Shade, and Memphis Willie Borum, absorbing ideas and techniques on guitar and especially the harmonica. In 1962 he moved to Chicago, seeking work, and there he played on the streets with Big Joe Williams and John

Lee Granderson and sat in with Muddy Waters and other great artists in the city's clubs. Musselwhite formed a band in 1966 and the following year released the album *Stand Back! Here Comes Charley Musselwhite's Southside Band.* Anchored by ex–Muddy Waters drummer Fred Below and debuting future blues-rock guitar star Harvey Mandel, the album displays Musselwhite's mastery of tone and big sound on the harmonica. Particular standouts on the album are "Help Me" and his version of the jazz-gospel piece "Cristo Redentor," which became his theme song. Between 1969 and 1975 he recorded for the Arhoolie label, marking one of his best periods as well as the debut on record of his guitar playing, which shows the influence of stylists like Big Joe Williams and John Lee Hooker. In 1979 he recorded a harmonica instruction album, *Harmonica According to Charlie,* that demonstrates his mastery of different playing positions on the instrument. His recordings for Alligator Records in the early 1990s, a period just after he freed himself from a heavy alcohol dependency, are also outstanding. In recent years, perhaps seeking new worlds to conquer, he has emphasized his guitar playing more and sometimes performed "unplugged." He remains very active on the American and international blues scenes.

Charley Patton (1891–1934): The quintessential Mississippi Delta blues stylist and the first blues star in this important regional tradition, Patton was already an itinerant musician by around 1912 and remained a professional in music for the rest of his life while still residing in the rural South. Patton's singing was rough and harsh, showing the influence of field hollers and perhaps of preachers and sanctified singers. He played guitar in the slide style with a knife and in the normal position but with much string snapping and other percussive effects. He was a master entertainer, frequently "clowning" with his instrument and creating a dialogue with himself through spoken asides during his singing. Between 1929 and 1934 he recorded over sixty songs and accompanied other artists. Patton's repertoire was predominantly blues, but it also included substantial components of ballads ("Frankie and Albert"), popular songs ("Running Wild Blues"), and spirituals ("Lord I'm Discouraged"). Most of his blues contained conventional themes of man-woman relationships, mixing traditional and original verses, but some dealt with topical themes ("High Water Everywhere") or were clearly autobiographical ("High Sheriff Blues"). Among his many protégés and disciples were such great blues artists as Willie Brown, Son House, and Howlin' Wolf, but his influence also extended to gospel artist Roebuck Staples, rock performers Captain Beefheart and John Fogerty, and proto–New Age guitarist John Fahey.

Professor Longhair (1918–1980): A New Orleans resident since infancy, Henry Roeland Byrd came to symbolize that city's piano blues tradition and influenced countless other players, including Fats Domino, Allen Toussaint, and Dr. John. He dropped out of school early and became a dancer and street entertainer, later playing piano in seedy neighborhood bars in New Orleans and around Louisiana. His local fame grew, and in 1949 his recording career began, as independent record companies started to tap into his city's deep musical talent pool. One of his first releases, "Bald Head," was a chart hit, the only one of his career. Longhair's songs were full of odd humorous themes, and his piano playing was equally "off-beat." He specialized in a great variety of boogie-woogie bass patterns, the most distinctive being his $3+3+2$-beat "blues-rhumba" rhythm, overlaid with extreme syncopation or lightning-fast triplets in the right hand. With one or two saxes and a rhythm section supplementing his piano, he recorded over the next few years such classics as "Mardi Gras in New Orleans," "Hey Now Baby," and "Tipitina." His singing voice had a wild, half spoken quality with croaking falsetto leaps and frequent nonsense syllables. His recordings were few in the late 1950s, but he had a local hit in 1959 with "Go to the Mardi Gras" and followed it in 1964 with another Mardi Gras song, "Big Chief," backed with a veritable "parade" of more than a dozen musicians. The blues revival was somewhat slow to discover his talent, but he made a major breakthrough in 1971 at the New Orleans Jazz & Heritage Festival. His career changed dramatically over the next decade, as he recorded several excellent albums and toured extensively. Professor Longhair died suddenly in his sleep in 1980, but he remains much revered in his home city, and his old records continue to be played on the radio every Mardi Gras season.

Ma Rainey (1886–1939): One of the greatest singers in the vaudeville style, Ma Rainey was also one of the first stage entertainers to adopt the blues into her repertoire. She claimed to have done this in 1902, and when her recording career began twenty-one years later, she soon became known as the "Mother of the Blues." She was born Gertrude Pridgett in Columbus, Georgia, the child of minstrel entertainers. By the age of fourteen she was appearing in shows, and at the age of eighteen she married entertainer William "Pa" Rainey, thus becoming Ma Rainey. They toured through the 1910s in tent shows and circus sideshows as well as on the southern vaudeville theater circuit, becoming known as the "Assassinators of the Blues." After her husband took sick, she headed shows on her own and continued to do so after his death. She dressed lavishly, wore diamonds in her teeth, and a necklace of gold coins, and toured in her own Pullman car. Between 1923 and 1928 she recorded nearly one hundred titles for Paramount Records, many of which she composed herself. Despite the records' annoying surface noise, her majestic voice, deep blues feeling, and exquisite sense of timing shine through.

Her recorded legacy undoubtedly includes some of the songs she had been singing in earlier years and thus provides one of the best indications of the sound of blues at the professional level in the first two decades of the twentieth century. Usually she was accompanied by a pianist, two to four wind instruments, and sometimes a banjo and/or drums. Her band members included some of the top names in jazz, such as Tommy Ladnier, Louis Armstrong, Johnny Dodds, and Kid Ory. On some of her sessions, however, she introduced accompaniments that were more typical of a southern barrelhouse or country supper, such as one or two guitars, banjo, solo piano, guitar and piano, or a jug band. Many of her songs were hits and were covered by later artists, including "Bo-Weavil Blues," "Moonshine Blues," "Last Minute Blues," and "Dead Drunk Blues." She continued to work in southern theaters and tent shows until 1935, when she retired to Columbus, Georgia, and purchased two theaters. When she died in 1939, Memphis Minnie recorded a tribute song, "Ma Rainey."

Jimmy Reed (1925–1976): The essence of simplicity in the blues, Jimmy Reed had the common touch and served as the starting point for many aspiring blues singers, black and white, in the 1950s and 1960s. He was born in the Mississippi Delta and learned guitar and harmonica from childhood friend Eddie Taylor, who became his longtime accompanist. Taylor and Reed's wife, who wrote many of his songs, played a big part in his success. In the late 1940s, Reed moved to Gary, Indiana, and played there and in Chicago in local bars. His opportunity to record came in 1953, and on his second session he had a big hit, "You Don't Have to Go." This record defined his sound for the rest of his career—a simple guitar part with Taylor playing a walking bass on second guitar, squeaky blasts on the harmonica, a mushmouthed vocal delivery, and lyrics that zeroed in on some essential characteristic of the man-woman relationship. The combination was irresistible. Hundreds of musicians incorporated his songs and his style into their repertoires. Reed stayed on the charts with "Ain't That Lovin' You Baby," "You Got Me Dizzy," and "Bright Lights, Big City." By the early 1960s he had developed a following with white listeners, one of the first Chicago-style bluesmen to do so, and soon he was playing at American rock venues and in Europe. His essential style never changed, thanks to the loyalty of Eddie Taylor, but the quality of his performances became variable by the mid-1960s due to alcoholism. In the 1970s, epilepsy was combining with his drinking to a devastating effect. Although he was unreliable on stage, he continued to get prestigious bookings on the strength of his earlier hits until he died in 1976. Although many blues artists have continued to perform and record versions of Jimmy Reed's songs, few have been able to combine all of the simple, basic elements that made him unique.

Bobby Rush (b. 1937): Perhaps the most original blues artist of the last two decades of the twentieth century, Bobby Rush has carved a niche for himself as a purveyor of neo-hokum blues mixed with elements of soul and funk. Possessing the energy of a man half his age, he puts on an old-time "chittlin' circuit" stage show. His success was a long time in coming. He was born Emmit Ellis, Jr., in a small town in Louisiana, the son of a preacher, but later changed his name to avoid embarrassment to his father. By the mid-1950s he was in Chicago and working on the fringes of the blues scene there. His occasional use of the harmonica on his more recent work is a reminder of this early phase of his music. He bumped around on the southern club circuit through the 1960s without major success until 1971 when a single titled "Chicken Heads" made it onto the charts. This record established his sound, a semi-recitative vocal set to a repeated bluesy guitar riff with

little harmonic development and lyrics full of sexual innuendo that drew upon African-American folk speech. The
record also established the larger-than-life persona of "Bobby
Rush," the simple, down-home man with oversized needs for
sex, food, and more sex. Northern audiences might have found
this imagery dated, offensive, or politically incorrect, but southern audiences ate it up. Rush called his style "folk-funk." He
continued to record for the Jewel label in the 1970s and had
success with "Bow-Legged Woman, Knock-Kneed Man" and
"Niki Hoeky." In 1979 he recorded the album *Rush Hour* for
famed Philadelphia producers Kenny Gamble and Leon
Huff, but he really hit his stride in the 1980s with a series of
albums for the LaJam label of Jackson, Mississippi. He showed
no signs of slowing down in the 1990s with albums on the
Ichiban and Waldoxy labels with titles like "I Ain't Studdin'
You," "One Monkey Don't Stop No Show," and "Hoochie
Man." He remains today one of the most satisfying and cul-
turally connected blues acts, very much up to date while
drawing on the deep roots of the blues.

Slim Harpo (1924–1970): In the 1940s and early 1950s James
Moore performed in the Baton Rouge area as Harmonica
Slim. He first recorded in 1955 in nearby Crowley, Louisiana,
for the Excello label as a harmonica accompanist to the popular Lightnin' Slim. In 1957 he finally had a chance to record
for Excello as Slim Harpo, and he would stay with the label for
the rest of his career. He had a regional hit with his first
record, "I'm a King Bee," later covered by the Rolling Stones.
Slim Harpo began playing guitar on his recordings and live
appearances, like Jimmy Reed wearing the harmonica on a
rack around his neck. His first national rhythm and blues hit
did not come until 1961 with "Raining in My Heart," in which
he adapted a New Orleans piano-based sound to a down-home
guitar-and-harmonica format. Harpo continued to turn out

fine records and hit the jackpot again in 1966 with "Baby Scratch My Back," which became a number one rhythm and blues record. Years after the last chart successes of John Lee Hooker, Lightnin' Hopkins, and Jimmy Reed, this was probably the last truly down-home blues record to do this well with black audiences. Harpo continued to have hits with dance-oriented pieces like "Shake Your Hips," "Tip On In," and "Te-Ni-Nee-Ni-Nu." Just as he seemed poised to become an international blues icon, Slim Harpo suffered a fatal heart attack in 1970 at the age of forty-six.

Bessie Smith (1894–1937): Considered by many fans to be the greatest of all blues singers, there is no doubt that Bessie Smith was the most popular and successful blues artist during the 1920s. She was born in poverty in Chattanooga, Tennessee, and, as a teenager, she began touring on the southern vaudeville circuit and worked on Ma Rainey's show in 1912 and again in 1915. Bessie Smith began her recording career in 1923 and recorded steadily for Columbia Records until 1931, making close to two hundred sides. All during this time she appeared in many stage shows and reviews throughout the North and South, generally as the headliner. She was usually accompanied on records by a pianist, often with one or two wind instruments. Her accompanists included some of the top names in jazz, such as Clarence Williams, Fletcher Henderson, Buddy Christian, Coleman Hawkins, Don Redman, Charlie Green, Buster Bailey, Louis Armstrong, and James P. Johnson. She also recorded duets with Clara Smith and the Birmingham Jubilee Singers, and in 1929 she made a film short of *St. Louis Blues,* acting out W. C. Handy's famous song. About a quarter of her songs were her own compositions. Her singing was powerful and featured a rough, growling quality in the middle of her range. Her flamboyant and often tempestuous personality was reflected in blues such as "Send Me to the 'Lectric Chair,"

"Them's Graveyard Words," and "Me and My Gin." During the 1920s she became a celebrated figure in the Harlem Renaissance as well as one of the few African-American singers to gain a substantial white following. Even in the South her weeklong vaudeville theater stints often included a show reserved for a white audience. The combination of the Depression, the breakup of her marriage, and alcohol problems caused her career to go into a decline, but in 1933 she recorded a comeback session of bluesy popular songs, among them "Gimme a Pigfoot" and "Take Me for a Buggy Ride," accompanied by a racially mixed jazz band that included Jack Teagarden and Benny Goodman. She continued to rebuild her career in cabarets and theaters, but her life ended tragically in an auto wreck near Clarksdale, Mississippi, in 1937.

Roosevelt Sykes (1906–1983): One of the most influential blues pianists and songwriters, an artist who recorded hundreds of tunes over six decades, Sykes is strangely underestimated by many modern fans of music. Perhaps it was that his songs and stylistic innovations became so widespread that they no longer were recognized as his own. Roosevelt Sykes was raised in West Helena, Arkansas, and settled in St. Louis in the 1920s. Both locations were centers of blues piano activity, but he also ranged up and down the Mississippi River, playing in logging camps and rough barrelhouses. His recording career began in 1929, and his first session included the classic "44 Blues," a song that became a test piece for other pianists. He was a master of fast boogies, but his greatest contribution to piano blues was as one of the pioneers of a style of slower blues. It featured a deep rumbling bass in the left hand consisting of a series of insistent single notes moving to different pitch levels while the right hand roamed freely and improvisationally over the keyboard, playing hornlike lines full of blues notes. Sykes composed many blues that became standards, including "Driving Wheel Blues," "Soft and Mellow," and "Mistake in Life." During his recording career, Sykes moved between St. Louis and Chicago, when he wasn't on the road somewhere down south. He went into a recording slump in the late 1950s but soon bounced back at the beginning of the next decade through recordings and personal appearances aimed at the folk and blues revival audience. He settled in New Orleans, where he spent his last years playing for tourists and making the occasional foray out to a festival.

Tampa Red (1904–1981): Born Hudson Woodbridge in Georgia, he was raised as Hudson Whittaker in Florida after his father died. When he moved to Chicago he became known as Tampa Red. He was called "The Guitar Wizard" and did as much as anyone in the blues field to popularize the steel-bodied resonator guitar and the slide technique. His slide playing was extended over long melodic lines rather than the shorter riffs of most other blues players. Beginning in 1928, Tampa Red recorded steadily and prolifically over a twenty-five year period in a variety of formats, always sounding up to date. In 1928 he formed a partnership with singer-pianist Thomas A. Dorsey (Georgia Tom), and the two worked as a duo, as accompanists to Ma Rainey, and as part of a jug band with vaudeville performer Frankie "Half Pint" Jaxon. Together with Jaxon they virtually invented the hokum style of blues with titles like "It's Tight Like That," "Jelly Whippin' Blues," and "What Is That Tastes Like Gravy." Dorsey turned to religion in 1932, going on to become a very successful gospel songwriter and publisher. Tampa Red soon found new piano partners and added a kazoo to his vocal and guitar sound. In 1936 he formed his Chicago Five, adding clarinet, second guitar, and bass. He used this format for three years, toward the end adding trumpet and tenor sax. In 1938 he reverted to the guitar-piano format, supplemented by bass and his kazoo. By 1940 he had switched to an electric guitar, and two years later he was using a drummer. During these years he had some of his biggest hits, including "Anna Lou Blues," "It Hurts Me Too," and "She Want to Sell My Monkey." His popularity continued into the early 1950s with hits like "Sweet Little Angel" and "She's a Cool Operator," as he kept a group of four to six musicians and competed with newcomers on the Chicago scene. His health turned poor in the mid-1950s. A comeback attempt with new recordings in 1961 was not particularly successful, and after more bad health he spent his last years in a rest home.

Koko Taylor (b. 1935): Born Cora Walton in Memphis, she left the South in 1953 with her husband, Robert Taylor, and headed for Chicago. There they visited local blues bars, and with her husband's encouragement Koko Taylor began to do guest vocals with the city's top artists. Her powerful voice with its distinctive growl soon came to the attention of producer Willie Dixon, who brought her to Chess Records after an initial single with another label. Just as he had done with Muddy Waters and Howlin' Wolf, Dixon wrote songs suited to Taylor's style and image, and she had hits in the mid 1960s with "I Got What It Takes" and "Wang Dang Doodle." She continued to record for the Checker subsidiary of Chess Records and turned out fine recordings in the late 1960s, such as "Insane Asylum" and "29 Ways," but with only slight commercial success. In 1975 she began recording for the Alligator label and helped it lead a successful revival of Chicago blues over the last quarter of the twentieth century. At first she had the female blues field almost to herself and was quickly dubbed "Queen of the Blues" (a title vacated by Dinah Washington some years earlier). Her growling vocal style served her well in a heavily male-dominated field, and she justified her reputation with albums such as *I Got What It Takes* and *The*

Earthshaker, on which she was backed by top-notch second-generation Chicago bluesmen. She continues to tour and make records that are consistently worthwhile.

Sonny Terry (1911–1986): One of the great blues harmonica virtuosos, this prolific artist enjoyed success with black audiences both before and after World War II and became one of the earliest blues representatives in the folk music revival movement from the 1940s to the 1980s. Saunders Terrell was born in Georgia and learned to play harmonica from his father. Accidents during his teenage years left him blind, after which he took music more seriously. In 1928 he moved to North Carolina and performed on the streets and in medicine shows. Sometime in the early 1930s Terry partnered with guitarist and singer Blind Boy Fuller. The two played in and around Durham, and in 1937 Terry became Fuller's regular harmonica accompanist on recording sessions. Terry went to New York City without Fuller in December 1938, to appear in the "From Spirituals to Swing" concert at Carnegie Hall as a representative of the southern folk blues tradition. There he was recorded by folklorist Alan Lomax for the Library of Congress, but he also made a commercial recording of two blues albums for Columbia Records that was issued in the company's classical series. Terry again made recordings under his own name in 1940 as by-products of Blind Boy Fuller sessions. When Fuller died in 1941, Terry joined forces with singer-guitarist Brownie McGhee, who recorded for a time as Blind Boy Fuller No. 2. Sonny Terry continued to make race records for independent companies in the 1940s and into the 1950s, usually with Brownie McGhee, and he began to show a gift for original songwriting. He had hits with such pieces a "Whoopin' the Blues" and "Dangerous Woman." By the middle of the 1950s he and McGhee were concentrating on the folk revival audience, recording for Folkways, Bluesville, and other specialty labels, and touring throughout America and Europe in a circuit of college concerts, coffeehouses, and festivals. After a falling-out with McGhee in the mid-1970s, Terry continued to tour and record sporadically until his death in 1986.

Big Joe Turner (1911–1985): If this singer didn't invent the role of "blues shouter," he certainly pioneered it and remained the style's greatest exponent over a long and prolific recording career. He was born and raised in Kansas City and got his start in the city's wide-open entertainment scene of the late 1920s and 1930s, sometimes working as a singing bartender. He was a big man with an equally big voice and could be heard over a swing band singing from behind the bar without a microphone. His voice came from deep in his massive chest and his diction was slurred, perhaps sometimes to cover his often salacious lyrics, but he had tremendous swing and could drive a band with his singing. By the mid-1930s he had become well known on the jazz circuit, working with bands out of Kansas City, but his big breakthrough came at the end of 1938 when he appeared at the "From Spirituals to Swing" concert in Carnegie Hall with Kansas City boogie-woogie pianist Pete Johnson. He began recording immediately thereafter and had success with "Roll 'Em Pete," backed by Johnson. He continued recording with small combos and other outstanding pianists of the time, including Joe Sullivan, Meade Lux Lewis, Sam Price, and Freddie Slack. Turner relocated to the West Coast in the 1940s and began to record for a series of independent labels there and in Chicago, Houston, and New Orleans. In 1951 he hooked up with New York City's Atlantic Records and began a period of even greater commercial success over the next decade. Unlikely as it may have seemed for someone in his forties, he became a rock and roll star in the genre's early days, having hits with "Honey Hush," "Shake, Rattle and Roll," and "Flip Flop and

Fly." In the 1960s Turner toured extensively and in the following decades he was a leading force in the revival of jump band blues on the West Coast.

Stevie Ray Vaughan (1954–1990): A guitarist who has inspired thousands of imitators and emulators, Vaughan in the 1980s built on the work of Eric Clapton and Jimi Hendrix from a previous generation. He was born and raised in Dallas, and took up guitar in the late 1960s, learning from his older brother, Jimmie, who has had a significant blues career of his own. After playing in garage bands around Dallas, Stevie Ray followed his brother and relocated to Austin, which was a more "happening" music scene in the early 1970s. By 1975 he had formed the band Triple Threat, which later evolved into Double Trouble, the band name he kept for most of the rest of his career. Without the benefit of a recording, these bands proved extremely popular on the Texas club scene, playing mostly blues with a bit of rock. Vaughan's big break came in 1982 at the Montreux Blues & Jazz Festival in Switzerland, where he and his band played a spectacular set. It created great excitement and resulted in an invitation to play lead guitar on David Bowie's *Let's Dance* album and another to record a blues session with Double Trouble. The latter resulted in the 1983 album *Texas Flood*, which had almost as great an impact on the rock world as the 1967 release of Jimi Hendrix's *Are You Experienced*. Vaughan also showed a gift for songwriting, and his "Pride and Joy" has become somewhat of a blues standard. The album went very high on the charts, as did albums in each of the next two years, *Couldn't Stand the Weather* and *Soul to Soul*. By 1986, however, he was having serious drug and alcohol problems and spent the next few years drying out. Seemingly rehabilitated, he recorded a fine album in 1989 titled *In Step*. The following year he recorded a reunion album with his brother, Jimmie, *Family Style*, which unfortunately turned out to be a posthumous release for Stevie Ray. In August of that year a helicopter carrying him from a concert in Wisconsin crashed, killing all on board.

T-Bone Walker (1910–1975): No artist was more responsible for creating the sound of electric lead blues guitar than T-Bone Walker. In addition, he was a prolific recording artist and an excellent singer and songwriter. He was born Aaron Thibeaux Walker and raised in Dallas, the stepson of a string band musician. Walker learned a variety of stringed instruments and helped the singer-guitarist Blind Lemon Jefferson get around the city. It was from Jefferson that he took his overall approach to guitar playing, featuring long single-note runs, pauses, held notes, and chord substitutions, but Walker would add a jazz sensibility, a greater harmonic knowledge, extraordinary showmanship, and improvisatory ideas of his own. Most important of all, he would add electronic amplification and the backing of a band. Walker's first appearance on record as an electric guitarist came in 1942 for the Capitol label, after he had relocated to the West Coast. "I Got a Break Baby" and "Mean Old World" gave him a hit record on the new label and displayed his ability to move easily between the shouting and crooning vocal styles that were becoming popular in the 1940s. During World War II he worked with big bands, and the year 1945 found him in Chicago recording for local labels with Marl Young's Orchestra and probably sowing seeds of the new guitar style among younger musicians in that blues-rich city. He soon returned to Los Angeles and in 1946 and 1947 recorded extensively for two local labels that would eventually be acquired by Capitol. Here he really hit his stride with hits like "Call It Stormy Monday" and "T-Bone Shuffle," along with other clever titles like "I Know Your Wig Is Gone" and "You're My Best Poker Hand." He toured widely in the late 1940s but did not record again until 1950, working with the

Imperial and Atlantic labels until 1957. Heavy alcohol consumption was causing trouble for Walker, and he recorded hardly at all for the next nine years, although he continued to perform on the West Coast and elsewhere. From 1966 until his death in 1975 he battled health problems but recorded a number of albums of varying quality, toured often, and finally got the respect he deserved as a pioneering blues stylist.

Dinah Washington (1924–1963): Although she was known as "Queen of the Blues," this artist, like Ray Charles, knew no genre limitations and had major success in the pop and jazz fields, not to mention forays into gospel and country music. Everything she sang, however, was infused with blues feeling. She was born Ruth Jones in Alabama but was raised in Chicago. As a teenager she sang with the Sallie Martin Gospel Singers, but she longed for popular stardom. Her ambition was tied to a terrific vanity and competitive spirit, matched with a gnawing insecurity about her appearance. Anecdotes about her fights, insults, and affairs with men are legion. She was married at least seven times, and had the audacity to insult Queen Elizabeth from a London stage, declaring herself the only true queen. In 1943, Ruth Jones came to the attention of agent Joe Glaser, who placed her as a vocalist with Lionel Hampton's band. Adopting the stage name of Dinah Washington and working with the songwriter Leonard Feather, she had immediate success with "Evil Gal Blues" and "Salty Papa Blues," two songs well suited to her personality. Her singing style was influenced by the then-popular Billie Holiday, but Washington's voice had a harder edge, almost a snarl, and most of her early repertoire was blues. She continued recording mostly blues through the 1940s, working with top jazz bands, such as those of Lucky Thompson, Gerald Wilson, Tab Smith, Chubby Jackson, Dave Young, Cootie Williams, Count Basie, Dizzy Gillespie, and Teddy Stewart.

In the 1950s she began increasingly to sing pop material and jazz standards, even covering several Hank Williams country tunes and having a hit with "Cold, Cold Heart." Still, a substantial portion of her recordings remained blues, and in 1958 she released an album of interpretations of old hits by Bessie Smith. In 1960 she had number one hits dueting with rising star Brook Benton on "Baby (You've Got What It Takes)" and "A Rockin' Good Way." She was still going strong, recording prolifically, and appearing at major jazz and pop venues, when she died in 1963, before her fortieth birthday, of an overdose of diet pills mixed with alcohol.

Muddy Waters (1913–1983): One of the most influential artists in blues history, McKinley Morganfield's career carried him from Mississippi Delta folk blues to electric Chicago combo blues and on into the field of rock and roll. He grew up on a plantation near Clarksdale, Mississippi, and soon came under the influence of bluesman Son House, mastering his slide guitar style. In 1941 and 1942 he was recorded in field sessions by folklorist Alan Lomax, performing solo blues and as a member of Son Sims's string band. The recordings documented an artist of immense potential and charisma, and the experience gave him the confidence and ambition to seek bigger things for himself in the music field. In 1943 he headed for Chicago, and by the following year he had an electric guitar and a small combo to back him up. His childhood nickname of "Muddy Water" became his name, Muddy Waters. With the help of reigning blues star Big Bill Broonzy, he scored a session with Columbia Records in 1946, which the company foolishly left unissued. The following year he showed up on the Aristocrat label, a predecessor of Chess Records. "I Can't Be Satisfied" and "I Feel Like Going Home," both with just his electric slide guitar and a string bass, were released in 1948 and were a double-sided hit record. Over the next two years he began to bring portions of his combo into the studio, including the fine singer-guitarist Jimmy Rogers who also had a recording career under his own name. Almost everything Muddy Waters recorded in the early 1950s was a classic of electric Chicago Blues, sung with passion and drawing from the rich Delta tradition but adding the power of the big urban beat and the playing of outstanding sidemen. "Screaming and Crying," "Rollin' and Tumblin'," "Honey Bee," and "Standing Around Crying" from this period are particularly outstanding. Other fine recordings through the end of the 1950s include "I'm Your Hoochie Coochie Man," "I Just Want to Make Love to You," and "Walking Through the Park." Muddy Waters fashioned an image of himself, often reflected in his song titles and lyrics, as the natural-born lover, the hoochie coochie man, and mojo worker. This image would later prove irresistible to young rockers discovering the blues in the 1960s and 1970s. He continued to make some good singles that appealed to black record buyers into the early 1960s, but by this time he had made inroads with white audiences as well. His overseas tours would play a major role in triggering an electric blues scene in England that would soon develop into a rock scene, and Muddy's songs became core repertoire items. He kept good bands together for the rest of his career, but tended to perform and record his old classics or other blues standards. By the time of his death in 1983, the blues revival was well under way, and Muddy Waters had played a large part in instigating it here and abroad.

Bukka White (1906–1977): Booker T. Washington White was one of the finest songwriters of country blues and an outstanding singer and slide guitar player. He was born near Houston, Mississippi, in the rural northeastern part of the state, but he also spent some of his early years in the Delta as a farmer and a musician. Unlike older musicians who had more varied

repertoires, White played mainly blues along with a few spirituals. In 1930 he recorded a blues and a spiritual record, the
highlight being "The Panama Limited," a train imitation
with speech and singing performed with slide guitar. In 1937
he killed a man in a barrelhouse fracas, and while awaiting
trial he recorded two blues in Chicago. "Shake 'Em on Down"
proved to be a hit, but whatever benefit it might have had for
his career was lost when he served a sentence in Mississippi's
notorious Parchman Penitentiary. There he was recorded by
John A. Lomax, who was documenting folksongs for the Library of Congress. Upon his release he returned to Chicago to
resume his commercial recording career and in 1940 recorded
twelve brilliant blues songs, helped by Washboard Sam. With
his rich singing voice and riffing guitar, he explored themes of
imprisonment, alcoholism, death, and depression, as well as
travel and partying. Great as they were, his records were not
commercially successful, and White settled in Memphis, doing industrial work and performing music on the side. His life
changed dramatically in 1963 when he was rediscovered by
two researchers from California. Bukka White was recorded
again and began a round of concert appearances and tours that
would take him all over the United States and Europe. His
voice had become rougher from years of hard living, but he
had developed an improvisational style of spontaneous composition that he called "sky songs" because he claimed to reach
up in the sky and grab them out of thin air. Bukka White enjoyed a long second career before passing away in 1977.

Robert Pete Williams (1914–1980): This highly introspective performer rose from obscurity and adversity to achieve a
reputation as a major blues artist in the last two decades of his
life. He was born in rural poverty and lived his entire life in
and around Baton Rouge, Louisiana. He learned guitar as a
youth, but through the 1950s his playing was mostly done at

small parties and gatherings of friends. In 1956 he was sentenced to Angola Penitentiary for murder and would have languished there if he had not been discovered by folklorist Harry Oster, who recorded him and was influential in his obtaining a parole. Williams's songs were very personal and often frightening in their depiction of wants, needs, and frustrations, combined with slashing guitar rhythms and minor scales. Among his masterpieces were "I'm Blue As a Man Can Be," "Thumbin' a Ride," and "I've Grown So Ugly." Yet he could also work extraordinary transformations on well-known standards such as "Louise" and "Matchbox Blues." It's doubtful that Williams ever could have had success as a commercial recording artist, but he found favor as a concert performer with folk and blues revival audiences in the United States and Europe, beginning in the mid-1960s. He made many recordings, and always maintained a high standard of performance and inventiveness, while constantly coming up with new material. He remains one of the most unique personalities and stylists that the blues has ever seen.

Sonny Boy Williamson (1914–1948): Very popular in his day, this artist was also the main architect of the modern blues harmonica sound. John Lee Williamson was born and raised in Jackson, Tennessee, and as a young man worked the joints in that city's Shannon Street and in nearby towns. He relocated to St. Louis in the mid-1930s and settled in Chicago sometime in the 1940s. Williamson began his recording career in 1937, backed by two guitarists. All six of the songs from this first session were hits, especially "Good Morning, School Girl," "Blue Bird Blues," and "Sugar Mama Blues." Williamson's success lay in his effective songwriting, his ability to drive the beat with his voice and harmonica, the unbroken stream of sound that he created between his voice and instrument, and harmonica playing that was full of blue notes and special timbral and percussive effects. By 1945 he had perfected the lineup of harmonica, guitar, piano, bass, and drums that would become the standard for Chicago Blues bands through the following decade. All that was lacking was for Williamson to play his harmonica through an amplifier to achieve electronic distortion, something that he actually did in Chicago clubs but was not able to put on records. He was poised to lead Chicago Blues to the next level in 1948 when he was murdered on the streets of the city, the victim of a mugging and beating as he walked home late at night following a performance at a tavern. Close to half of his recorded songs have continued to be performed by other artists, and his singing and playing styles have been widely imitated.

Sonny Boy Williamson II (1912–1965): Aleck "Rice" Miller adopted the name of another great blues harmonica player, although he was an outstanding musician in his own right. Miller was born in the Mississippi Delta to a very religious family from whom he was estranged early in life when he decided to become an itinerant blues musician. By the early 1930s he was traveling around Mississippi and perhaps other parts of the South with a belt containing numerous harmonicas in different keys, calling himself "Harp Blowin' Slim" or "Little Boy Blue." During this decade he performed with the top tier of blues singer-guitarists, such as Robert Johnson, Big Joe Williams, and Robert Nighthawk, as well as up and coming artists like Elmore James and Robert "Junior" Lockwood. He was clearly working to create a small-combo sound and to bring the harmonica into the mainstream of Deep South blues. In 1941 he began broadcasting on radio station KFFA in Helena, Arkansas, sponsored by King Biscuit Flour. He was heard by thousands of sharecroppers throughout the Delta region of Arkansas and Mississippi, which resulted in a broad regional reputation. Around this time he adopted the name of

Sonny Boy Williamson. His reputation reached Lillian Mc-Murry of Trumpet Records in Jackson, Mississippi, and in 1951 she persuaded him to record for her company. Backed by a small combo of two electric guitars, piano, and drums, Sonny Boy's "Eyesight to the Blind" was an immediate hit and a southern juke joint classic, featuring wonderful tone coloring on the harmonica, blasting distortion by the band, an infectious dance beat, and poetic lyrics that seemed to flow spontaneously from the singer's imagination. Over the next three years he became the Trumpet label's star, having hits with tunes like "Sonny Boy's Christmas Blues," "Mighty Long Time," and "From the Bottom." In 1955 his recording contract was sold to Chess Records, and he continued to record hits for them over the next ten years, including "Don't Start Me to Talkin'," "Keep It to Yourself," and "Help Me." From 1963 to 1965 he toured often in Great Britain and Europe and fronted the Yardbirds with Eric Clapton, Eric Burdon and the Animals, and Chris Barber's Jazz Band, lending blues credibility to the early efforts of these artists. His health declined and in 1965 he returned to Helena, where he died.

SIX

The Music

The performances described below should by no means be taken as a list of the greatest recorded blues of all time, although they are a good representation of the greatest. They also represent the range of blues styles over the past century. These artists and songs both overlap with and extend the lists in chapters 5 (The Performers) and 7 (Blues on CD). In this chapter we highlight individual performances in a bit more detail.

Above all else, blues music is about conveying personal feeling and, in so doing, reaching others and establishing a sense of life-affirming solidarity. Not every blues performer can muster up a great level of feeling and translate it into a great performance, nor does feeling necessarily correlate with technical virtuosity, versatility, and compositional skill. Some of the performances described in this chapter are quite simple in respect to these qualities, yet they achieve a uniqueness that no one has ever been able to match. Of course, feeling and sensitivity do often drive an artist to compose poetic lyrics and achieve innovative vocal and instrumental virtuosity. These qualities are on display in many of the songs listed here, but are only starting points. There are hundreds more excellent blues recordings by these and many other fine artists.

3 O'Clock Blues, B.B. King: It's hard to believe this was recorded way back in 1951, for almost all of the elements of contemporary soul blues are here. The only thing missing is the electric bass, which had not yet entered popular music, and the drums and piano, barely audible here, would figure more prominently if the recording were mixed today. This is the young B.B. King with his first record hit, displaying a two-octave range and moving in and out of a falsetto voice. Almost every syllable glides between two or more notes, and one syllable actually covers six notes. A massive horn section lays down a harmonic bed and a slow rhythmic groove, letting King's voice float freely over the top. His guitar does the same, answering his vocal lines with improvised statements of bell-like clarity. These lonesome cries from the soul, expressed by both his voice and guitar, have drawn millions of fans to his side over the years and influenced hundreds of musical followers.

All Your Love, Magic Sam: Sam Maghett was one of the leading representatives of the "West Side" sound that arose in the Chicago Blues scene of the late 1950s, grafting the modern electric lead guitar onto a small-combo format, often without any horns. Although a piano and electric bass are listed in discographies, they are inaudible in this, Magic Sam's 1957 debut recording, and all that can be heard are drums, Sam's tremolo-laden lead guitar, producer Willie Dixon's close-miked acoustic bass, and a second guitar playing rhythm and bass figures in the background. With the exception of this second guitarist, the recording sounds like an early version of a "power trio." The rhythm has a staggering quality, and the first two vocal lines of every stanza move between two blue notes, the flat seventh and blue third, giving the listener a sense of hearing someone who is on the edge of breakdown.

Ay-Tete-Fee, Clifton Chenier: The strange title of this song is a record company executive's attempt to render the singer's Creole French "Hey Petite Fille" ("Hey Little Girl"). This piece gets us close to the birth of zydeco music. Chenier practically screams the vocal, alternating stanzas in French and English, while playing a raucous amplified piano-accordion. He sounds like someone not just from another culture but from another planet. Zydeco music is reasonably familiar today, but what must people outside the Creole community have thought of this record when it first appeared in 1955? A piano and guitar provide rhythm and harmony, while the drums accent the offbeats and a bass plays a Caribbean rumba figure, adding to the exotic quality of Chenier's singing and accordion playing. A version of this song entirely in English was recorded six years earlier by New Orleans pianist Professor Longhair, but Chenier has taken it to the swamps.

Black Night, Charles Brown: Brown had one of the most distinct and intimate singing styles in the blues, and this slow song is a great vehicle for it. His piano is spare behind his crooning vocals, but he takes a dazzling break, ranging all over the keyboard. As fine as his playing is, the real instrumental stars in this number one rhythm and blues hit from 1950 are guitarist Johnny Moore and tenor sax man Maxwell Davis. It's not that they play so many notes, it is that every one is appropriate to the sad and lonely mood that Brown sets up. Moore punctuates the vocal with jazzy chords emphasizing the blue notes, while Davis bends long notes in the lower register. This is cocktail hour blues for someone who is drinking alone.

Blue Yodel No. 8 (Muleskinner Blues), Jimmie Rodgers: This song of a levee camp worker has become a standard in country music, popularized in recent decades by Bill Monroe and none other than Dolly Parton, but this 1930 recording by Jimmie Rodgers is the original. His performance here suggests a man from a "redneck" background seriously trying to reconcile the differences in black and white music. His guitar playing is much of the time confined to chordal background, but every now and then he breaks out into finger-picked melodic lines in the manner of his black counterparts. His singing shows him to be absolutely comfortable with the loose timing of the blues, and his yodeling mixes typical Alpine melodic figures with falsetto leaps drawn from the black field holler tradition. Jimmie Rodgers pointed the way, and country music is still trying to work out these musical contradictions.

Blues with a Feeling, Little Walter: Walter was a notorious brawler, and here it sounds like he is going a round with the recording microphone. His singing and harmonica playing are right in the listener's face. This is classic Chicago electric blues from 1953. Walter crowds and occasionally overloads the microphone with his vocal peaks of emotion and draws out incredible nuances with his harmonica playing. Two-note chords subtly change character as his tonal emphasis moves between the two ends. The guitar playing of brothers Louis and Dave Myers is a simple medium shuffle but brilliant in the way they lock together in a walking figure with a melodic lead on top, reinforcing Fred Below's drumming. Chicago Blues didn't get much better than this.

Bo Diddley, Bo Diddley: This is another aspect of Chicago Blues that belonged entirely to this artist, who used the song to announce his arrival on the scene. Recorded in 1955, it caught the first wave of rock and roll fever and allowed the artist to make a living as a rocker to the present day. This song, however, also portends a new direction for the blues, although few other artists have gone as far down the road Bo Diddley set out on. He tunes his guitar to an open chord and turns on the tremolo switch, playing few chord changes but concentrating instead on a ferocious syncopated rumba rhythm, reinforced by nothing but drums and maracas. The latter instrument had great potential in blues, and it is surprising that few other musicians followed Bo Diddley in this sound. This truly original artist found some African musical roots overlooked by others and built a style around them.

Boogie Chillen, John Lee Hooker: Like Bo Diddley, Hooker was another rhythmic genius of electric blues guitar. This half-spoken piece from his first recording session in 1948 proclaims the singer's coming of age as he drops in at "Henry's Swing Club," but it also turned out to be the coming of age of a new type of blues music, one that gave precedence to rhythm, percussion, and "groove" instead of melodic and harmonic complexity. Hooker's Mississippi roots are evident here, as he plays a series of riff variations on the guitar, stomps his feet percussively, and pushes the tempo. Only once during a break is there a suggestion of a chord change. Otherwise, Hooker plays varying clusters of notes chosen from a pentatonic scale that includes two blue notes. His rhythm is a distillation of "swing" that was being played at the time by bands of upwards of ten musicians. This piece was the start of a modern musical movement that is still growing.

Bull-Doze Blues, Henry Thomas: Almost nothing is known about Henry "Ragtime Texas" Thomas, but recent research suggests that he was born in northeast Texas in 1874, making him a member of the generation that created the blues form. This piece from 1928 could well stand for the first full-fledged blues. His strummed guitar outlines the twelve-bar form with its standard three-chord harmony, while his verses consist of a single line repeated three times. During breaks he plays the panpipes, a set of tuned reed whistles held on a rack around his neck, a nineteenth-century folk instrument with African sources, here placed in the service of a new twentieth century African-American music. His simple lyrics are about travel and the hobo's search for a better place where he'll "never get bull-dozed." This is Henry Thomas's own secular "freedom song."

Caldonia, Louis Jordan: Jordan was at the forefront of a movement that started in the late 1930s, uniting blues and jazz by reducing the size of big bands, simplifying the arrangements, and putting the emphasis on blues vocals. By the time of this 1945 recording Jordan and his Tympany Five were at the height of their popularity, and "Caldonia" proved to be one of their biggest hits. It opens with a piano boogie-woogie chorus, reinforced by the bass and drums. Then two tenor saxophones, one of them Jordan's own, come in for a riffing chorus, followed by another with an added trumpet. Now that the full band has been heard, Jordan enters with a rapping vocal about his hardheaded woman, Caldonia. His singing contains squeaks and screams, mannerisms that would show up a decade later in early rock and roll. The exuberance, joy, and humor in this and other performances made Jordan one of blues's first crossover successes.

Cold Sweat, James Brown: In 1967, when "soul blues" seemed to be the predominant black contemporary style, the blues revival explored the music's history, and blues-rock went psychedelic, emphasizing long and loud improvised guitar solos. A new blues sound was emerging from deep in the ghetto: It was the sound of funk, and it was trying to take blues in a new direction. "Cold Sweat" is the seven-minute tour de force that introduced it. The harmony is stripped down to a single chord, now and then transposed up a fourth, with only passing references to other chords. The piece is also minimalist in other respects, being basically a series of riffs consisting of Brown's vocal ejaculations and responses by a tight massive seven-piece horn section. The other instruments function essentially as a rhythm and percussion section. Brown's vocals consist largely of grunts and screams—pure emotion, though nonetheless tuneful if one listens carefully.

Crossroads, Cream: Cream and the Jimi Hendrix Experience were the two important power trios of British blues-rock music (although Hendrix was an American). To give themselves a full sound they featured loud volume, heavy distortion and reverb on the electric guitar and electric bass, and "busy" drumming. In other words, the bass and drums were not just parts of a background rhythm section but were designed to capture the listener's attention along with the guitar and vocals. This 1968 live performance is based on Robert Johnson's solo vocal and acoustic guitar recording of "Cross Road Blues" made thirty-two years earlier. Cream regularizes Johnson's extended lines to an even twelve bars and his quirky duple-triple rhythms to straight pounding eighth note beats, with Clapton also singing on the beat. In all of this they have discarded many of the qualities that made Johnson's original a great piece of music. On the other hand, they have added fiery guitar soloing of great virtuosity, an interesting original riff figure, and bass playing and drumming that go far beyond the usual roles of these instruments in the blues. Clapton comes into his own as a vocalist on this piece, perhaps inspired by the passion of Johnson's original recording. This is how millions of new American and British fans experienced blues in the late 1960s.

Evil Blues, Li'l Son Jackson: Jackson is one of the many great blues artists whose original body of work is undeservedly overlooked by today's fans and critics. This is a 1949 solo performance with lightly amplified guitar that alternately demonstrates both of the main styles of Texas players, one featuring a steady thumping single-note bass overlain with treble melodic figures, and the other a kind of proto-lead playing featuring string bending, pauses, held notes, and long improvisational melodic lines. Jackson sings of disturbing thoughts about race, religion, family, and man-woman relationships, throwing in some odd dissonant harmonies on the guitar. The result is utterly distinctive, and this artist deserves a place alongside John Lee Hooker, Lightnin' Hopkins, and Arthur "Big Boy" Crudup as one of the geniuses of solo blues to emerge in the 1940s.

Evil Gal Blues, Dinah Washington: This is Dinah Washington's first big hit from her first recording session as a featured artist in 1943. It combines the best of jazz and blues of the day. The song was written expressly for her by producer and jazz critic Leonard Feather and is perfect for her sassy, stabbing vocal style. The Lionel Hampton Orchestra is reduced here to a jump band of seven musicians, and only pianist Milt Buckner is heard prominently, underpinned by drums and a bass that plays boogie figures. Hampton's vibes, a muted trumpet, a clarinet, and tenor sax are added in different combinations on each chorus, but once the singer enters, the attention is focused on her. Dinah Washington had been an obscure vocalist attached to Hampton's famous orchestra until this song broke and launched her successful career.

Eyesight to the Blind, Sonny Boy Williamson II: From the early jug bands to modern electric small combos, southern blues bands have displayed a wonderful democratic quality. All of the instruments help to build both the rhythm and the melody, and no individual claims too much attention at any one time. Heaven knows, Sonny Boy Williamson was trying to hog the spotlight on this, his 1951 debut recording. He seems desperate to share his feelings about his woman with the world, spewing out a breathless torrent of words and warbling harmonica responses. The woman's loving causes the blind to see, the dumb to talk, and a dying man to rise up off his deathbed. Pianist Willie Love and a drummer and two guitarists are right with Sonny Boy on this one, creating a powerful drive. This piece beautifully conveys the atmosphere of a Saturday night in a Delta juke joint half a century ago.

'Fore Day in the Morning, Roy Brown: Brown was one of the many blues shouters who emerged in the 1940s and without a doubt one of the most distinctive in the lot. His rich voice matches the power of any great operatic tenor. With drama and precise diction he wails the tale of a man abandoned by his woman. Brown's vocal lines march melismatically up and down a very long scale, and he is a master of bending tones and striking blue notes, especially the flatted fifth. On this 1948 recording he is backed by a seven-piece jump band of musicians from his native New Orleans. The trumpet and two saxophones mostly play as a section, leaving most of the lead work to the fine piano of Leroy Rankins, although an electric guitar comes to the fore toward the end of the piece. Roy Brown and his band were known as the "Mighty Mighty Men" with good reason.

Grinder Man Blues, Memphis Slim: Pianist Peter Chatman possessed a formidable technique, applied here in a style pioneered by Roosevelt Sykes. This 1940 recording is one of his first, and he is accompanied only by a string bass player. His left hand plays swing triplets deep in the bass, except on a solo break where it comes up higher on the keyboard. It is constantly moving in varied one-measure rising stepwise figures full of passing notes, including the flat fifth and sixth, while his right hand plays a contrasting rhythm of sixteenth notes ranging over several octaves. This is virtuoso blues piano at its best. Memphis Slim's image of an itinerant meat grinder as a great lover may be disturbing to some modern sensibilities, but it was typical of blues at this time.

Honky Tonk Train Blues, Meade Lux Lewis: The rhythms of trains inspired early solo blues guitarists, harmonica players, and pianists. Lewis was a powerful keyboard wizard from Chicago, and this is his masterpiece. He recorded it many times in his career, but his original 1927 version is arguably his greatest. His left hand plays walking bass eighth notes with a bit of swing, while his right hand plays a stream of variations, including swing eighth notes in rhythm with the left hand, triplets, and syncopated figures that give a sense of rhythmic disjunction. At times the listener can not tell which hand is keeping the main beat. The joy of this piece is the way the two hands pull apart and come back together rhythmically. This is boogie-woogie piano at its best in one of its earliest recorded examples.

I Ain't Gonna Let You See My Santa Claus, Victoria Spivey: The singer's double entendre image verges on being a single entendre if one knows of Victoria Spivey's obsession with sexual themes in her songs. She tells her cheating man off in no uncertain terms, singing with great verve and backed by a powerful blues pianist and three jazz masters on trumpet, clarinet, and bass. New Orleans trumpeter Lee Collins is particularly outstanding on this 1936 marriage of blues and jazz. Spivey was one of the few vaudeville blues singers whose career survived the Great Depression, even if she did have to step in the gutter now and then. She's in charge here, with top-notch musicians raring to do her bidding.

I Don't Live Today, Jimi Hendrix: Blues music had long been improvisational, but in 1967 it became experimental in the hands of Jimi Hendrix, his British band members (bassist Noel Redding and drummer Mitch Mitchell), and his producer and engineer. Through guitar overdubs, feedback, and other devices, some known only to himself, Hendrix created a blues that displays not merely variation from one chorus to another but actual musical development. Contrary to normal blues practice, it is the voice that responds to the guitar here. Using a powerful descending riff, Hendrix performs twelve-bar choruses with minimal harmonic development, singing about the dullness of a life that seems little different from death. Suddenly the melody jumps up a fifth, as Hendrix himself seems to jump up out of a pit, singing the song's title phrase and playing an improvised guitar solo, only to fall back in a complete rhythmic breakdown. He recovers, and the tempo speeds up, with the band playing at double time. The piece seems to break apart again, as it fades out with Hendrix asking "Are you experienced?" This is psychedelic blues at its earliest and best.

I Feel Good, Little Girl, Junior Kimbrough: Recorded in 1982, this is an example of a dance-oriented blues style that emerged in the Mississippi hill country, east of the Delta. It relies on insistent guitar riffs and minimal chord changes. In fact, there is only a brief hint of a change to the subdominant chord in

Kimbrough's instrumental breaks in this piece. Junior Kimbrough created dronelike anthems with unusual structures and managed to get his band members to learn these songs. This one has only a single stanza of fifteen bars that is repeated several times with instrumental breaks. Bassist George Scales plays a variant of Kimbrough's guitar part in a lower register, and drummer Calvin Jackson replicates the guitarist's rhythmic phrasing to create a powerful dance and trance groove.

I Just Want to Make Love to You, Muddy Waters: Recorded in 1954, this is a nearly irresistible invitation to lovemaking. Muddy Waters sets his woman on a pedestal, building her up and making her feel good with his promises of devotion reinforced by a series of insistent riffs on a single chord. By the time he switches to the subdominant chord, he knows she is his. Bassist Willie Dixon composed this song and produced the recording. This is Muddy Waters's classic lineup. Pianist Otis Spann supports Muddy's guitar riff, while drummer Fred Below and Little Walter, playing a big chromatic harmonica, create an eerie sense of inevitability. Muddy Waters shouts and growls his way through this tour de force, showing why he was considered the king of Chicago Blues.

I Pity the Fool, Bobby Bland: Bland begins this song singing calmly, stating that he pities the fool who loves a certain woman. Suddenly we learn that the fool is none other than the singer, as he bursts out screaming about the people who are standing around watching him make a fool of himself. Bland is the picture of utter humiliation in this frightening outburst, sounding like he is going to do harm to himself or somebody else. This is powerful soul blues at its emotional best. The 1960 performance is greatly enhanced by the arrangement of Joe Scott, featuring twin trumpets as part of a six-piece horn section. The relentless quarter-note beat is broken up by the jagged lead guitar lines of Wayne Bennett.

Keep On Chooglin', Creedence Clearwater Revival: Led by the brilliant John Fogerty, this group of four white boys from the San Francisco Bay area managed to achieve a remarkable down-home blues sensibility. In this insistent one-chord riff piece one hears elements of Fred McDowell, Howlin' Wolf, and a host of other Mississippi blues guitarists and singers. Recorded in 1969, it seems to be an alternative to the "boogie music" concept developed a couple of years earlier by another California band, Canned Heat, from the music of John Lee Hooker, who was also a guitarist originally from Mississippi. This tune is basically a juke joint dance piece, revved up for performance in a rock ballroom or at an outdoor festival. The tempo accelerates over the course of seven-plus minutes, and we hear extended solos on harmonica and guitar with some psychedelic feedback. This is blues for a new audience, drawing tastefully on the music's deep roots.

Key to the Highway, Jazz Gillum: Gillum isn't usually placed in the first rank of blues artists, but he was one of the stars of the Chicago recording scene in 1940. Wherever he belongs in the hierarchy, he certainly rose to the occasion on this song, making it a much-covered classic. Gillum plays wailing harmonica only on instrumental choruses, and the main attraction is his rich bass singing, complemented by Big Bill Broonzy's crisp playing on a big Gibson guitar and a bass to drive the beat along. This is an eight-bar blues about the eternal theme of leaving. In this case the singer is running because "walking is much too slow." Blues singers have been traveling with this song ever since.

Merry Christmas, Pretty Baby, Jessie Mae Hemphill: The deepest roots of blues combine with modern studio technology on this 1984 recording. The descendent of several generations of rural Mississippi musicians, Hemphill sings in a melismatic style not far removed from the field holler. Her electric guitar is simple and rhythmic, with a touch of feedback, moving between tonic and subdominant chords behind the singing and answering the vocal phrases with repeated riffs that emphasize the flat third and seventh blue notes. She plays a tambourine with her foot and adds two more layers of percussion with overdubbed snare and bass drums. The rhythms are drawn from fife and drum music passed down within her family and played at community picnics. This is self-created fusion music, traditional and contemporary at the same time.

Mississippi Swamp Moan, Alfred Lewis: This extraordinary performance from 1930 illustrates how the blues can employ the full palette of tonal resources, both vocal and instrumental. Many of the sounds heard here would barely be considered musical in the western tradition. Lewis was a harmonica player, recorded in Chicago, about whom nothing else is known. He sings traditional blues lines in a falsetto voice, sometimes through the reeds of the harmonica itself, giving his singing a buzzing quality. The harmonica completes his lines in descending bluesy phrases in the high register, with his sound on the instrument being alternately squeaky and warbling. The interaction of singing and playing is so tight that it seems as if man and instrument are one being. This is the African concept of instruments as voices at work in the blues.

Moanin' at Midnight, Howlin' Wolf: Here is the sound of a West Memphis cinder block juke joint captured in a studio in

1951 by Sam Phillips, the producer who would later discover Elvis Presley. Phillips always maintained, however, that Howlin' Wolf was the greatest artist he ever recorded. The sound here is overwhelming, especially when one considers that this was only a trio, or really just a duo when Wolf put down his harmonica and sang. Willie Johnson's guitar is cranked up all the way and terribly distorted, as it no doubt had to be if it were to be heard in its normal setting. Fortunately Phillips realized that this quality was part of the aesthetic of the music and let it stand. Willie Steele plays a simple drum kit like a washboard inside a big resonating tub. Although this song uses the three-line blues form, it is basically a series of riffs without chord changes. Wolf's voice matches the guitar's distortion, rising like some sound out of the bowels of the earth. After scaring his listeners to death for three minutes, he announces at the end that he is going to bed!

The Mojo, J. B. Lenoir: Jimmy Reed's records are best known for introducing walking bass figures on guitar to Chicago Blues, but fellow Mississippian J. B. Lenoir was playing them several years earlier. On this 1953 recording for a small independent Chicago label, Lenoir plays a ferocious boogie beat, ably supported by Sunnyland Slim's piano and a bass and drums, while J. T. Brown wails in response on the tenor saxophone. The latter instrument was more commonly heard in jazz orchestras and jump bands, but here it fills a role usually occupied by a harmonica. Lenoir had a distinctive high voice that some mistook for a woman's. He tells of a visit to New Orleans, mixing images of the city's nightlife and its reputation for voodoo activity. This is rough and gritty electric blues, direct from the clubs of southside Chicago.

My Country Man, Big Maybelle: The singer praises her farming man with corns on his hands and "a whole lot of energy."

The imagery may be rural, but the performance style is urban and up to date for 1952. Big Maybelle had a voice to match her size, and she lets it out here, growling and shouting her way through the lyrics yet never failing to be tuneful. The recording is all hers, but she is greatly aided by the arrangement of bandleader and songwriter Leroy Kirkland and a crew of seven jazz musicians. The pianist plays a basic rhythmic boogie-woogie, reinforced by a tight horn section of trombone, tenor, and baritone saxophones. Their sound is deeper than that of the usual horn section, perhaps to match the singer's range. An electric guitar with a bit of distortion provides the only real lead instrumental work, but it never draws attention away from the singer and her song. The performance is tight and thoroughly professional, representing the best of jump blues.

On the Road Again, Canned Heat: This song and its singer and arranger, the introspective Alan Wilson, were unlikely candidates for pop success, but it is a tribute to the expansive and experimental tastes of rock fans that it stayed high on the charts for seven weeks in 1968. This is psychedelic blues-rock that benefits from studio overdubbing technology. It achieves its effect, however, purely from natural sounds rather than loudness, distortion, and feedback. This one-chord song is based on Floyd Jones's 1953 recording in a minimalist Chicago style much influenced by Howlin' Wolf. Wilson maintains the harmonic simplicity of the original but gives it a boogie beat with his guitar, taken from the sound of John Lee Hooker, which Larry Taylor doubles on the electric bass in a lower register. The eerie quality of the original is conveyed by Wilson's high-pitched, reedy voice and his deep harmonica playing. Throughout the piece one hears a drone sound from an Indian tamboura, representing the popular interest of the time in Eastern mysticism and music. Floyd Jones sang of the lonely traveler on the open road, but Wilson's version is every bit as much about a journey in the mind.

Poor Man's Blues, Bessie Smith: In 1928, more than a year before the stock market crash, the Great Depression was already being felt in black America. In this original composition Bessie Smith has created perhaps the greatest expression of protest in the blues. She manages to go beyond personal, racial, and gender concerns to speak for the poor and downtrodden men and women throughout America, all this when she was at the height of her popularity and financial success. Addressing her song directly to "Mister Rich Man," she asks him to open up his heart and mind, reminding him of the poor man's service to America in World War I, which many had called "the rich man's war and the poor man's fight." Her ability to growl and bend notes is in full display here, seconded on every line by Joe Williams's trombone, while in the background Porter Grainger on piano and Bob Fuller and Ernest Elliott on clarinet and saxophone lay down a thick, soupy harmony that sometimes wavers ambiguously between tonic seventh and subdominant chords. The combination is magnificent, and three-quarters of a century later, one can't fail to be moved by Bessie Smith's plea.

Prison-Bound Blues, Leroy Carr: This 1928 recording was one of the first hits for the duo that established the piano-guitar sound in the blues. Carr plays thick rhythmic chords on the piano along with right-hand arpeggios and occasional lead figures, but most of the soloing is done by guitarist Scrapper Blackwell. He bends strings and plays in both upper and lower registers in a proto-lead style that he created prior to the invention of the electric guitar. Carr's plaintive singing and songwriting skill are on display here. A handful of verses perfectly sum up the sense of defeat of a prisoner sent up for a long stretch and abandoned by the woman he loves.

Roll Over Beethoven, Chuck Berry: Chuck Berry's home city of St. Louis was an early center of ragtime music, and there is perhaps a hint of that old genre in this piece with its even eighth notes on Berry's guitar, the boom-chack beat on the drums, and Berry's syncopated singing. But there was nothing old about the theme of this 1956 song or the genre it introduced—rock and roll. More than anyone else in the 1950s, Chuck Berry chronicled the lifestyle of an emerging adolescent demographic, and he did it using blue notes, the blues form, and blues instrumentation. Berry's singing here is more of a recitative chant, but it is delivered with great enthusiasm. And what great lyrics, what great guitar playing, and what a great beat!

See See Rider Blues, Ma Rainey: The "Mother of the Blues" is in top form here, accompanied by some of the best players in jazz, so it's no wonder that this 1924 recording became an enduring hit. Her majestic voice paints a simple picture of abandonment and revenge, with every space filled in by a front line of Louis Armstrong on cornet, Charlie Green on trombone, and Buster Bailey on clarinet. These were "first call" session musicians for vaudeville blues recordings of the era, and it's not hard to see why, as each one has a distinct voice to match Rainey's. A piano and banjo fill out the rhythm. Ma Rainey didn't use a lot of mannerisms and dramatics. The emotion and richness of her voice were enough to proclaim her stature.

The Sky Is Crying, Elmore James: Two tenor saxophones lay down a thick background for Elmore James's passionate singing and slide guitar on this achingly slow blues, recorded in Chicago in 1959. The production by Bobby Robinson is superb, as the studio room seems to come alive, practically revealing the vibration of the singer's vocal cords and letting the listener hear the scraping of the slider against the guitar strings, all heavily amplified. Piano, bass, and drums fill out the sound. The whole song is an outpouring of emotion. The singer's woman has left him, the sky is crying, and tears are flowing in the street and out the singer's door. The descending slide figure on the guitar seems to suggest more tears falling down. The singer's voice, a cross between a cry and a scream, adds to the mood of sadness.

Stop and Listen Blues, Mississippi Sheiks: The Sheiks were a family string band, but here they are reduced to just two members, singer-guitarist Walter Vinson and violinist Lonnie Chatmon. This 1930 recording shows how an instrumental format of the nineteenth century was adapted to the new blues music. Vinson's melody and guitar part are drawn from those of "Big Road Blues" by fellow Mississippi bluesman Tommy Johnson, but Vinson adds more popping of the bass strings against the neck of the instrument. Chatmon plays a more complex paraphrase of Vinson's vocal melody in a high register on the violin, answering his lines with improvised phrases. The violin had a lot of potential for playing blue notes, but it ceded its place at the forefront of nineteenth-century black folk music to the harmonica and saxophone as blues and jazz became predominant in the twentieth century.

Sue, Bobby Rush: The master of neo-hokum blues provides almost nine minutes of vocal foreplay here in this 1982 hit. It starts with a conversation with the singer's mother in which he tries to tell her what his girlfriend, Sue, does for him. Then he proceeds to tell us, building up our anticipation until the culmination in a surprise ending. Much of his panting vocal is spoken, breaking out into occasional sung rhymes that draw on traditional blues rhetoric and folk speech. All this is set to an insistent guitar riff backed by bass, drums, and keyboard synthesizers. The one-chord riff carries us back to the deepest roots of the blues as well as to a contemporary funk sound. With material like this, Bobby Rush has kept the blues fresh on the chittlin' circuit over the last few decades in the face of blues-rock and nostalgia trends.

Sweet Home Chicago, Robert Johnson: Johnson is best known today for his slide guitar blues and his themes of supernatural encounters, but he was best known during his short lifetime for more upbeat songs like this 1936 recording. Johnson plays a walking bass figure derived from the left hand of boogie-woogie piano blues. Some fifteen years later it would show up on electric guitar in Chicago Blues recordings of people like J. B. Lenoir and Jimmy Reed. Johnson's lyrics in this recording don't make a great deal of sense, but the beat and vocal refrain are so compelling that it doesn't matter. Hundreds of blues singers have subsequently performed versions of this song, often substituting their own lyrics.

T-Bone Shuffle, T-Bone Walker: This is a blues given a jazz treatment by a fine jump band in 1947. Walker's voice is simply one more instrument in a series of solo spots. The piano, bass, and drums establish a simple shuffle boogie rhythm, followed by a twelve-bar chorus featuring Walker's long-lined electric guitar, then followed by another from tenor sax player Hubert Myers. Walker sings a chorus, urging his baby to let her hair down and have a "natural ball." He follows with two louder and more insistent choruses on the guitar, bending a string on nearly every note, and then goes back to singing. Next comes the culminating instrumental section, a duet between trumpeter George Orendorff and Walker on guitar, now bending two strings at a time. He ends with another vocal chorus. T-Bone Walker established the sound of jazzy lead electric guitar in the blues during the 1940s, and one can hear echoes of his phrases in the later work of Chuck Berry and hundreds of other players.

Terrible Operation Blues, Georgia Tom and Jane Lucas: This is actually a hokum dialogue skit in which the doctor and female patient re-enact an "operation" followed by a description of what was removed (four monkey wrenches and a bale of hay, among other things). It's hard to believe that within two years of this 1930 recording Georgia Tom would launch his career as Thomas A. Dorsey, the "Father" of gospel music. He certainly isn't very reverent in this masterpiece of sexual double entendre as he tells his patient to take off her underwear. He plays a bluesy ragtime pattern on the piano, while Big Bill Broonzy leads with a lively guitar on this delightful romp. Dorsey may be best known for his gospel compositions, but hokum has had a prominent place in the blues ever since he introduced it.

Texas Flood, Stevie Ray Vaughan: This 1982 recording lasts over five minutes, mainly because Vaughan supplements his three stanzas of singing with the same number of instrumental choruses. Although he is best known as an influential blues-rock guitarist, his singing should not be overlooked. His vocal timing is excellent, and he displays a voice all his own without sounding like he is trying to replicate someone else's mannerisms, a fault of many white blues singers of the modern era. Credit should also go to bassist Tommy Shannon and drummer Chris Layton for the fine rhythmic groove they provide on this slow blues. Unlike many "power trios" who try to bowl the listener over with a wall of sound, these musicians give each other and the audience some breathing room so that the song itself as well as Vaughan's guitar soloing can be appreciated. The piece was composed and first recorded by Larry Davis in 1958 and represents a long line of blues on themes of natural disasters.

That's All Right, Elvis Presley: Elvis was nineteen years old when he recorded this piece in 1954, a version of a song recorded eight years earlier by Mississippi bluesman Arthur "Big Boy" Crudup. Whether or not this was the first rock and roll record, as some have argued, it was the first record release of Presley's career, and he was to become the biggest star in the early period of the new genre. Elvis's recording is no better than Crudup's, but what is significant is that this effort by a young white boy from Memphis was no worse either, for Crudup had been a star in the blues field and a major creative stylist. Elvis sounds completely comfortable singing the blues, and already signs of his distinctive style are evident, such as his long, slow slides into some notes. On the instrumental side, the recording shows vestiges of country music, with Presley's rhythmic strumming on an acoustic guitar, Scotty Moore's electric lead guitar in the style of Merle Travis, and Bill Black's oom-pah bass. This hybrid record was a hit with white and black listeners alike, and with it a major new sound, based in the blues, was launched.

Tipitina, Professor Longhair: This 1953 recording could only have come from New Orleans, and probably only from the odd creative genius of Professor Longhair. His eight-bar blues is an invitation to his girlfriend to join him in partying, delivered in his unique half-spoken style, interspersed with what are either nonsense words or some secret code. Longhair sets up a $3 + 3 + 2$ rumba boogie riff on the piano with his left hand, while the right hand plays melodic eighth-note figures, sometimes switching to triplets to create a fascinating rhythmic complexity. The bass player hits straight quarter notes, while the drummer plays a parade beat, giving the whole thing the flavor of a Mardi Gras celebration. Tenor and baritone saxes merely fill out the harmony with long, soft held notes. While he drew deeply from his city's well of musical traditions, Professor Longhair was one of a kind.

Viola Lee Blues, Cannon's Jug Stompers: Cannon's Memphis unit plays jug band music at its best. The star of this 1928 recording is vocalist and harmonica player Noah Lewis, who sings verses about homemade whisky, the courtroom, and prison. We never learn who Viola Lee was, but somehow one gets the impression she was involved in the singer's plight. Lewis's singing is plaintive, and his harmonica has a lovely pure and penetrating tone. He was the first in a lineage of great west Tennessee harmonica players that included Hammie Nixon, Big Walter Horton, and John Lee "Sonny Boy" Williamson. The abundant instrumental choruses feature wonderful interplay between Lewis's harmonica and the kazoo and jug. Band leader Gus Cannon on the banjo and a guitarist ably march the rhythm along.

Walkin' the Dog, Rufus Thomas: It's not hard to imagine this 1963 Memphis recording as a modern version of a jug band, with Lewie Steinberg on bass and Floyd Newman and Gilbert Caple on baritone and tenor saxes substituting for jug, kazoo, and harmonica. Trumpet, organ, electric guitar, and drums add further thick layers of melodic, harmonic, and rhythmic complexity. But the star is vocalist Rufus Thomas, the "World's Oldest Teenager," a veteran 1940s blues shouter who started in minstrel shows and survived as a performer long enough to see the twenty-first century. He was known for humorous novelty blues on animal themes like this one. It was a top ten hit on both the rhythm and blues and pop charts!

What'd I Say, Ray Charles: When this was released in 1959, it was the first dose of soul music that many Americans had heard. It's a continuous performance of over six minutes, and it starts off as a rocking instrumental blues with Charles on the relatively new electric piano along with a bassist and a drummer who taps heavily on the cymbal. It's pleasant enough, but it really starts to build when Charles comes in with his singing. A four-piece horn section is added, and it's getting hot when Charles abruptly stops playing. This results in vociferous complaining by the Raelettes, who were standing by all the time, getting worked up by Charles's passionate singing. He jumps back into the piece, and from this point on he moans, sighs, and screams in sexual ecstasy, answered by the Raelettes, while the drummer works out on the cymbal and toms and the horns blast away. Around the country there were calls to ban this piece from the airways, but it became a top ten hit anyway and number one on the rhythm and blues chart.

When You Get Home, Write Me a Few Little Lines, Fred McDowell: McDowell was one of the greatest discoveries of the blues revival. In his first recording session in 1959 he was in his mid-fifties, but he sounds like a much younger man. This song was recorded on location in Como, Mississippi, by folklorist Alan Lomax, and the artist is surrounded by family, friends, and fellow musicians, who can be heard enjoying themselves to his music. He plays the guitar at a breakneck tempo that accelerates over the course of the performance, laying down a series of riffs in the slide style. McDowell's slider is both a melodic and percussive device as it scrapes over the strings. His singing is equally strong and intense, as he delivers traditional verses about loneliness and separation, culminating in the news that his woman has died. Meanwhile, his guitar sounds the rhythm of life.

Wild Women Don't Have the Blues, Ida Cox: This singer leaves no doubt about who is the boss in her relationships with men, and she advises other women to be like her. "You never get nothing by being an angel child," she proclaims. In this original composition, recorded in 1924, Ida Cox uses the twelve-bar form but fills it up with long verses. Nevertheless, pianist Lovie Austin, cornetist Tommy Ladnier, and clarinetist Johnny Dodds find places to insert their sounds. These were some of the top accompanists of vaudeville blues singers, and their beautiful tone can be appreciated in spite of the surface noise of this early recording. Cox's tart voice and clear diction also cut through, making this an enduring classic of the style.

Woman Woman Blues, Ishman Bracey: This 1930 recording is practically a definition of the sound and meaning of the blues. Bracey was a singer-guitarist from Jackson, Mississippi, who later became a Baptist preacher. In a two-line blues, extended with repeated guitar riffs, he uses just about every possible technique on his instrument to play blue notes and achieve percussive effects. His playing alternates between lush major harmonies and violent, wrenching blue notes on bent strings. His singing also presents contrasts between a sweet falsetto and a voice that sounds like it has been dragged out through clenched jaws. Bracey's traditional verses alternate themes of love and cruelty. Beauty and ugliness are blended here and distilled to a fine art.

Blues on CD

The record business these days is such that blues CDs go in and out of store display bins with alarming rapidity. Unfortunately, this is generally not because they sell in such huge quantities that the stores can't keep them in stock. Instead, most good blues music enjoys modest sales that extend over a long period of time as new fans continue to discover the music's enduring quality. Record stores, on the other hand, are largely geared to selling the current "hits." Older items are taken off the shelves to make room for the flood of new releases that hopefully will generate some quick sales. The record companies, in turn, often let the slower-selling items go out of print permanently or temporarily when their stock is sold. The Curious Listener may find record stores convenient for surveying current releases. For the older and hard to find items, however, one should look for a reliable music mail order service or smaller specialty record stores.

Most blues up to the 1960s, and in many cases much later,

were released as 78 and 45 r.p.m. "singles." The listener thus experienced the sound of an artist for only three or six minutes at a time. When LPs and CDs began to appear, sequencing the music on an extended series of tracks, it became apparent that most blues artists had a sound limited by the concise character of the blues form itself and by their own personal style, their "bag of tricks" that they applied in more or less the same way to many tunes in their repertoire. Blues performers generally don't possess the compositional and improvisational versatility and the harmonic knowledge of, say, jazz musicians. They usually perfect their style early in their career and stick with it. Thus, it is easy for the first-time listener to blues to become bored with the apparent lack of variety of any one artist over a series of recorded tracks. He or she must learn to listen to the music a bit differently, appreciating the artist's degree of feeling, the subtle variation in melody, tone, and rhythm, the striking poetry and directness of communication of the song, and the emotional connectedness between the artist and the song, between voice and instruments, and between the song and a cultural environment.

One good way to begin blues listening is through anthologies, and several are listed in this chapter. These allow the listener to sample a variety of artists and styles and pick out favorites to explore later in more depth. They also sometimes present great music by artists who never recorded enough material for a complete CD or who recorded a few great tracks in the midst of other more ordinary efforts. All the anthologies listed here offer fine and varied music, and have lengthy and authoritative notes containing background on the artists and songs. The majority of the CDs listed here, however, concentrate on a single artist. Some are box sets; others are single CDs. A few present the complete recorded works of an important artist, while others present an artist's greatest recordings or greatest hits, his or her work for a particular record company, a significant phase of an artist's career, or recordings that were originally released together as an album that has by now achieved milestone status. If the price of some of the larger packages seems daunting, the same music is usually available on single CDs. Whatever the case, the Curious Listener should seek out CDs with good sound quality and authoritative booklet notes. The items listed below usually meet these criteria, but there are often equally good alternative packages that allow the listener to explore the music of these artists in greater or less depth.

There should be one word of caution in regard to a few of the items listed here. In the case of some early recordings from the 1920s and 1930s the original masters have been lost, and the reissues had to be prepared from dubbed copies of issued records, some of which were worn. In some cases only a single worn copy of a great piece of music exists. In other cases the masters themselves suffer from surface noise or the limitations of early recording technology. We must either put up with these factors or not hear this music at all. They affect, for example, the entire recorded output of such great blues artists as Ma Rainey, Blind Lemon Jefferson, and Charley Patton, and the prewar recordings of Skip James. Enjoy them as you would any other antique or work of art that has suffered a bit from the ravages of time.

The fifty CDs or sets listed here by no means purport to be the fifty greatest blues CDs ever made, but they are a good start, and they provide much historical and stylistic variety. Actually, the work of almost all of the artists mentioned in this book, particularly those featured in the previous two chapters, is well worth exploring in depth. Through exploring the many records that are now available, reading the literature on blues, getting advice from other fans and collectors, making a few mistakes, but also discovering many hidden gems, the Curious Listener will find the music that is worth hearing again and again and the artists who are worth hearing in depth.

Afro-American Folk Music from Tate and Panola Counties, Mississippi, Various (Rounder): These field recordings from 1942 and 1969–71 document the range of folk music in the northwest corner of Mississippi, allowing the listener to understand the blues in its broader musical, historical, and social context. There are blues performances with guitar and one-string "diddley bow" by Othar Turner, Ranie Burnette, and Compton Jones, along with other tracks containing fife and drum bands, a string band, a family percussion group, panpipes, banjo, work songs, children's songs, and a gospel song.

The Anthology, Bobby "Blue" Bland (Duke-Peacock/MCA): The best of Bland's work from 1952 to 1982 on the Duke, ABC, and MCA labels is presented on two CDs. His voice is sometimes smoldering, sometimes blazing on the selections, many of which landed high on the rhythm and blues charts. The early tracks also benefit from the fine arrangements of band leaders Bill Harvey and Joe Scott and the guitar of Wayne Bennett. From about 1970 onward the arrangements and material sometimes get a bit too "sweet," but Bland never strays far from the peak of soul blues feeling in his singing. His falsetto cries later became rough vocal squalls, and both techniques can be heard here.

Best of Canned Heat, Canned Heat (Capitol): This CD gives a good portrait of this popular band, including their hits, from their most important period of 1967 to 1970. "On the Road Again," "Fried Hockey Boogie," and "Boogie Music" present the rhythmic groove, adapted from John Lee Hooker, that they popularized. "Bullfrog Blues" and "Rollin' and Tumblin'" are prewar blues given tasteful electric band treatments. "Same All Over," "Time Was," and "Amphetamine Annie" demonstrate some real songwriting skills, and "Let's Work Together" is a delightful cover that will make anyone nostalgic for the sixties.

The Best of the Memphis Jug Band, Memphis Jug Band (Yazoo): This raucous unit with shifting personnel recorded more songs between 1927 and 1934 than any other jug band of the era. The excellent selection on this CD concentrates on the blues side of their repertoire and includes songs that were covered by folk and blues-rock groups in the 1960s, such as "K. C. Moan," "Cocaine Habit Blues," and "Stealin' Stealin'." Three different jug players, each with a different style, are heard, along with Ben Ramey's manic, nonstop kazoo. Guitar and harmonica, and sometimes other instruments, round out the sound.

Big, Bad & Blue, Big Joe Turner (Rhino): Joe Turner was a blues survivor whose recording career took him through six decades and many styles of accompaniment. As a vocalist, however, he changed little. He was a big, swaggering shouter from Kansas City, who could drive a band with his voice and who had a way with blues of sexual innuendo. These three CDs take us from the beginning (1938) to practically the end (1983) of his career. More than a third of the material is devoted to his tenure with Atlantic Records in the 1950s, when he went so far as to achieve rock and roll stardom, and it includes such hits as "Honey Hush," "TV Mama," "Shake, Rattle and Roll," and "Flip, Flop and Fly." But there are also wonderful recordings from earlier years with boogie-woogie pianist Pete Johnson and various jump bands. The great artists who back him up on these tracks are too numerous to mention. Turner's career was a glorious march through much of the history of the blues, with forays into jazz and rock.

The Birth of Soul, Ray Charles (Atlantic): These three CDs cover the artist's period with Atlantic Records from 1952 to 1959, when he joined the passion of gospel music to the power of the blues to create what the title of this set proclaims. The first disc reveals him as somewhat of a cross between a shouter and a crooner but with bits of the soul vocal style beginning to emerge. He shows himself to be a fine blues pianist, and several tracks have outstanding guitar by Mickey Baker. By the end of 1954 Charles was a full-fledged soul blues singer, recording "I Got a Woman," which opens the second disc. This and the final disc cover the next five years, in which he perfected the style, culminating in such classics as "Hallelujah I Love Her So," "Lonely Avenue," and "What'd I Say." There are many more in this set just as great as these.

Blind Lemon Jefferson, Blind Lemon Jefferson (JSP): The listener will have to make an effort to hear the music through the surface noise of some of these tracks, but it will be well worth it. Jefferson was a master of guitar-accompanied blues and the sub-genre's biggest star. These four discs contain everything he recorded in his brief career (1926–29). The guitar playing, especially on the first two discs, is simply dazzling. Many of the pieces seem to contain constant improvisation. His singing displays great freedom and a huge melodic range, and there's wonderful poetry in many of his verses. Jefferson takes anyone who is willing to really listen into a world that few today could imagine, a world of dirt roads, city street corners, prisons, grinding poverty, and mistreating men and women. Out of horror, he made beauty.

Blue Bird Blues, Sonny Boy Williamson (Bluebird): This disc takes us through Williamson's entire recording career from 1937 to 1947, and in it we hear the artist evolve from being a harmonica player with a couple of country blues guitarists to the leader of a proto-electric Chicago blues band. We also hear a batch of songs that would become blues standards, such as "Good Morning, School Girl," "Sugar Mama Blues," and "Hoodoo Hoodoo." Besides Williamson's formidable talent as a harmonica player, singer, and songwriter, we hear many other blues stars of the period backing him up. These include down-home blues guitarists Big Joe Williams, Robert Lee Mc-Coy, Henry Townsend, and Yank Rachell, Chicago blues guitarist Big Bill Broonzy, Washboard Sam, pianists Joshua Altheimer, Blind John Davis, and Eddie Boyd, bassists Ransom Knowling and Willie Dixon, and drummer Judge Riley.

Blues, Jimi Hendrix (MCA): Many of Jimi Hendrix's rock tunes turn out on closer inspection to be extensions of the blues form. There is no doubt, however, that the eleven tracks assembled here are blues. They come from studio outtakes, informal sessions, concert recordings, and jams. Although they are odds and ends, they are far from throwaways, and taken together they shed plenty of light on the solid blues foundation of this extremely influential artist. Naturally the focus is on electric guitar pyrotechnics, but we also get to hear the artist solo with acoustic guitar on the opening track, "Hear My Train a Comin'." Two of the tracks are songs from Muddy Waters and one is from Albert King; the rest are Hendrix originals. Although most of these tracks were not released on his commercial albums, they are more focused than many of the tracks that were.

The Blues, Various (Smithsonian/Sony): This is an excellent four-CD compilation, with each disc covering a decade of blues from the 1920s to the 1950s, while the last three tracks make a dash toward the 1980s. There is a certain amount of duplication with other single-artist discs recommended here, but many other important artists are sampled, which will probably lead the listener to want to hear more. Among the latter are Sara Martin, Furry Lewis, Sleepy John Estes, Big Joe Williams, Tampa Red, Peetie Wheatstraw, Wynonie Harris, and Otis Rush, to name just a few.

Blues Masters, Jimmy Reed (Rhino): The elements of Reed's style are simple and unmistakable—the walking bass figures played by second guitarist Eddie Taylor, the squeaky harmonica fills, and the slurred vocals. But what catchy songs he composed (with lots of help from his wife) and what a catchy delivery! Hundreds of artists have covered "Big Boss Man," "Honest I Do," "Ain't That Lovin' You Baby," and the other hits gathered here, but none as well as the original versions. Good blues can be complex and performed by virtuosos, but it doesn't have to be. Reed had the common touch, and his songs will last for many generations.

Butt Naked Free, Guy Davis (Red House): Davis is one of several younger black musicians who have emerged in recent years with a style based in the older traditions of acoustic blues and folk music. While he is more or less a revivalist in his sound, his repertoire is largely original. This CD, released in 2000, is one of his best efforts. He is free of the self-conscious mannerisms and the vocal and instrumental exaggerations of so many revivalists, both black and white, and sounds comfortable with his material. This in turn makes him convincing, like a good actor. It should come as no surprise, then, that his own background is in acting and that he is the son of actors Ossie Davis and Ruby Dee. Songs like "Waiting for the Cards to Fall," "High Flying Rocket," and "Sugarbelle Blue" display a gift for songwriting to go with his singing and guitar-playing talent.

The Chess Box, Chuck Berry (Chess/MCA): Anyone who thinks that being a rock and roller somehow made Chuck

Berry not a blues artist will realize from these three CDs that he simply created a different kind of blues. He infused the blues form with storytelling and described more succinctly than any social historian American working-class life and the emergence of an adolescent demographic in the 1950s and 1960s. His great hits are here—"Maybellene," "Johnny B. Goode," "Back in the U. S. A.," and many others—but there are also many straight blues along with oddities like "Havana Moon" and "Thirteen Question Method." The instrumentation is blues, the guitar playing spectacular, the poetry brilliant, and the performances energetic. Even the selections from the early 1970s, when Berry was already firmly a part of the nostalgia circuit, have much to recommend them.

The Chess Box, Bo Diddley (Chess/MCA): Bo Diddley is another artist more often associated with rock and roll than blues, but like Chuck Berry he also simply created a new sound in blues. It draws on African and Caribbean rhythmic and harmonic ideas and ones that the artist took from deep levels of folk tradition, including children's songs and sanctified shouts. The most innovative pieces are classics like "Bo Diddley," "Bring It to Jerome," "Mona," and "Say Man," but these two CDs also contain many wonderful examples of Chicago electric blues, such as "You Don't Love Me" and "Diddy Wah Diddy." In the manner of boxer Muhammad Ali, Bo Diddley celebrates himself in most of his songs, but we never resent it because of his humor. Jerome Green's maracas playing on most of these selections is a special treat and gives Bo Diddley's music a unique, rhythmic flavor.

The Chess Box, Howlin' Wolf (Chess/MCA): These three CDs present material from 1951 to 1973, which spans most of this great artist's recording career. For someone whose roots ran so deep in Mississippi blues and who didn't begin to record until he was past the age of forty, Howlin' Wolf was a surprisingly versatile artist. Besides deep riff–based blues like "Smokestack Lightnin'" and "I Asked for Water," there is the topical "The Natchez Burnin'," more sophisticated Willie Dixon compositions like "Wang Dang Doodle" and "Three Hundred Pounds of Joy," and a workout with British blues-rockers on "The Red Rooster." Wolf sounds strong and fresh at all stages of his career, and there is always that unearthly voice. He was an intimidating presence in the blues and made others play his music his way.

The Chess Box, Muddy Waters (Chess/MCA): These three CDs cover a huge span of Muddy Waters's career, from 1947 to 1972. Although they are missing his earlier Mississippi field recordings. Still, the Mississippi roots are in evidence in classics like "I Can't Be Satisfied," "Louisiana Blues," and "Still a Fool," and there is plenty of great electric slide guitar playing throughout these selections. Willie Dixon's songwriting enters the picture at the end of the first disc with "Hoochie Coochie Man" and continues with great songs like "I'm Ready" and "You Shook Me." What is surprising, however, is the number of great songs composed by Muddy Waters himself, such as "Long Distance Call," and "My Home Is in the Delta." Muddy's bands contained many great sidemen, and here we get to hear the talents of Little Walter and James Cotton on harmonica, Otis Spann and Pinetop Perkins on piano, Willie Dixon on bass, Fred Below and Willie Smith on drums, and Jimmy Rogers, Pat Hare, Earl Hooker, Buddy Guy, Sammy Lawhorn, and others on guitar.

The Cobra Records Story, Various (Capricorn): This is the story of a short-lived (1956–58) Chicago blues label founded by gangland figure Eli Toscano, who was found floating in Lake Michigan shortly after he sold the company to pay gambling debts. Cobra and its affiliate Artistic label are best known for pioneering the "West Side" blues sound that fused spectacular electric lead guitar and melismatic soul singing with the Chicago small-combo format. That sound is abundantly represented on these two CDs by Otis Rush, Buddy Guy, and Magic Sam, but there are also fine selections by Big Walter Horton, Harold Burrage, Betty Everett, Sunnyland Slim, Shakey Jake, and Ike Turner. The success of many of these tracks is due in part to producer and bass player Willie Dixon.

The Complete Aladdin Recordings, Lightnin' Hopkins (Aladdin/EMl): Hopkins recorded for so many labels over his long career that it would be difficult for anyone to put together a retrospective survey of his entire output. He was consistently creative, however, and rarely turned out anything that was less than excellent. These two CDs come from the beginning of his recording career, 1946–48, and present him at his very best. Even when borrowing from earlier artists, his songs have a wonderful, spontaneous feeling and are full of great poetry. He sings in a melismatic style not far removed from a field holler and plays electric guitar in a proto-lead style but without the support of a band. These are blues for listening more than for dancing, although a few pieces like "Lightnin's Boogie" have plenty of rhythm. There are also several wonderful selections featuring Thunder Smith on piano.

The Complete Early Recordings of Skip James, Skip James (Yazoo): This Mississippi artist recorded eighteen tracks in 1931 that stand apart from everything else in the prewar blues era for their weird sound that mixes a heavy dose of brooding melancholy with occasional outbursts of manic exuberance. Nothing James recorded in his rediscovery career (1964–69) matches them, although his later work would stand very tall if it weren't for these early masterpieces. His voice moves eerily in and out of the falsetto range, and his guitar is usually in a strange minor tuning. The fast tempos of some of his pieces are astounding. There is a certain defiance in his music, as if he knew that he was an unappreciated genius. If his guitar music is not enough, there are five tunes that have him accompanying his singing with piano. His style on that instrument is equally strange, full of starts and stops, foot stomping, and wild one-handed rampages over the keyboard.

The Complete Okeh Sessions 1952–55, Big Maybelle (Epic/Legacy): What a voice this singer had! She is heard here, early in her recording career, with orchestras under the direction of Leroy Kirkland, Denny Mendelsohn, and Quincy Jones. These groups contained excellent jazz musicians, including trombonists Alfred Cobbs, Eli Robinson, and Billy Byers, saxophonist Sam Taylor, guitarist Mickey Baker, and drummers Herbie Lovelle and Panama Francis. Even bluesman Brownie McGhee makes an appearance on guitar. "Gabbin' Blues," "Rain Down Rain," and "One Monkey Don't Stop No Show" are good representatives of Maybelle's varied moods. Her "Whole Lotta Shakin' Goin' On" is the song that later launched the career of rocker Jerry Lee Lewis. She sings her heart out on every selection.

The Complete Recordings, Robert Johnson (Columbia): If ever there was a blues artist whose music deserves to be heard in its entirety, it is Robert Johnson. The task is actually not too difficult, as all of his songs fit on two CDs. None contain anything besides his singing and guitar playing, but they are quite a varied lot. They include riff-based pieces with slide guitar like "Walking Blues" and "Preaching Blues" and up-to-date numbers reflecting urban musical trends, such as "Phonograph Blues" and "Little Queen of Spades." Johnson's mood also swings between the exuberance of "They're Red Hot" and "Terraplane Blues," the tenderness of "Love in Vain" and "Honeymoon Blues," the despair of "Drunken Hearted Man" and "Cross Road Blues," and the horror of "Stones in My Passway" and "Hellhound on My Trail." This is absolutely essential material.

Complete Recorded Works, 1930–1936, Little Brother Montgomery (Document): Montgomery was one of the greatest blues pianists and a singer with a pleading voice from deep in the tradition. He was able to shape every one of his songs into an artistic gem while preserving the integrity of his source or his original idea. He was so on top of his music and repertoire that he recorded eighteen of these selections in a single day and still managed to make each one of them sound fresh. This CD includes three versions of his classic "Vicksburg Blues," as well as two other songs that would become standards: "Frisco Hi-Ball Blues" and "The First Time I Met You." Other outstanding numbers are "Santa Fe Blues," "Chinese Man Blues," and the three piano solos that conclude this CD.

Crossroads, Eric Clapton (Polydor): The trouble with retrospective box sets released during an artist's lifetime is that they don't anticipate the possibility that the artist will have a further period of creativity and popularity. Clapton has done just that since this four-CD set was released in 1988. Nevertheless, it contains a good chunk of his best material, starting in 1963, including tracks as a member of the Yardbirds, John Mayall's Bluesbreakers, Cream, Blind Faith, and Derek and the Dominos, as well as many under his own name. Most are blues tunes, and the others are bluesy rock. His spectacular guitar playing in extended solos is the main attraction, but his singing comes into its own in this material, and it should not be underrated. The influences of Robert Johnson, B.B. King, Otis Rush, and a host of other guitar greats are evident here. Clapton is respectful but never reverential, and his own style emerges early on.

The Definitive Blind Willie McTell, Blind Willie McTell (Columbia/Legacy): The Georgia twelve-string guitarist was at the height of his powers on these recordings made between 1929 and 1933. They cover two CDs and include solo performances as well as accompaniments to singer Ruth Willis and duets with longtime partner Curley Weaver. These songs demonstrate the breadth of McTell's repertoire, ranging from deep blues ("Broke Down Engine Blues") to hokum ("It's a Good Little Thing") to ragtime ("Georgia Rag") to spirituals ("Don't You See How This World Made a Change"). McTell sang and played with great sensitivity and precision, and each selection is a beautifully polished performance.

Deluxe Edition, Koko Taylor (Alligator): Koko Taylor was part of the Chicago blues scene in the 1960s, a protégé of producer Willie Dixon, but in spite of a couple of hit records, she always seemed to get squeezed out of the spotlight by the male stars like Muddy Waters and Howlin' Wolf. Her career didn't achieve sustained success until she joined the Alligator label, where she has stayed to the present day. This CD is a retrospective of her Alligator recordings, which are consistent in their quality. Taylor's rough growl and her stance as a woman not to be messed with may make her seem one-dimensional, but one has to admit that it's quite a dimension! Her singing style has inspired many wannabes, *but she is the real thing.* This CD also gives the listener an opportunity to hear many fine sidemen representing the second and third generations of electric Chicago blues.

Driftin' Blues, Charles Brown (Aladdin/EMI): Brown recorded in Los Angeles for the Aladdin label briefly in 1945 and then for an extended period from 1948 to 1956 in a group that enjoyed remarkable stability. Sometimes billed as Johnny Moore's Three Blazers, it consisted of Brown on vocals and piano, Moore on electric guitar, and Eddie Williams on bass, supplemented from 1950 onward with a drummer and tenor saxophone player. On his last Aladdin session Brown recorded in New Orleans with the studio musicians who usually backed Fats Domino and other local stars. This CD is an excellent representation of this period in Brown's long career and includes most of his early hits, such as "Driftin' Blues," "Trouble Blues," and "Hard Times." Brown's group brought jazz and classical elements to the blues, leading it in the direction of "art" music yet never abandoning spontaneity and feeling. This music is at the opposite end of the blues stylistic spectrum from that of contemporary artists like Howlin' Wolf, but it captures moods that the harder and louder artists never expressed.

Empty Bed Blues, Bessie Smith (Asv Living Era): Smith's complete recordings from 1923 to 1933, 160 songs plus a few alternate takes, are available in a series of box sets on the Columbia label, and her serious fans and collectors may want to head straight there. Meanwhile, this CD, containing thirty-one tracks, is an exceptionally well-chosen selection. Some CD treatments of female vaudeville blues singers focus more on the talents and jazz pedigrees of their male accompanists, but this one puts the emphasis solidly on the singer and her best songs, some of which were her own compositions. The obligatory selections are here—"Downhearted Blues" (her first recording), "St. Louis Blues" (with Louis Armstrong), "Back-Water Blues," and "Empty Bed Blues"—but there are many other gems like W. C. Handy's "Yellow Dog Blues" and "Do Your Duty." Bessie Smith's reputation for greatness has never faded since the 1920s, and she stands today at the highest level in the field.

The Excello Singles Anthology, Slim Harpo (Hip-O): This Louisiana artist's entire recording career from 1957 to 1969 was with the Excello label, and these two CDs gather all of his singles in one complete set. Harpo stayed on the jukeboxes and on radio long after other down-home blues artists had faded from sight or crossed over to the blues revival scene. Like Jimmy Reed, with whom he is often compared, his sound was simplicity in itself, although no one has been able to do it better. He sang in a nasal voice and played adequate harmonica and sometimes guitar as well. Drums and a second guitar or bass completed the basic lineup, with piano and one or two saxophones moving in and out of his various recording groups. Harpo's early hits, like "I'm a King Bee," "Rainin' in My Heart," and "Shake Your Hips," have some wonderful rhythmic grooves, but he does surprisingly well late in his career with added production and arrangement in Nashville sessions. He even manages to give distinctive treatments to such pop standards as "Mohair Sam" and "Folsom Prison Blues," both with added horn sections.

Free Again, Robert Pete Williams (Original Blues): Williams will be an acquired taste for some listeners. His singing has a stark, jagged quality, frightening in its intensity, that is not softened by the knowledge that this man served time in the Louisiana State Penitentiary for murder. His guitar playing is also jagged and often in minor keys, sometimes very slow but with a relentless beat on the faster numbers, which he preferred. Most of all, his singing, playing, and songwriting were utterly original and highly spontaneous. His music is primitive art in the best sense. His moods at the time of performance are evident, and they are mostly moods of loneliness, aimlessness, and impending death, as in "Almost Dead Blues," "A Thousand Miles from Nowhere," and "Hobo Worried Blues." When Harry Oster made these field recordings in

1960, Williams was on parole, working long hours in semi-slavery on another man's farm, not allowed to leave the state to pursue musical opportunities. Fortunately he finally made good, both in his life and his musical career.

Hoodoo Lady (1933–1937), Memphis Minnie (Columbia/Legacy): Memphis Minnie is best known for her guitar duets with her husbands, Kansas Joe and Little Son Joe. None of that music is heard here; instead, we have the pleasure of hearing her fine guitar playing on its own in several tracks, as well as in various combinations with piano, mandolin, string bass, drums, and clarinet. Minnie always sets the pace with bouncy, strutting, hip-shaking rhythms all her own. Some of the selections, all made in Chicago, have the flavor of jug band music from back in Memphis. Her voice is harsh and direct, as is her imagery in such songs as "Ice Man (Come On Up)," "Keep On Eatin'," and "My Butcher Man." Songs like "Man, You Won't Give Me No Money" can lead to debates as to whether she was a proto-feminist or simply a hustler. Whatever the case, she held her own over a long career in a male-dominated blues scene.

King of the Blues, B.B. King (MCA): B.B. King has continued to record and perform since this four-CD career retrospective set was released in 1992. Some important recordings are missing here, especially from his earliest period (1949–61), which is covered in a mere nine selections, but otherwise this is a pretty good representation of the music of this prolific artist. He has been extraordinarily influential, both as a singer in the gospel-influenced soul style and as an electric lead guitarist, and many of his songs have become standards in the repertoires of others. This is a nice selection of big hits, undeservedly lesser-known tracks, and "guest star" collaborations with leading figures of the jazz, pop, and rock worlds. There isn't much that B.B. King hasn't done in the blues, or hasn't done very well, and most of it is represented here.

King of the Blues Guitar, Albert King (Atlantic): Albert King was always a fine artist, but these seventeen tracks from 1966–68 are his best, thanks in part to the support of the Stax Records house musicians, Booker T. and the MGs and the Memphis Horns. By the end of this period King was becoming part of the blues-rock world, and it would soon be reflected in his long guitar solos. His playing is more concise on these tracks, most of which appeared as three-minute singles. His smoky voice is also strong and convincing on songs like "Laundromat Blues," "Oh, Pretty Woman," and "As the Years Go Passing By." It's easy to see why rockers both admired and felt intimidated by him.

Martin Scorsese Presents the Blues: A Musical Journey, Various (Hip-O): This five-CD set is part of a massive blues documentary project that also includes television and radio programs, a Web site, a book, and an educational component. The music here mostly rises above the clichés that pervade the other material, only falling down in the selections that are closely geared to the films' attempts to anoint certain trends as the present and future of the blues. Barring these exceptions, which account for no more than 10 percent of the set's 116 tracks, this is an extremely well chosen group of recordings covering the music's history. Most of the greatest blues artists are represented with some of their best-known pieces, and there are many tracks that were historic milestones, such as Mamie Smith's "Crazy Blues," Pine Top Smith's "Pine Top's Boogie Woogie," and B.B. King's "The Thrill Is Gone." This set is as good a place to start as anywhere and a good way to turn others onto the blues.

Mean Old World: The Blues from 1940 to 1994, Various (Smithsonian/MCA): This four-CD set overlaps somewhat with the time period (but not the selections) of the other Smithsonian set, *The Blues,* but it places greater emphasis on the postwar years. White blues artists are not included, however, in this set's concept of the blues, except in a few rare instances as sidemen, and even rock and rollers like Chuck Berry and Little Richard fail to find a place here. On the other hand, this set gives some space to shouters and crooners, soul blues singers, and acoustic blues discoveries, who are often neglected in such surveys. For what it covers, it contains well-chosen selections, many of them big hits in their day, with excellent performances by important artists.

The Mercury Blues 'n' Rhythm Story, 1945–1955, Various (Mercury): The Mercury label became best known for jazz and pop music, but in its earliest years it recorded a surprising amount of blues of excellent quality. Over two hundred tracks are gathered here on eight CDs. Jazzy jump bands, shouters, and crooners are heavily represented on this label, such as Dinah Washington, Julia Lee, Ella Johnson, Eddie "Cleanhead" Vinson, Jimmy Witherspoon, and Screamin' Jay Hawkins, just to name the best known. In fact, this is one of the best surveys of that much neglected phase of blues history. But Mercury also recorded prewar veterans like Sippie Wallace, Helen Humes, St. Louis Jimmy, Big Bill Broonzy, and Memphis Slim, along with new down-home artists like Lightnin' Hopkins and Smokey Hogg, and emerging rhythm and blues stars like Professor Longhair and Johnny Otis. Surprisingly, for a company that was based in Chicago, Mercury recorded little of the emerging electric combo style of that city, although there are a few excellent tracks by Sunnyland Slim and Robert Jr. Lockwood. This set contains many other treasures by little-known artists deserving greater attention.

The Modern Downhome Blues Sessions: Arkansas & Mississippi 1951–1952, Volume 1, Various (Ace): Blues musician Ike Turner led Modern Records label owner Joe Bihari on a tour of the Deep South juke joint blues scene just after the music had gone electric. The results are presented here, and they rival in importance and quality the field recordings made in the same territory by Alan Lomax and other folklorists, perfectly filling in a gap between Lomax's field trips of 1942 and 1959. These tracks are absolutely stunning in their raw intensity. Elmore James is the only artist of any notoriety, and he only has two selections here. The real stars are Drifting Slim, Junior Brooks, Sunny Blair, Houston Boines, Charley Booker, Boyd Gilmore, and Ernest Lane.

Mother of the Blues: 1923–1928, Ma Rainey (EPM Blues Collection): There are many CDs containing selected tracks by this artist, and the serious collector will probably want to get all of the approximately 100 songs she recorded, as her stature rivals that of Bessie Smith. The seventeen songs on this single CD are an especially good sample of her work in various formats, including jazz band, jug band, and piano-guitar duet. Some of her best work is heard here, including "Moonshine Blues," "Barrel House Blues," and "Oh Papa Blues." Accompanists are among the top names in jazz of the period, including Louis Armstrong, Charlie Green, Kid Ory, and Coleman Hawkins. All mothers deserve respect, and no one has ever had anything but the highest praise for this "Mother of the Blues."

Poet of the Blues, Percy Mayfield (Specialty): Mayfield's songwriting skills can impress us so much that we lose sight of what a great singer he was. In the same way that a good tenor will leap easily to a higher register, Mayfield's voice moved in and out of the low end of his range. He was smooth, but his style gave an ominous edge to his singing, which suited the often gloomy subjects of his lyrics. "Life Is Suicide," "Hopeless," and "Wasted Dream" are not the exceptions but rather are typical titles. One doesn't mind, however, so polished is the singing and songwriting, along with the arrangements and playing of the Maxwell Davis Orchestra with its almost unvarying lineup of three saxes, piano, guitar, bass, and drums.

Rock Me Mamma, Arthur "Big Boy" Crudup (Bluebird): As a singer and guitarist, Crudup was a low-down Mississippi bluesman of the first rank, his voice sounding like it was ringing across a cotton field and his guitar intoning rhythmic riffs with few chord changes. However, he was a songwriter of considerable sophistication and sensitivity, and many of his compositions have become standards, pieces like "Rock Me Mamma," "That's All Right," and "My Baby Left Me." Some of his greatest lyrics actually are found in his lesser-known songs, such as "Black Pony Blues," "Give Me a 32-20," and "I'm Gonna Dig Myself a Hole." Crudup is important not merely because Elvis Presley liked his songs, but because he actually anticipated by several years the sound of early rockabilly music, both in his beat and in his instrumentation of electric guitar, bass, and drums.

Screamin' and Hollerin' the Blues: The Worlds of Charley Patton, Charley Patton and Others (Revenant): Patton is another artist who will be an acquired taste for some listeners, in part because of the surface noise on his recordings. But one also has to get used to his rough voice, his nearly incomprehensible lyrics, and the unfinished quality of many of his songs. What makes him great, then? It is the utter spontaneity and passion of his music, his total involvement in what he is doing. There's also the breadth of his repertoire, an unforgettable voice, a beautiful touch on the guitar, and some verses of re-markable social insight. Each song reveals something new with every listen. This set of seven CDs is quite expensive, due to its packaging that includes the equivalent of two books of written documentation. Patton's own recordings would fit on three CDs, but this box contains recordings of his musical associates, such as Son House, Willie Brown, Louise Johnson, and Buddy Boy Hawkins. These were artists of more or less equal stature, which is to say they were among the greatest.

The Sky Is Crying, Elmore James (Rhino): This CD is a career retrospective of an important artist whose music successfully made the transition from Mississippi to Chicago and seemed to be headed in the direction of blues-rock at the time of his sudden death in 1963. It begins with his first recording, "Dust My Broom," made in Mississippi in 1951 and based on an earlier recording by Robert Johnson, and ends with tracks from the early 1960s made in Chicago, New Orleans, and New York City. While his first recording has Sonny Boy Williamson II playing harmonica, James abandoned this sound almost immediately and began to record with one to three saxophones and sometimes a trumpet. The combination of horns with his high-volume electric slide guitar worked well and helped to modernize the musical elements that James brought with him from the South. He left the world with many powerful recordings, some of the best of which, including many of his hits, are here.

Smokin' in Bed, Denise LaSalle (Malaco): Denise LaSalle might be viewed as the female counterpart to Bobby Rush. Both specialize in sexual double entendre songs, mostly self-composed, and both have been stars on the chittlin' circuit and southern black radio for several decades. This CD, released in 1997, is representative of the consistently interesting recordings she has made in recent years for Malaco Records of Jackson, Mississippi. Tracks like the album's title song and "Dirty Old Woman" give a good idea of her main theme. The recent trend of nostalgic songs about blues itself is represented by "Juke Joint Woman" and "Blues Party Tonight," while "Never Been Touched Like This" and "If I Don't Holler" contain hip-hop remix treatments.

Steppin' on the Blues, Lonnie Johnson (Columbia/Legacy): Johnson continued to perform and record fine music for nearly forty years after he made the selections on this CD, but his early work (1925–32), represented here, is his greatest. He was a guitarist of extraordinary versatility, able to perform stunning instrumental solos like "Playing with the Strings," duets like "Guitar Blues" with jazz guitarist Eddie Lang, or "6/88 Glide" with pianist John Erby, and then turn around and play pure country blues behind the field holler vocals of Texas Alexander. Johnson was no slouch as a vocalist either, or as a songwriter, as he demonstrates in tunes like "Mean Old Bedbug Blues" and "Got the Blues for Murder Only." For good measure there's a double entendre duet with vaudeville star Victoria Spivey, "Toothache Blues." About the only things missing are representative selections displaying Johnson's considerable talents on violin and piano. But he's best known as a guitarist, and one who had a great influence on later electric lead stylists. That side of his music is gloriously and abundantly revealed here.

Strong Persuader, Robert Cray (Mercury): Blues reflected intellectualism and middle-class sensibilities in the 1940s and 1950s in the work of such diverse artists as Charles Brown, Josh White, Percy Mayfield, and Chuck Berry, and perhaps something similar was afoot in the 1980s with the rise to prominence of Robert Cray. Coming from Tacoma, Washington, and growing up in the post–Civil Rights era, he performs and composes an "integrated" type of blues that doesn't seem aimed at any particular racial audience. Yet in a stylistic sense it is solidly based on the soul blues developed in the ghettoes and on the chittlin' circuit some decades earlier by artists like B. B. King and Albert Collins. Cray is his own man, however, as a vocalist, lead guitarist, and songwriter, exploring the complex psychological dimensions of his subjects in songs like "I Guess I Showed Her" and "Right Next Door (Because of Me)." This fourth CD of his career, released in 1986, shows his style fully matured, with his four-piece band supplemented in fine fashion by the Memphis Horns.

Take This Hammer, Leadbelly (Bluebird): Leadbelly was the first performer of unquestioned authenticity to become a star in the folk music revival. These recordings were made for RCA Victor in 1940, and on half of them he is paired with the immensely popular Golden Gate Quartet. The idea behind these collaborations was to recreate the sound of southern prison worksongs, and it works beautifully. With Leadbelly's churning twelve-string guitar and his and the quartet's lusty singing, these expressions from the margins of society are turned into high art. They include some of Leadbelly's best known pieces, such as "Pick a Bale of Cotton," "Midnight Special," and "Rock Island Line." The remaining half of the twenty-six selections consists of solo blues, including favorites such as "Good Morning Blues" and "Easy Rider" and a wonderful paean to "New York City," his adopted home. Some of these songs recall the earliest sounds of folk blues, while others go back even further into nineteenth-century folk music.

Texas Flood, Stevie Ray Vaughan and Double Trouble (Epic/ Legacy): The original 1983 release of this album had almost as much popular impact as an earlier debut album from 1967 by

Jimi Hendrix. Both were in a "power trio" format of electric guitar, electric bass, and drums, but Vaughan is less psychedelic and stays closer to basic blues structures. This CD release is supplemented with a studio outtake from the original sessions, a brief interview of the artist, and three live recordings from 1983. Vaughan and his band members work together beautifully to create a full sound and some fine grooves. For several years prior to this debut, they had had opportunities to observe, sit in with, and back up some of the top contemporary blues artists, and it shows here. Vaughan's guitar disciples are often criticized for their excesses, but his own playing is quite tasteful and no less spectacular.

Texas Songster, Mance Lipscomb (Arhoolie): This CD combines most of two old albums, one from Lipscomb's first recording sessions in 1960 at his home in Navasota, Texas, and another made four years later at a coffee house in Berkeley, California. At age sixty-five when he first recorded, Lipscomb hardly sounded ready for retirement, nor does he later on when entertaining young hippies. He sings in a rich country voice and plays guitar in a typical thumping Texas style with a strong beat. He has a broad repertoire, mostly blues but with interesting folk ballads, versions of old popular songs, ragtime numbers, and spirituals. Around 1910, blues in the South existed within this larger spectrum of music, and this CD carries us right back to that era.

They Call Me the Fat Man, Antoine "Fats" Domino (Imperial/EMl): Anyone who thinks of Fats Domino only as a crooner of soft ballads hasn't heard much of the man. That can easily be rectified by listening to the four CDs that comprise this set, and they reveal him to be quite a fine blues artist. Of course, it's blues from New Orleans, and that means that it's mixed with jazz and pop elements. His walking bass rhythms on the piano are smooth and relaxing, and one often doesn't realize how much he's doing with his right hand in the higher range. This set contains about half of the material he recorded for the Imperial label from 1949 to 1962, including his big hits of the 1950s. Virtually all were recorded in his native city with top session musicians and his musical arranger Dave Bartholomew. The material is consistently delightful and includes undeservedly lesser-known blues like "The Fat Man" and "Don't Lie to Me," old folksongs like "Bo Weevil" and "The Rooster Song," and, of course, "When the Saints Go Marching In."

The Ultimate Collection: 1948–1990, John Lee Hooker (Rhino): Even though he still had another eleven good years to go, this is a career retrospective of a great and prolific artist's work, packed into two CDs. It covers all of his phases, including his riveting early solo sides, his building of a small combo with bass and drums, his reversion to acoustic guitar for a "folk" audience, his work with Chicago blues stars, and his collaborations with leading jazz and rock figures. Hooker himself doesn't really change. Everything else is built onto his solo style with its powerful guitar rhythms and free-form structures with few chord changes. It's a tribute to his many accompanists that they were able to follow him and respect the integrity of his music. When all is said and done, however, Hooker is at his best and most creative in his solo pieces or with the bare minimum of accompaniment. There is plenty of that side of his music here, and much more awaits the Curious Listener on other CDs.

When the Sun Goes Down: The Secret History of Rock & Roll, Various (Bluebird): These four CDs, also sold separately, contain selections from the vast catalogue of blues recorded by the RCA Victor company from the 1920s to the early 1950s. The set starts with Robert Petway's primal Mississippi chant, "Catfish Blues," and ends with proto-rock and roll by Little Richard. Many of the tracks, in fact, are the original versions of blues that were covered by rock artists from the 1950s onward. All phases of the blues from this period, except the great shouters and crooners of the 1940s, are well represented, including stars like Big Bill Broonzy and Washboard Sam and more obscure but equally outstanding artists like Bessie Tucker and Julius Daniels. Some of the special delights of this set are oddities like the vocal quartet rendition of "Dixie Bo-Bo" by the Taskiana Four, Mississippi Sarah's jug playing with Daddy Stovepipe on "If You Want Me, Baby," and the Hall Johnson Choir's remarkable version of "St. Louis Blues."

EIGHT

The Language of Blues

Every type of music needs a terminology, both for its performers and for those who seek to appreciate or understand it. Of the words and phrases listed below, some are standard technical terms for describing music of any sort. Others are particular to the blues and related types of music (folk, jazz, etc.). They include terms used by the musicians and ones often used by commentators in the literature on blues. They describe characteristics of the music itself, performance techniques, instruments, roles of musicians, and aspects of the social environment of the blues.

AAB: A shorthand description of the most common stanza pattern of the blues. The letters represent the three lines (verses) of this pattern. The first line (A) is repeated (the second A), followed by a different, usually rhyming, line (B).

Ballad: A type of folksong that tells a story with a chronological development, usually sung in the third person about some important person or event. "Ballad" has a completely different meaning in the world of popular music, where it describes a sentimental love song, usually sung in the first person at a slow or moderate tempo.

Bar: *See* Measure.

Barrelhouse: A barrelhouse is a place where drinking, dancing, and music, usually of a rough and rowdy type, take place. The term is probably derived from barrels of whiskey or beer, which sometimes double as barstools. "Barrelhouse" can also be used to describe the type of music typically heard in such a place, and it can be used as a verb to describe the behavior encountered there. *See also* in chapter on Varieties of Blues.

Beat: The insistent pulse that musicians create and that the listener to music feels. The beat functions as a time-keeping reference for musicians and dancers.

Blue Note: A note characteristic of blues singing and playing that falls between the flat and natural pitches of a scale degree. It can occur as a neutral pitch between these two pitches, as a wavering between them, or as an upward slide from flat toward natural.

Boogie-Woogie: A type of blues based on a riff, usually played in the lower register. It is especially associated with piano blues. *See also* in chapter on Varieties of Blues.

Bottleneck: The neck of a bottle can be worn by a guitar player on the finger to slide over the strings, creating a whining sound. *See also* Slide Guitar.

Chord: Three or more notes sounded at the same time to produce a harmony. By extension, the term can be used to describe the harmony that is implied by two notes sounded at the same time or by a sequence of notes within a melodic line.

Chord Changes: These are harmonic shifts from one chord to another.

Combo: From "combination." A small group of musicians, consisting usually of three or more players.

Cover: A performance or recording of a hit song previously recorded by another artist. The term usually implies some degree of imitation of the original hit.

Degree: One of seven pitch levels in a scale. These levels in their "natural" form are the familiar *do-re-mi-fa-sol-la-ti* and are numbered one through seven. Most of these degrees can also be sounded "flat" or "sharp," which are levels midway toward the next lowest or next highest scale degree. *See also* Blue Note.

Duple Rhythm: A rhythm that occurs in evenly spaced groupings of two or four.

Falsetto: A high-pitched "head voice" produced by male singers, above the normal vocal range.

Frottoir: A scraping percussion instrument used in zydeco music. Derived from the washboard, it is a corrugated aluminum vest worn over the player's neck or shoulders and scraped rhythmically with thimbles worn on the fingers.

Griot: A member of a social caste in some West African societies, whose occupational role includes entertainment and music. In their itinerant existence, low social status, performance of songs of social commentary, and use of stringed instruments, they resemble blues singers. Their music is one of the historical sources of the blues.

Harmony: The sounding of notes at two or more different pitches at the same time, usually creating an agreeable effect on the listener.

Harp: A term used by blues musicians for the harmonica.

Heterophony: The performance of a melodic line by two or more players or singers at the same time with slight variation between them. The variation can occur in both pitch and rhythm.

Holler: A type of solo singing in black American folksong tradition, performed under conditions of work in fields, levee construction, and other rural occupations. The singing is typically free-form, strident, sometimes wordless, and infused with blue notes. Used for both communication and self-expression, hollers were an important ingredient in the earliest blues.

Improvisation: Spontaneous creation of music, either by combining preconceived and traditional elements or entirely from the imagination.

Interval: The space between two pitches, usually counted in degrees (e.g., a flat third, a fifth, etc.).

Jug: A jug is a ceramic, glass, or metal vessel used as a bass instrument in a jug band. The player forms the notes with the voice while expelling air into the vessel, which acts as a resonator. Prototypes of the instrument are found in some forms of African music. *See also* Jug Bands in chapter on Varieties of Blues.

Juke: Also spelled *jook*. This is a term of uncertain etymology, possibly from "chock," a type of homemade beer. A juke house or juke joint is a small honky-tonk, often a converted residence, where drinking, music, and dancing take place. The term can also be used as a verb to describe these activities. A jukebox is a coin-operated record player, a machine that came to replace live music in juke houses.

Kazoo: A type of instrument especially associated with jug bands. It is a small tubelike enclosure, usually made of metal, with an opening covered by a thin membrane of animal skin, tissue, or plastic wrap. The player inserts the tube into the mouth and creates sounds with the voice, causing the membrane to vibrate and distort the sound with a buzzing quality. Prototypes of the kazoo are found in African music.

Lead: This term refers to the most prominent vocal or instrumental line within a group, the one that carries the main melody.

Measure: A minimal unit of meter in a tune. In written notation a measure is bounded by vertical bar lines on the staff. Hence a measure is sometimes called a "bar."

Medicine Show: A type of entertainment once commonly found in southern towns. A "doctor" would organize a show consisting of dancers, musicians, and comedians, and travel from town to town, using the entertainment to draw an audience that would then listen to his sales pitch for his "medicines." Blues singers and jug bands were often hired for these shows.

Melisma: The singing of one syllable over two or more pitches.

Melody: The main vocal or instrumental line of a tune.

Meter: A grouping of pulses, all of the same duration, that serves as the basic organizational unit for the temporal portion of a piece of music. For example, a 4/4 meter would be a grouping of four quarter-notes. Usually the meter remains the same throughout a tune.

Modulation: Shifting of a melody from one tonal center to another.

Mojo: A term from the world of magic and hoodoo, often encountered in blues lyrics. A mojo or "mojo hand" is a charm worn or carried by a person that confers luck or success in dealing with others. The term is of uncertain etymology, possibly from the Spanish *mal de ojo,* meaning "evil eye," i.e., a charm to ward off the evil eye, often represented visually by an eye in the palm of a hand.

Note: A musical sound at a particular pitch. Sometimes, by extension, the term can describe a series of different pitches joined together in a continuous sound.

One-String Bass: A string or rope attached to the bottom of an inverted tub or bucket, tightened by a stick that extends from the rim of the bucket to the end of the string. The player strikes the string while varying its tension with the stick to create different pitches. The bucket acts as a resonator. Since a washtub is often used in constructing this instrument, it is sometimes called a "washtub bass." Prototypes are found in African music.

Parallelism: A type of harmony in which two or more voices or instruments perform the same melodic line, keeping a constant interval between them. This technique is especially common in African music.

Pitch: The measurement of the sound wave of a musical note in vibrations per second. The pitch sounds higher as the number of vibrations increases.

Race Record: A phonograph record of music by black performers marketed to the black community. This term was in use from the 1920s to the 1940s, although the underlying concept continues to the present day.

Revival: Renewed or increased interest in an older type of music that is thought to be dead or dying. The interest can come either from within or outside the community that originally created and nurtured the music. A blues revival, growing out of earlier revivals of folk music and New Orleans jazz, reached its peak in the 1960s, resulting in the rediscovery of many older performers and an expansion of the blues audience.

Rhythm: The patterning or grouping of beats in music, creating a sense of motion.

Riff: A short, repeated melodic-rhythmic phrase. Many blues tunes contain an identifying or "signature" riff.

Scale: The differently pitched notes used in a tune. Most blues scales range between four and seven notes, although blue notes give them added flexibility.

Sheet Music: A printed version of a song, sold commercially.

Shuffle: A rhythmic pattern common in blues since the 1930s. It is usually viewed as a triple pattern with the second beat unstated, played at a medium or fast tempo.

Skiffle: A dialect form of "scuffle." The term came to mean a type of loosely performed music, often on homemade instruments, characteristic of jug and washboard bands.

Slide Guitar: The technique of sliding a hard, smooth object over the strings of a guitar to produce a percussive whining sound. The object can be a pocket knife or a bottleneck, a small glass bottle, or a metal tube worn on the player's finger. The technique is especially common in blues from the Deep South.

Songster: Originally a term used by black Americans to designate someone known as a singer, usually with a large repertoire of songs. In the literature on blues it has come to mean a singer with a diverse repertoire of blues and other types of songs designed for varied audiences and occasions.

Stanza: A grouping of verses into a unit. A song usually contains several stanzas, each sung to the same or a similar melody. The most common blues stanza pattern is the three-line AAB form.

Swing: This term generally refers to a rhythmic feeling somewhere between duple and triple. For some, however, it merely means any rhythm that excites the senses and induces a feeling of motion.

Syncopation: The accenting of off-beats, that is, notes that fall between the regular steady pulses or "beat" of a tune. Correspondingly, some of the main beats are often left unaccented.

Tempo: The speed of a tune, measured by the number of beats per minute. In blues the tempo sometimes accelerates over the course of a performance.

Tonal Center: The fundamental pitch on which a scale is based. It is the first degree of the scale and is essentially the note commonly called *do*.

Triple Rhythm: A rhythm that occurs in evenly spaced groupings of three. Sometimes in blues the second beat is silent, resulting in a "shuffle" rhythm.

Twelve-Bar Blues: A standard blues pattern consisting of twelve measures (bars). The three-line AAB pattern is typically twelve bars in length.

Verse: A line of text in a song.

Washboard: The common household object used as a musical instrument by scraping over its ridges with thimbles worn on the fingers. It was a popular rhythm instrument in blues into the 1940s, when it was replaced by the drum set. The washboard survives in an evolved form as the frottoir in Zydeco music.

Washtub Bass: *See* One-String Bass.

Resources for Curious Listeners

While the music itself constitutes the primary body of resources, the listener's appreciation and understanding of blues can be greatly enhanced by consulting what is available on the subject in print and over the internet. Because many listeners approach blues from a cultural and/or temporal distance, they are aided by knowing something about the lives of the performers, their sociocultural background, their interactions with one another, the origins of the music, its relationship to other types of music, and its place in communities, daily life, and larger patterns of culture and history. Since the 1960s, and especially since the 1990s, there has been an explosion of printed and other resources. Some of them, of course, reflect little more than enthusiasm and half-baked opinion, but there are many fine informative and interpretive works, with more appearing every year. Some of the best are listed on the following pages.

Books

A few of these books go out of print from time to time, but usually they reappear, sometimes in an updated edition. By far the main preoccupations of writers on the subject have been the history of the blues or particular phases of it and the lives of performers. There are now several dozen excellent biographies and autobiographies of blues personalities. Only a few are listed below in order to give space to other works that reflect the broader scope of blues literature.

A Blues Bibliography, Robert Ford: Published in 1999 and 800 pages in length, this book is a very useful resource for the serious researcher. The vast majority of the works listed are biographical and are arranged alphabetically under the name of the artist. Other sections deal with instruments, record labels, blues reference sources, regional variation, and lyrical and musical analysis. At the end is a helpful author index.

Africa and the Blues, Gerhard Kubik: An eminent scholar of African music with vast fieldwork experience delineates clearly the elements of blues that are traceable to that continent, even to specific African regional musical traditions. He shows how these elements were synthesized in the United States to form the blues genre several generations after contact with Africa was broken off and how the blues scale and blue notes were created out of African tonal practices. The discussion is technical at times but written clearly and free of jargon. Of special interest is the description of how American blues has influenced certain emerging African popular music styles in recent years. The work dispels a lot of ill-informed and romantic writing on the subject.

All Music Guide to the Blues, 3rd ed., Vladimir Bogdanov, Chris Woodstra, and Stephen Thomas Erlewine, eds.: This is a massive (755 pages of small print) and up-to-date (2003) survey of blues on compact disc, arranged by artist. Almost every blues CD in or out of print is described and evaluated by competent reviewers. At the end of the book are several useful essays on various styles and phases of the music that highlight the most important artists.

Bessie, Chris Albertson: Bessie Smith was the most popular and, in the opinion of many, the greatest vaudeville blues singer of the 1920s. There have been several books written about her, but this is by far the most thorough. It is based on her recordings, contemporary press accounts, and the reminiscences of family members, friends, and fellow singers and musicians. Her troubled life, her loves, and her controversial death are recounted in detail.

Big Bill Blues, William Broonzy: Compiled from a series of letters from Broonzy to Belgian fan Yannick Bruynoghe, this is one of the few autobiographies actually written by a blues artist, as opposed to those written with a collaborator or pieced together from interview responses. In this sense, it is valuable as Broonzy's unfiltered representation of himself. Accepted as such, it is a delightful read, rich in anecdote and tall tale, but as a factual account it needs to be read with caution. When he wrote it in the 1950s, Broonzy was presenting himself as the last of the old-time folk blues singers. Thus he downplays his great commercial success over the previous two decades.

Big Road Blues, David Evans: Subtitled "Tradition and Creativity in the Folk Blues," this is a study of how blues are learned, composed, and transmitted in a folk tradition. Based on analysis of early records by artists like Charley Patton and Tommy Johnson and the author's fieldwork in Mississippi and Louisiana in the 1960s and 1970s, it demonstrates the creative use of lyrical and musical formulas and the transmission of blues within a local tradition. The book also examines the earliest accounts of blues at the beginning of the twentieth century and the reactions of scholars and writers to the emergence of this new folksong genre.

Black Pearls: Blues Queens of the 1920s, Daphne Duval Harrison: The world of vaudeville blues and the women who sang it is described in this study. It presents the glamour as well as the tough working conditions of the theaters and the recording studios, the lyrics of the songs, and the lives of the most important singers. The book contains chapters on Sippie Wallace, Victoria Spivey, Edith Wilson, and Alberta Hunter, based on interviews conducted by the author.

Blues and Gospel Records 1890–1943, 4th ed., Robert M. W. Dixon, John Godrich, and Howard W. Rye: This is the "Bible" of prewar blues record collectors. It provides all the details of every commercial and field recording of blues, gospel, and related types of folk music by African-American artists through 1943—recording location, date, instrumentation, accompanying musicians, record labels, and release numbers—with indexes of song titles and accompanists.

Blues Fell This Morning: Meaning in the Blues, Paul Oliver: First published in 1960 and revised thirty years later, this is a pioneering study of blues lyrics, mostly of the prewar era. Oliver relates the themes of blues to their sociocultural background in African-American rural and urban life. Among the topics explored are work, travel, love, sex, magic, the supernatural, gambling, violence, punishment, natural disasters, and current events.

Blues from the Delta, William Ferris: Based on the author's fieldwork in Mississippi in the 1960s, this book shows how blues functions in a community context and in the lives of its performers and audience. Some of the topics explored here are the sense of fellowship among musicians, the place of blues within the climate of tense racial relations, and the meanings of the songs. Blues is presented as a living tradition rather than a vestige of a historical style.

Blues Legacies and Black Feminism, Angela Y. Davis: The author sees reflections of a proto-feminist ideology in the lives and songs of blues women of the 1920s and later. She shows how they created roles for themselves that were generally far more independent than those of other American women of the time, both black and white, and how they contested both racial discrimination and male domination. Despite a great emphasis on the singers' personal needs and desires, Davis finds expression of black and female solidarity in their songs. The lyrics of all of the recordings of Ma Rainey and Bessie Smith are transcribed and analyzed from this perspective, as is the career of later jazz singer Billie Holiday.

Blues Records 1943–1970, Mike Leadbitter and Neil Slaven (Volume 1); Mike Leadbitter, Leslie Fancourt, and Paul Pelletier (Volume 2): These volumes are the "Bible" of postwar blues recordings, at least up to 1970. Discographical information is organized alphabetically by artist and includes dates and places of sessions, accompanying artists and instruments, song titles, and labels and release numbers. Unlike the prewar blues discography, these volumes contain no indexes.

Blues Traveling, Steve Cheseborough: Anyone who is thinking of combining a love of blues with tourism will want this
book. It is a guide to locations of blues interest in Mississippi,
a state that has probably contributed more blues artists per
capita than any other. Locations include towns where prominent artists were born or lived, burial sites, juke joints, places
mentioned in songs, and other significant spots related to the
music or its cultural and historical background. Several regional tours (by car) are laid out.

Blues with a Feeling: The Little Walter Story, Tony
Glover, Scott Dirks, and Ward Gaines: Little Walter was the
most influential blues harmonica player of the postwar era
and, in the opinion of many, the greatest player on that instrument of all time in the blues field. This study of his life
and music is meticulously researched through surviving doc-
uments and press accounts, interviews of family members,
friends, and fellow musicians, and the artist's recordings. It
provides a fascinating look at the Chicago and down-home
blues scenes from the 1940s through the 1960s. Walter's brilliant musicianship and artistic sensitivity stand in contrast
with his heavy drinking, womanizing, and pugnacious personality.

Children of the Blues, Art Tipaldi: This is one of the few
books to provide an in-depth examination of the blues revival of the past four decades. It does so in a series of artist
profiles based on interviews by the author. From those who
got their start in the 1960s, like Taj Mahal, John Hammond,
Jr., and Charlie Musselwhite, through Robert Cray, to children of veteran artists Luther Allison, Johnny Copeland,
and Jimmy Rogers, plus many others, this book focuses on
the continuities between older and younger generations of
blues.

Down in Houston: Bayou City Blues, Roger Wood: Many people believe that blues reached a high point in black America in the 1950s and that from the 1960s onward the torch was gradually passed to white musicians and their mostly white audiences. Through interviews and a narrative account, Wood reveals a still-vital African-American blues scene in Houston. Enhanced by James Fraher's beautiful photography, the book examines the personalities and places that make up the city's blues life. Few of the artists are well known nationally, but locally they are heroes.

Father of the Blues, W. C. Handy: Handy was the first successful popularizer of the blues and had an impressive career as a band leader, performer (on cornet and guitar), songwriter, publisher, and spokesperson for the worth and importance of this music. This book is his autobiography, published in 1941 after nearly four decades of involvement with the blues. It traces his early career in minstrel bands in the 1890s, his encounters with folk blues in the Mississippi Delta, his success as a songwriter and publisher in Memphis, and his struggles in the commercial music world of New York City.

I Am the Blues, Willie Dixon with Don Snowden: Dixon was another great blues songwriter, active especially from the 1940s through the 1960s, who also became a spokesperson for the music. This book recounts his life, which took him from Mississippi to Chicago to California, eventually to become somewhat of a world citizen. It also gives thoughts on songwriting and life in general from one of its great observers and poets.

The Land Where the Blues Began, Alan Lomax: Lomax began a lifetime of researching blues in 1933 on a field recording trip with his father and published this reminiscence sixty years later. It concentrates mainly on his work in the state of

Mississippi and chronicles his encounters not only with the blues but a whole range of folk music, including work songs, spirituals, ballads, fiddle tunes, fife and drum bands, and much more. The author takes a novelistic approach and is sometimes careless with details, but the depth of his experience, particularly in the early years, is unparalleled, and his general observations must be taken seriously.

The Life and Legend of Leadbelly, Charles Wolfe and Kip Lornell: Huddie Ledbetter had a remarkable career that took him from playing music in the backwoods of the Louisiana-Texas borderland, through prison sentences in the penitentiaries of both states, to concert tours throughout America and a role as the country's first authentic professional folk singer. The authors do a remarkable job of reconstructing his life, including very elusive details of his early career, through analysis of his recordings and interviews, press accounts, and interviews of family members, friends, and fellow musicians. Leadbelly was a complex character who overcame problems in his social environment and his own sometimes rough personality to become one of the most important and honored figures in American music of the first half of the twentieth century.

Nothing But the Blues, Lawrence Cohn, ed.: This is a collection of essays on different historical and stylistic phases of the blues, each by a different author. Together they constitute a history of the blues, although inevitably some important developments fall through the cracks between the essays. This is a large format coffee-table book with wonderful historical photos, yet it is also an authoritative account of the music's history.

Queen of the Blues: A Biography of Dinah Washington, Jim Haskins: Dinah Washington was immensely popular and had considerable crossover success with white audiences, but she suffered from terrible insecurity and compensated for it in ways that were not always productive. Her friends and musical associates contribute a substantial collection of anecdotes, bringing her career into focus. This is someone who really had the blues!

Roosevelt's Blues, Guido van Rijn: Although most blues are about man-woman relationships, there are some that deal with larger issues and current events. During the presidency of Franklin D. Roosevelt (1933–1945), many blues were recorded on themes of hard times, government efforts to improve the economy and provide work, and the events of World War II. The author examines virtually all of these songs, organizing them according to their themes, and shows how they reflect the opinions of the black community as well as the personal concerns of the singers.

Seems Like Murder Here: Southern Violence and the Blues Tradition, Adam Gussow: The author examines blues songs, autobiographical accounts of blues artists, and literary works with blues themes to explore violence in the blues and its relationship to larger historical patterns of violence, both perpetrated on black Americans and perpetrated by them on one another. Lynching, juke joint killings, race riots, and other acts of violence all figure here, interwoven with blues themes and blues contexts. The author makes a correlation and connection between the increase of lynching in the 1890s and early twentieth century and the rise of the blues genre.

Sounds So Good to Me: The Bluesman's Story, Barry Lee Pearson: From interview statements, this book draws a composite portrait and biography of the "bluesman," following performers and their music from the Deep South to northern cities and the international concert scene. Within this composite, the individuality of each artist emerges, as great singers also reveal themselves to be great storytellers. Following brief life histories of two artists who made the transition from rural Mississippi to Chicago, the book contains chapters about the interview as a "performance," childhood music learning experiences, blues and religion, the blues life, recording experiences, and career ups and downs.

The Story of the Blues, Paul Oliver: A British scholar, Oliver was already writing about blues in the 1950s and is now the dean of blues writers, having authored several books on the subject. This is his history of the blues. Published in 1969, it is now woefully out of date, but it still remains the best general history of the music up to the advent of the 1960s blues revival.

Their Eyes Were Watching God, Zora Neale Hurston: Hurston was a great American literary figure but also an important folklorist and scholar, who did fieldwork on blues, folk music, and storytelling in African-American communities in the South. This novel, first published in 1937, is based in part on her field experiences. It recounts the adventures of a young woman who leaves a boring but relatively secure life to take up with an itinerant juke joint blues musician. It was one of the first novels with a blues theme and remains the best, a true classic of American literature.

Urban Blues, Charles Keil: While other researchers in the 1960s were beginning to reconstruct the history of the blues, Keil was studying it as contemporary black popular culture. At the time, B. B. King and Bobby Bland were the top blues artists in black America, and Keil studies them as models of the urban bluesman. Chapters deal with the artist's place within the music business, performance style, and the artist's broader social role. Particularly enlightening are Keil's discussion of the concept of "soul" and his comparison of the bluesman to the preacher. First published in 1966, this book remains a classic of social analysis of music.

Woman with Guitar: Memphis Minnie's Blues, Paul and Beth Garon: One of the few female blues singers to accompany herself on an instrument, Memphis Minnie remains an attractive figure to many up-and-coming women blues singers. Through her music and her personality she managed to create a prominent place for herself over a thirty-year period in a world that was heavily male dominated. Based on her many recordings and the reminiscences of people who knew her, this book chronicles her career and assesses its place in American music.

The World Don't Owe Me Nothing, David "Honeyboy" Edwards, with Janis Martinson and Michael Robert Frank: Edwards is a bluesman whose career covers more than seventy years and stretches from the Mississippi Delta to Chicago and on to world stages. A fine but secondary figure as an artist, he is in the first rank as a storyteller. Edwards knew and performed with an amazing number of important figures in the blues—Big Joe Williams, Charley Patton, Robert Johnson, and Little Walter, just to name a few—and has an incredible memory for detail. This man's life is no less than the story of the blues, and no account gives better insight into the psychology of the music than this book.

Magazines

Here are the major blues magazines in the English language. Many American blues societies publish newsletters, some of which have increasingly come to resemble magazines offering more than local or regional coverage. There are also articles and features of blues interest in many magazines devoted to pop music, jazz, rock, record collecting, and specific instruments, especially the guitar.

Blues & Rhythm: This British magazine is directed especially to blues record collectors, with some coverage of gospel, soul, and rhythm and blues. Each issue contains columns on special topics, notes and queries, and concert and festival reviews.

Blues Revue: This American magazine is very much oriented to the current blues revival scene, devoting about equal attention to white and black artists. Each issue usually has a cover story on some currently popular artist. There are also columns and op-ed pieces, many of them written by performers, tips and instructional guides for musicians, and concert reviews.

Juke Blues: Each issue of this British magazine typically contains four or five artist profiles, ranging among early historical figures, obscure but still active artists, and currently popular stars. There are also reports from various blues centers in the United States and gospel, soul, and jazz sections.

Living Blues: America's oldest blues magazine was founded in 1970 in Chicago and later moved to the University of Mississippi. It is dedicated to blues as an African-American musical tradition with an emphasis on currently active artists. A typical issue contains three or four artist interviews or profiles. Other features are reports from the field, editorials, and radio charts.

Websites

Blues Websites, especially ones devoted to individual artists and record companies, are being created daily. Most can be accessed by a simple web search or through links at The Blue Highway, Blues World, or BluesLand. Some other interesting informational sites are also listed here.

The Blue Highway (www.thebluehighway.com): This is an all-purpose blues Website with many links, containing a chat room, radio listings, essays, tributes to blues greats, artist profiles, news, record labels, festivals, and shopping.

The Blues Foundation (www.blues.org): The foundation serves as an umbrella organization for local and regional blues societies and as an advocate for the music. It produces an international amateur blues talent contest, the Handy Awards recognizing excellence in the field, a "Blues in the Schools" program, and a convention devoted to the blues industry. It has also established a Blues Hall of Fame. The Website also lists blues clubs, affiliated organizations, and blues societies.

Blues World (www.bluesworld.com): This is a link to many specialized blues Websites devoted to record labels, festivals, books, magazines, obituaries, tourism, interviews, photos, discographies, opinion, and all sorts of neat stuff!

BluesLand (www.bluesland.net): This site features news, blues on the radio, bibliography, photos, and links to other blues sites.

BluesNet (www.bluesnet.hub.org): Here is an extraordinary blues bibliographic database, containing over ten thousand items.

Cleanhead's Blues & Jazz Page (www.bluesandjazz.net/discographylinks.html): For the serious researcher and record collector, this site contains many excellent discographies, discographical essays, and record label histories related to blues and jazz.

European Blues Association (www.euroblues.org): This British-based site contains blues news and information on the organization's events and its Archive of African-American Music.

Junior's Juke Joint (www.deltablues.net): Anthropologist and blues enthusiast John L. Doughty, Jr., takes the intrepid internet tourist to juke joints in isolated corners of Louisiana and Mississippi, with photos, anecdotes of visits, descriptions of the music, food, people, the juke joints themselves, and news of local festivals.

Roots and Rhythm (www.rootsandrhythm.com): This is a gigantic shopping mall for records, books, and videos of blues and other types of American and worldwide "roots" music.

Year of the Blues 2003 (www.yearoftheblues.org): This massive and ongoing project features monthly events in different locations, television programs, a radio series, education initiatives, and much more.

Documentaries

The history of blues is generally better related in books and articles, but even the worst of blues films are valuable if they contain good performance footage and artists talking about their own lives and music. The following items focus on the music and musicians and are representative of some of the better film efforts.

A Well Spent Life, Les Blank and Skip Gerson, dirs.: This is a loving portrait of Mance Lipscomb, a Texas sharecropper, songster, and blues musician. Blank and Gerson really got to know their subject well, and it shows here, as Lipscomb talks about his life and its relationship to his music. There is hardly any footage of folk blues from the first half of the twentieth century, especially in its natural setting, so this 1971 production is the next best thing.

The Blues Accordin' to "Lightnin'" Hopkins, Les Blank and Skip Gerson, dirs.: Hopkins was one of the great poets of the blues, and he used this film as an opportunity to expound his wisdom, his humor, his jive, and his great music. We see him at home in Houston and in a return to his birthplace out in the country.

Chicago Blues, Harley Cokliss, dir.: Dick Gregory narrates this attempt to show the history and variety of blues in Chicago, from survivals of rural blues to electric urban combos. Produced in 1971, it contains some powerful footage by Johnnie Lewis, Floyd Jones, Muddy Waters, Buddy Guy, Junior Wells, and J. B. Hutto.

Deep Blues, Robert Mugge, dir.: There were still many fine traditional blues performers in Memphis and Mississippi in the early 1990s. If one ignores the annoying commentary of blues-rock star Dave Stewart and journalist Robert Palmer, there is plenty of great performance footage here by Uncle Ben Perry, Booker T. Laury, R. L. Burnside, Jessie Mae Hemphill, Junior Kimbrough, Jack Owens, and others.

Devil Got My Woman: Blues at Newport 1966, Alan Lomax, dir.: The Newport Folk Festival of 1966 had an extraordinary array of Mississippi blues talent: Skip James, Son House, Bukka White, and Howlin' Wolf (by way of Chicago). Folklorist Alan Lomax assembled them in a relaxed atmosphere, with gospel guitarist Rev. Pearly Brown added for contrast, and captured some great performances along with their banter as they jockey for status and supremacy.

The Land Where the Blues Began, Alan Lomax, dir.: Put together mostly from footage made in Mississippi in 1978, this is a companion to Lomax's book of the same title. There is stunning performance footage, much of it shot in a natural context at house parties and picnics, not only of blues but of older traditions of fife and drum music and other folk instruments.

Legends of Country Blues Guitar, Vestapol Productions: This is a series of performances by some of the great figures of solo blues guitar, assembled from various sources between the 1950s and early 1970s. Mississippi John Hurt, Son House, Reverend Gary Davis, Big Bill Broonzy, Robert Pete Williams, Mance Lipscomb, Henry Townsend, Brownie McGhee, and Josh White are seen and heard when they were still in or near their prime. There is no context for this concert footage, but the music itself is riveting. A musician can especially learn a lot from studying these performances.

Piano Players Rarely Ever Play Together, Stevenson Palfi, dir.: This is one of the best attempts to show the continuities and changes in blues tradition. Three generations of New Orleans blues piano players, Tuts Washington, Professor Longhair, and Allen Toussaint, are gathered together to perform and discuss their styles of music. They comment on the changing New Orleans music scene and one another's playing and deliver some fine performances, both separately and together.

St. Louis Blues, Dudley Murphy, dir.: The acting ranges from sublime to stiff, and the plot is corny, but where else does one get to see the great Bessie Smith in her prime? In this fifteen-minute short made in 1929 she sings and enacts the "plot" of W. C. Handy's immortal blues composition. The Harlem club scenes are priceless, and Bessie is at her best, despite some rather odd backup by a choir. The great pianist James P. Johnson, who accompanied her on some of her records, is also seen and heard. Because it's not very long, this film is often marketed together with other historical works of black cinema.

About the Author

David Evans began teaching in the Anthropology Department of California State University, Fullerton in 1969. In 1978, he joined the faculty at The University of Memphis and has been Professor of Music there ever since. He designed and has directed its ethnomusicology Ph.D. program—the only American doctoral program with a specific specialization in southern U.S. folk and popular music. He is the author of several books, including *Big Road Blues: Tradition and Creativity in the Folk Blues* (University of California Press, 1982), based on his fieldwork. He has contributed book chapters and entries on various aspects of the blues, including major biographical studies of Bukka White and Blind Willie McTell, and chapters in the *Blackwell Guide to Blues Records, Black Women in America,* and *The Blues: A Bibliographic Guide.* He has produced over forty LP and CD recordings and has written liner notes for over eighty others. Evans is also a performer (blues vocal and guitar) and has toured throughout the United States, Europe, and South America, as well as recording two CDs. He was honored with a 1981 Grammy Award nomination for his booklet notes to *Atlanta Blues: 1933,* and he won a Grammy in 2003 for his notes to *Screamin' and Hollerin' the Blues: The Worlds of Charley Patton.*

Index

Ace, Johnny, 63, 104

Acoustic blues, 60–61, 81, 116. *See also* Country blues; Folk blues

AF of M. *See* American Federation of Musicians

"African Opera Series," 21

African/European musical syntheses, 12–15

Afro-American Folk Music from Tate and Panola Counties, 194

Afro-Caribbean music, 77

"Ain't That Lovin' You Baby," 148, 198

Alexander, Texas, 124, 213

Ali, Muhammad, 199

"All I Could Do Was Cry," 130

"All Your Love," 114, 166–167

Allison, Luther, 56, 100

"Almost Dead Blues," 206

Altheimer, Joshua, 35, 106, 197

"America the Beautiful," 112

American Federation of Musicians (AF of M), 39, 77

American Folk Blues Festival, 52, 119

Ammons, Albert, 38, 65, 100, 138

"Amphetamine Annie," 195

Anderson, Jelly Roll, 45

The Animals, 53, 66, 121, 164

"Anna Lou Blues," 153

The Anthology, 194

Are You Experienced, 121, 156

Armstrong, Louis
  blues records and, 24
  Johnson, Lonnie, and, 132
  Rainey, Ma, and, 147, 182, 210
  Smith, Bessie, and, 150, 205

Arnold, Kokomo, 33, 100, 133

"As the Years Go Passing By," 135, 208

Austin, Lovie, 115, 189

"Avalon Blues," 51, 128

Axis: Bold As Love, 121

"Ay-Tete-Fee," 113, 167

"Baby (You've Got What It Takes)", 159

"Baby Don't You Love Me No More," 110

"Baby Scratch My Back," 149

"Baby Seals Blues," 21

"Back Door Man," 127

"Back in the U.S.A.," 199

"Back-Water Blues," 205

Bailey, Buster, 150, 182

Baker, Lavern, 100

Baker, Mickey, 196, 202

"Bald Head," 145

Ballads, 18, 220
  white v. black, 16–17

Banjo Joe. *See* Cannon, Gus
Barbeque Bob, 71
Barber, Chris, 164
"Barnyard Boogie," 134
Barrel House Annie, 45
"Barrel House Blues," 210
Barrelhouse blues, 61, 64, 65, 220. *See
    also* Boogie-woogie
Bartholomew, Dave, 77, 216
Basie, Count, 38, 158
Bastin, Bruce, 35
"Beale Street Blues," 30
The Beatles, ix, 75
Bechet, Sidney, 38
Beck, Jeff, 120
Belfour, Robert, 73
Bell, Alexander Graham, 9
Bell, Ed, 71
Below, Fred, 144, 168, 176, 200
Bennett, Wayne, 177, 194
The Benny Goodman Sextet, 38
Benton, Brook, 159
Berry, Chuck
    blues-rock and, 53, 62, 66
    career of, 101–102
    CD collection of, 198–199
    Dixon, Willie, and, 117
    middle-class sensibilities and, 213
    rock's origins and, 46, 182
    Walker, T-Bone, influence on, 185
Besman, Bernie, 123
Best of Canned Heat, 194–195
The Best of the Memphis Jug Band, 195
Big, Bad & Blue, 195
Big Bill and the Memphis Five, 76
"Big Boss Man," 198
"Big Chief," 146
Big Maybelle, 43, 64, 179–180, 202
    career of, 102–103
"Big Road Blues," 183
Big Three Trio, 117
Bihari, Joe, 210
The Birth of Soul, 196
The Black Ace, 45
Black, Bill, 186
Black Bob, 33, 106
"Black, Brown, and White," 106

"Black Gal," 113
"Black Mare Blues," 106
"Black Night," 107, 167–168
"Black Pony Blues," 116, 211
"Blackjack," 112
Blackwell, Francis "Scrapper," 30, 49, 68,
    110, 181
Blair, Sunny, 210
Blake, Blind, 30, 72, 100, 106
Bland, Bobbie "Blue," 48, 78, 176–177,
    194
    career of, 103–104
Blind blues singers, 30–31, 72
Blind Faith, 114, 203
Blind Lemon Jefferson, 196
Block, Rory, 61
Bloomfield, Mike, 50, 101
Blue Bird Blues, 196–197
"Blue Bird Blues," 162
"Blue Night Blues," 111
Blue notes/scales, 4, 83–84, 92, 93, 220
"Blue Shadows," 136
"Blue Tail Fly," 106
Blue yodel, 6, 61–62
"Blue Yodel No. 8," 168
Bluegrass, 6, 62
Blues. *See also* Blue yodel; British blues;
    Chicago blues; Classic blues; Country
    blues; Deep South blues
    acoustic, 60–61, 81, 116
    African retentions in, 87–88, 89, 91,
        105, 178
    African-American vernacular in, x
    authenticity and, xv
    barrelhouse, 61, 64, 65, 220
    black audience and, xiv, xvi, 48, 56, 78,
        104, 122–123, 140
    combos, development of, 40–42, 43, 44
    commercial/hit music v., x
    contemporary, 47, 59–60
    country and western music and, 6, 97
    definition of, 1–2
    double entendre in, x, 96, 118, 142,
        174–175, 185, 212
    down-home, 42
    earliest, 17–19
    east coast, 71–72

electric guitar and, 40–41
experience v. form, xi
as expression of daily life, xv
festivals, 54, 60
field research and, 50
folk, 61
formal characteristics of, 3–4, 13,
  16–17, 64, 83–97, 219
future of, 56–57
geographical terms and, 60
golden age of, 43
gospel influence on, 44–45, 78, 96–97,
  104, 112, 119, 122, 126
harmony, 89–91
improvisation, 92–94
influence of, ix, xiii–xv, xviii
instruments used in, 13, 35, 87–89, 89,
  92, 93–94
international, 54, 62
jazz and, 5–6, 40, 41, 59, 60, 63, 64, 65,
  66, 69, 75–76, 76, 77, 78, 80, 92, 94,
  111, 116, 124, 130, 132, 136, 139, 147,
  150, 151, 155, 157, 158, 172, 175, 185,
  205
jazz/rock v., 5
lyrics, 94–97
mainstream popular culture and, 7–8
major record labels and, 42
modern, 54–57
museums, 55
musical origins of, 13–17
nicknames, 45
1940s, 39–42
1950s, 42–44, 46–47
1960s, 47–54
notes/scales, 83–84
origins of, ix, 2, 5, 9–17
pop music and, 10, 19, 40, 41, 47, 63,
  64, 65, 97, 103, 130, 158, 159
professionalism and, 5, 10
psychedelic, 54, 180
radio and, 26, 42–43, 46, 122–123
rap and, 97
record collecting, 28–29
recordings of, early, 22–23, 24
records, reissue of, 51, 55
records/CDs, an overview, 191–194

revival, 49–52, 55, 75, 101, 119, 128,
  134, 138, 140, 146, 154, 160, 188, 225
rhythm, 93
rock and, 62–63, 92, 94, 97
in the schools, 55
sheet music and, 21
social origins of, 11–13
societies, 55
soul music and, 48–49
spontaneous nature of, xi
subject matter, 3
terminology, 59–60, 219–227
tonality v. major/minor system, 4–5
tourism, 55, 67
urbanization and, 39, 40
vaudeville, 19–20, 24–26, 31, 61, 62,
  74, 80, 100, 142, 189
verse form, 85–87
West African precedents for, 13–15
west coast, 80–81
white, 62
white audiences and, 23, 40, 46, 49, 56,
  75, 134, 138, 148, 151
white musicians and, 50, 56, 62, 136,
  143, 144
Word War II and, 39
Blues, 197
The Blues, 197, 209
"Blues Before Sunrise," 111
Blues crooners, 63, 81, 100, 209
Blues Foundation, 55
Blues Heaven Foundation, 118
Blues Masters, 198
"Blues Party Tonight," 213
Blues revival, 51–52, 55, 75, 101, 119, 128,
  134, 138, 140, 146, 154, 160, 188, 225
Blues rhumba, 145
Blues shouters, 63–64, 81, 100, 173, 209
Blues Unlimited, 53
"Blues with a Feeling," 168
Blues World, 53
Bluesbreakers, 114
Bluesbreakers with Eric Clapton, 114
Blues-rock, 62–63, 81, 100–101, 102, 118,
  144. *See also* British blues; Cream;
  Hendrix, Jimi; King, Albert;
  Vaughan, Stevie Ray; White blues

"Bo Diddley," 105, 169, 199
"Bo Weevil," 216
Bobbie Cadillac, 45
"Bobo Stomp," 111
Bogan, Lucille, 100
Boines, Houston, 210
Bolden, Buddy, 9
"Boogie Chillen," 123, 169
Boogie music. *See* Canned Heat
Boogie with Canned Heat, 108
Boogie-woogie, 40, 42, 61, 64–65, 76, 89, 101, 155, 170, 195, 220. *See also* Lewis, Meade Lux; Professor Longhair
pop music and, 139
Booker, Charles H., 21
Booker, Charley, 210
Booker, James, 77
Booker T. and the MG's, 50, 52, 135, 208
Books/magazines, 229–240
"Boom Boom," 124
Borum, Memphis Willie, 143
Bouchillon, Chris, 79
"Bo-Weavil Blues," 147
Bowie, David, 156
"Bow-Legged Woman, Knock-Kneed Man," 149
Boyd, Eddie, 197
Bradford, Perry, 21, 22, 23
Bradshaw, Tiny, 76
"Bright Lights, Big City," 148
"Bring It to Jerome," 199
British blues, 65–66, 67, 81, 160, 200
British Invasion, 53, 66, 77
"Broke Down Engine Blues," 204
Brooks, Junior, 210
Broonzy, Big Bill
blues combo and, 35–36
career of, 105–107
city blues and, 68
Civil rights and, 97
country blues and, 38
Georgia Tom and, 185
Gillum, Jazz, and, 177
rhythm and blues and, 209
rock and roll and, 217
as stylist, 33

Waters, Muddy, and, 159
Williamson, Sonny Boy, and, 197
Brown, Charles, 40, 63, 111, 167–168, 204–205, 213
career of, 107–108
Brown, Clarence "Gatemouth," 41, 45, 80, 100
Brown, J. T., 179
Brown, James, 49, 54, 62, 78, 100, 104, 170–171
Brown, Nappy, 63
Brown, Roy, 63, 100, 173
Brown, Ruth, 43, 64, 78, 100
Brown, Willie, 126, 133, 145, 212
Buckner, Milt, 172
Buckwheat Zydeco, 81
Buford, Mojo, 46
Bull City Red, 38, 118
"Bull Cow Blues," 106
"Bull-Doze Blues," 170
"Bullfrog Blues," 194
Bumble Bee Slim, 33, 45, 111
Burdon, Eric, 164
Burnette, Ranie, 194
Burnside, R. L., 56, 71, 73, 100
Burrage, Harold, 201
Burrell, Kenny, 112
Butt Naked Free, 198
Butterbeans, 45
Butterbeans and Susie, 80, 100
Butterfield, Paul, 50, 53, 62, 101
Byers, Billy, 202

"Cadillac Assembly Line," 135
"Caledonia," 170
"Call It Stormy Monday," 157
"Call My Job," 135
"Candy," 103
Canned Heat, 28, 53, 62, 65, 177, 180–181, 194–195
career of, 108–109
Canned Heat, 108
Cannon, Gus, 49, 143, 187
career of, 109–110
Cannon's Jug Stompers, 75, 109, 187
Caple, Gilbert, 187
Captain Beefheart, 145

Carr, Leroy, 30, 61, 68, 107, 133, 181–182
   career of, 110–111
"Carried Water for the Elephant," 110
Carter, Bo, 74
"Catfish Blues," 108, 217
"Celeste Blues," 138
Cephas, John, 72
"Chains of Love," 104
Chandler, Chas, 121
Charles, Ray, 31, 78, 104, 130, 158, 188, 196
   career of, 111–112
Charters, Samuel, 49, 69, 110
Chatman, Christine, 102
Chatman, Lonnie, 183
Chavis, Boozoo, 81
Chenier, Clifton, 81, 167
   career of, 112–113
The Chess Box (Bo Diddley), 199
The Chess Box (Chuck Berry), 198–199
The Chess Box (Howlin' Wolf), 199–200
The Chess Box (Muddy Waters), 200
Chicago blues, 100. *See also* Guy, Buddy;
   Little Walter; Waters, Muddy;
   Williamson, Sonny Boy
   British Invasion and, 77
   Canned Heat and, 108
   CD compilation of, 200–201
   deep south blues and, 70
   Diddley, Bo, and, 105, 199
   Hooker, John Lee, and, 216
   influence on white artists, 44
   James, Elmore, and, 129, 212
   Lenoir, J. B., and, 179
   Little Walter and, 139
   Musselwhite, Charlie, and, 143
   origins/development of, 43–44, 66–68
   revival of, 153
   Rush, Bobby, and, 148
   swamp blues and, 79
   urban blues and, 80
Chicago Blues All-Stars, 118
Chicago Bob, 45
"Chicago Bound Blues (Famous
   Migration Blues)", 115
Chicago Five, 36, 152
"A Chicken Ain't Nothin' But a Bird," 134

"Chicken Heads," 148
"Chinese Man Blues," 203
Chittlin' circuit, xv, 48, 120, 135, 148, 184
Chris Barber's Jazz Band, 164
Christian, Buddy, 150
Christian, Charlie, 136
City blues, 68, 80
Civil Rights movement, 47–48, 64, 97, 121
Clapton, Eric, 53, 56, 66, 120, 135, 156,
   164, 171–172, 203–204
   career of, 113–115
Clara Smith and the Birmingham
   Jubilee Singers, 150
"Clarksdale Moan," 28
Classic blues, 80. *See also* Vaudeville
   blues
Clayton, Doctor, 46, 78, 100
Cobbs, Alfred, 202
The Cobra Records Story, 200–201
"Cocaine Habit Blues," 195
"Cold, Cold Heart," 159
"Cold Sweat," 170–171
Cole, Nat "King," 40, 63, 103, 107, 111
Coleman, Jaybird, 71
Collins, Albert, 56, 80, 100, 120, 214
Collins, Lee, 175
Como, Perry, 103
The Complete Aladdin Recordings, 201
*The Complete Early Recordings of Skip
   James,* 201
The Complete Okeh Sessions 1952-55, 202
Complete Recorded Works, 1930-1936, 203
The Complete Recordings, 202–203
Contemporary blues, 68–69, 80, 100
Cooder, Ry, 61
Cooke, Sam, ix, 122
Copeland, Johnny, 56, 80
Cotton, James, 200
Couldn't Stand the Weather, 156
Council, Dipper Boy, 118
The Count Basey Orchestra, 38
Country and western music, 111, 112
Country blues, 40, 61, 69, 70, 71, 72, 73,
   77, 100
   revival of, 49–52
The Country Blues (Charters), 49, 69
Country music, 6

Country rock, 6
Cousin Joe, 100
Covers blues. *See* Country blues
Cox, Ida, 25, 32, 38, 81, 189
    career of, 115–116
"Crawling King Snake Blues," 124
Cray, Robert, 101, 213–214
Crayton, Pee Wee, 41, 80
"Crazy Blues," 22, 208
Cream, 53, 114, 171–172, 203
Creedence Clearwater Revival, 177
Creole blues. *See* zydeco
"Cristo Redentor," 144
"Cross Road Blues," 133, 171, 203
Crossroads, 203–204
"Crossroads," 114, 171–172
Crudup, Arthur "Big Boy," 42, 172, 186,
    211
    career of, 116–117
Crump, Jesse, 115
"Crying Time," 112
Curtis, King, 120

Daddy Stovepipe, 217
"The Dallas Blues," 21
Damn Right, I've Got the Blues, 120
"Dangerous Woman," 154
Daniels, Julius, 217
Davis, Blind Gary, 118
Davis, Blind John, 106, 197
Davis, Guy, 56, 61, 101, 198
Davis, Larry, 186
Davis, Maxwell, 167, 211
Davis, Ossie, 198
Davis, Reverend Gary, 72, 73
Davis, Walter, 33
de la Parra, Fito, 109
"Dead Drunk Blues," 147
"Dead Presidents," 118, 139
"Death Letter Blues," 115
Dee, Ruby, 198
Deep South blues, 70–71, 71, 73, 106
The Definitive Blind Willie McTell, 204
Delafose, John, 81
Delta blues, 70–71. *See also* Deep South
    blues
Deluxe Edition, 204

Derek and the Dominos, 114, 203
"Devil Got My Woman," 131
Diddley, Bo, 46, 53, 67, 117, 140, 169, 199
    career of, 104–105
"Diddley Daddy," 105
Diddley-bow, 14
"Diddy Wah Diddy," 105, 199
"Dimples," 124
"Dirty Old Woman," 213
Disco, 122
Disraeli Gears, 114
"Dixie Bo-Bo," 217
Dixon, Willie
    career of, 117–118
    Clapton, Eric, and, 114
    Howlin' Wolf and, 127
    King, B. B., and, 119
    Magic Sam and, 166
    as songwriter/producer, 176, 200, 201
    Taylor, Koko, and, 153, 204
    Waters, Muddy, and, 176, 200
    Williamson, Sonny Boy, and, 197
"Do Your Duty," 205
Doctor John, 77
Dodds, Johnny, 115, 147, 189
Domino, Antoine "Fats," 45
    CD set of, 215–216
    New Orleans blues and, 77
    Professor Longhair's influence on, 145
    rhythm and blues and, 78
    rock and roll and, 100
    white audience and, 46
"Don't Answer the Door," 136
"Don't Lie to Me," 216
"Don't Make Me Pay for His Mistakes,"
    122
"Don't Start Me to Talkin'," 164
"Don't Throw Your Love on Me So
    Strong," 135
"Don't You *See* How This World Made a
    Change," 204
Dopsie, Rockin', 81
Dorsey, Thomas A., 7, 73, 152, 185. *See
    also* Georgia Tom
Double Trouble, 156
Douglas, Kid, 142
"Down Home Blues," 69, 122

"Downhearted Blues," 205

Down-home blues, 42, 43, 48, 69, 100, 106, 116, 143, 149–150

Doyle, Little Buddy, 45

Dr. John, 145

"Driftin' Blues," 104, 107, 205

Driftin' Blues, 204–205

Drifting Slim, 210

"Driving Wheel Blues," 152

"Drunken Hearted Man," 133, 203

"Drunken Spree," 131

"Dry Spell Blues," 126

Dupree, Champion Jack, 52

"Dust My Broom," 129, 212

Dylan, Bob, 38, 53, 63, 142

Early Downhome Blues (Titon), 69

The Earthshaker, 153–154

East Coast blues, 71

Edison, Thomas, 9

Edwards, David "Honeyboy," 34

Eisenhower, Dwight D., 134

Eldridge, Roy, 116

Electric Ladyland, 121

Electric Mud, 54

Electric Wolf, 54

Electrical recording
field trips and, 27
invention of, 26

Ellington, Duke, 24, 132

Elliot, Ernest, 181

Empty Bed Blues, 205

"Empty Bed Blues," 205

Erby, John, 213

Eric Clapton, 114

Estes, Sleepy John, x, 36, 49, 71, 100, 198

"Ethel Mae," 117

Everett, Betty, 201

"Evil Blues," 172

"Evil Gal Blues," 158, 172–173

"Evil-Hearted Woman," 111

The Excello Singles Anthology, 206

"Eyesight to the Blind," 164, 173

Fahey, John, 145

"Falling Rain Blues," 132

Family Style, 156

"Farther Up the Road," 104

"The Fat Man," 216

Feather, Leonard, 158, 172

Ferguson, H-Bomb, 45, 63

Ferris, William, 35

Field recordings, 32, 34, 36

Films, 229–245

"First Time I Met the Blues," 119

"The First Time I Met You," 203

Fitzgerald, Ella, 134

The Five Breezes, 117

Fleetwood Mac, 66

"Flip, Flop and Fly," 155, 195

"Floating Bridge," x

Fogerty, John, 145, 177

Folk blues, 72. *See also* Acoustic blues;
Country blues; Down-home blues
recordings of, 26–31

Folklorists, 34–35

"Folsom Prison Blues," 206

Ford, T-Model, 45

"'Fore Day in the Morning," 173

"44 Blues," 151

"Forty-Four," 127

Francis, Panama, 202

"Frankie," 128

"Frankie and Albert," 145

Franklin, Aretha, 38

Free Again, 206–207

Fresh Cream, 114

"Fried Hockey Boogie," 108, 194

"Frisco Hi-Ball Blues," 203

"From Spirituals to Swing," 36, 50, 106, 116, 138, 154, 155

"From the Bottom," 164

Fuller, Blind Boy, 30, 36, 72, 154
career of, 118–119

Fuller, Blind Boy, No. 2, 45, 119, 154

Fuller, Bob, 181

Fulson, Lowell, 41, 80, 100

Funderburgh, Anson, 80

Funk, 7, 105, 171

Fuqua, Harvey, 129, 130

Future Blues, 109

"Gabbin' Blues," 103, 202

Gaither, Little Bill, 33, 111

Gamble, Kenny, 149

Gant, Cecil, 40, 63, 100

"Georgia on My Mind," 112

"Georgia Rag," 141, 204

Georgia Tom, 30, 68, 73, 74, 152, 185

"Get a Little, Give a Little," 123

"G.I. Jive," 134

Gillespie, Dizzy, 158

Gillum, Jazz, 33, 68, 106, 177

Gilmore, Boyd, 210

"Gimme a Pigfoot," 151

"Give Me a 32-20," 211

Glaser, Joe, 158

"Go to the Mardi Gras," 146

"Going to Germany," 110

"Going up the Country," 108

The Golden Gate Quartet, 38, 138, 214

"Good Biscuits," 143

"Good Morning Blues," 214

"Good Morning, School Girl," 162, 197

"Good Rockin' Daddy," 129

Goodman, Benny, 38, 151

Gordon, Jimmie, 33

Gordon, Rosco, 104

Gospel blues, 73

Gospel music. *See also* Dorsey, Thomas A.
   blues and, 6–7, 31, 96–97
   blues shouters' roots in, 64
   Civil Rights movement and, 48
   gospel blues v., 73
   House, Son, and, 145
   King, B. B., and, 44, 136
   soul blues and, 78

"Got the Blues," 131

"Got the Blues Can't Be Satisfied," 128

"Got the Blues for Murder Only," 213

Grainger, Porter, 181

Granderson, John Lee, 143–144

The Grateful Dead, 75

"Graveyard Bound Blues," 115

Great Depression, 31–33, 74, 81, 111,
   115, 151, 175, 181

Green, Charlie, 150, 182, 210

Green, Jerome, 199

Green, Lil, 35, 100

"Grinder Man Blues," 174

Griots, 14–15, 221

"Guitar Blues," 213

guitar, electric, importance of, 40–42, 44

Guitar Slim, 45, 100

Guthrie, Woody, 79

Guy, Buddy, 44, 56, 67, 119, 140, 200, 201

The Hall Johnson Choir, 217

"Hallelujah I Love Her So," 112, 196

Hammond, John, 36, 38, 138

Hammond, John, Jr., 50, 61

Hampton, Lionel, 158, 172

Handy awards, 55

Handy Brothers Music Company, 21

Handy, W. C., 9, 10, 19, 20, 21, 23, 30,
   103, 150, 205

"Hard Time Killin' Floor Blues," 131

"Hard Times," 107, 205

Hare, Pat, 200

The Harlem Hamfats, 35, 68, 74, 76,
   100, 101

Harlem Renaissance, 151

Harmonica According to Charlie, 144

Harmonica Slim, 149

Harpo, Slim, 48, 79, 206
   career of, 149–150

Harris, Corey, 56

Harris, Peppermint, 45

Harris, Wynonie, 40, 63, 100, 198

Harvey, Bill, 194

"Haunted Blues," 143

"Havana Moon," 199

"Hawaiian Boogie," 129

Hawkins, Buddy Boy, 212

Hawkins, Coleman, 116, 150, 210

Hawkins, Screamin' Jay, 209

Hayes, Clifford, 75

The Healer, 124

"Hear My Train a Comin'," 197

Heath, Percy, 112

Heavy metal, 7, 62

Hegamin, Lucille, 81

"Hellhound on My Trail," 203

"Help Me," 144, 164

Hemphill, Jessie Mae, 71, 73, 100, 178

Hemphill, Sid, 34

Henderson, Fletcher, 24, 150

Henderson, Rosa, 100

Hendrix, Jimi
  blues background of, 54
  blues-rock and, 62, 171
  British blues scene and, 66
  career of, 120–122
  Clapton, Eric, and, 113
  King, Albert, influence on, 135
  recordings of, 175, 197
  Vaughan, Stevie Ray, and, 156, 215
"Hey! Bo Diddley," 105
"Hey Joe," 122
"Hey Now Baby," 145
"Hideaway," 114
"High Flying Rocket," 198
"High Sheriff Blues," 145
"High Water Everywhere," 145
Hill, Bertha "Chippie," 25, 32
Hill Country Blues, 73
Hill, King Solomon, 28
Hill, Z. Z., 56, 69
  career of, 122–123
Hinton, Milt, 116
Hip-hop, 213
"Hit the Road Jack," 112
Hite, Bob, 28, 108, 109
"Hobo Blues," 124
"Hobo Worried Blues," 206
Hogan, Silas, 79
Hogg, Smokey, 45, 209
Hokum blues, 68, 74, 142, 152, 183, 185, 204
The Hokum Boys, 74
Holiday, Billie, 40, 63, 158
Hollers, 16
Holy Blues, 73
"Honest I Do," 198
"Honey Bee," 96, 160
The Honey Dripper, 45
"Honey Hush," 155, 195
"Honeymoon Blues," 203
"Honky Tonk Train Blues," 138, 174
Honky-tonk, 6
"Hoochie Coochie Man," 200
"Hoochie Man," 149
"Hoodoo Hoodoo," 197
Hoodoo Lady, 207
"Hoodoo Lady," 143

Hoodoo Man Blues, 119
Hooker, Earl, 100, 200
Hooker, John Lee
  blues revival and, 48, 150
  British musicians and, 53
  Canned Heat influenced by, 65, 108, 109, 177, 180, 194
  Deep South blues and, 71
  free verse, use of, 86, 92
  influence of, 42, 56, 144
  Jackson, L'il Son, compared to, 172
  recordings of, 169, 216
  style of, 42, 125
Hooker 'n' Heat, 109
"Hopeless," 211
Hopkins, Sam "Lightnin' "
  blues revival and, 48
  career of, 124–125
  down-home blues and, 43, 69, 150
  free verse, use of, 92
  Jackson, Son, compared to, 172
  Jefferson, Blind Lemon, and, 41–42
  recordings of, 201, 209
  Texas blues and, 79, 80
Horton, Big Walter, 139, 187, 201
"Hot Fingers," 132
"House Rent Stomp," 106
House, Son, 28, 34, 38, 49, 51–52, 71, 78, 108, 133, 145, 159, 212
  career of, 125–126
"How Long—How Long Blues," 110
"How Many More Years," 127
Howard, Rosetta, 35
Howell, Peg Leg, 71
Howlin' Wolf
  British blues and, 66
  Brown, Charles, v., 205
  Canned Heat influenced by, 180
  career of, 126–127
  Chicago/South Side blues and, 67, 143
  Creedence Clearwater Revival influenced by, 177
  Dixon, Willie, and, 117, 153
  Hendrix, Jimi, influenced by, 120
  nickname of, 45
  Patton, Charley, influence on, 145
  psychedelic blues and, 54

Howlin' Wolf (continued)
  recordings of, 178–179, 199–200
  as stylist, 44
  Taylor, Koko, and, 204
  white musicians and, 53
Huff, Leon, 149
Humes, Helen, 38, 209
Hunter, Alberta, 23, 32, 81
Hunter, Ivory Joe, 61, 63, 100
Hurt, Mississippi John, 45, 49, 51
  career of, 127–128

"I Ain't Gonna Let You See My Santa
    Claus," 174–175
"I Ain't Studdin' You," 149
"I Asked for Water," 200
"I Can't Be Satisfied," 159, 200
"I Can't Stop Loving You," 112
"I Don't Live Today," 121, 175
"I Feel Good Little Girl," 175–176
"I Feel Like Going Home," 159
"I Got a Break Baby," 157
"I Got a Woman," 196
I Got What It Takes, 153
"I Got What It Takes," 153
"I Guess I Showed Her," 214
"I Just Want to Make Love to You," 160,
    176
"I Keep the Blues," 111
"I Know Your Wig Is Gone," 157
"I Need Someone (To Love Me)", 122
"I Pity the Fool," 176–177
"Ice Man (Come On Up)", 207
"Ida Red," 101
"If I Don't Holler," 213
"If I Get Lucky," 116
"If You Want Me, Baby," 217
"I'll Take Care of You," 104
"I'm a King Bee," 149, 206
"I'm a Man," 105
"I'm Alabama Bound (The Alabama
    Blues)", 19
"I'm Blue As a Man Can Be," 162
"I'm Gonna Dig Myself a Hole," 211
"I'm Gonna Move to the Outskirts of
    Town," 134
"I'm in the Mood," 124

"I'm Movin' On," 112
"I'm Ready," 200
"(I'm Your) Hoochie Coochie Man," 118,
    160
In Step, 156
"In the Evening When the Sun Goes
    Down," 107
"Insane Asylum," 153
Ishman, Bracey, 189
The Isley Brothers, 120
"It Ain't No Use," 122
"It Hurts Me Too," 153
"It's a Good Little Thing," 204
"It's My Life, Baby," 104
"It's Tight Like That," 30, 152
"I've Got a Woman," 112
"I've Grown So Ugly," 162

Jackson, Bull Moose, 63, 76, 100
Jackson, Calvin, 176
Jackson, Chubby, 158
Jackson, John, 72
Jackson, Li'l Son, 43, 80, 100, 172
Jackson, Milt, 112
Jackson, Papa Charlie, 45, 74, 106
James, Elmore
  career of, 128–129
  Johnson, Robert, influence on, 36, 44
  recordings of, 182–183, 210, 212
  South Side blues and, 67
  Williamson, Sonny Boy II, and, 163
James, Etta, 64, 78
  career of, 129–130
James, Skip, 49–50, 51, 133, 201
  career of, 130–131
Jaxon, Frankie "Half Pint," 74, 80, 100,
    152
Jazz, 5–6, 12
Jefferson, Blind Lemon
  career of, 131–132
  country blues and, 18, 30
  Hopkins, Lightnin', and, 41, 124
  influence of, 29
  Johnson, Lonnie, compared to, 27
  King, B. B., influenced by, 136
  Leadbelly and, 131, 137
  lyric themes of, 31

nickname of, 45
recordings by, 196
Texas blues and, 80
Walker, T-Bone, and, 41, 157
"Jelly Whippin' Blues," 152
Jim Crow laws, 11, 25
The Jimi Hendrix Experience, 121, 171
Jimmy James and the Blue Flames, 121
"John Henry," 106
John Mayall and the Bluesbreakers, 53, 203
"Johnny B. Goode," 199
Johnny Moore's Three Blazers, 107, 205
Johnson, Blind Willie, 73
Johnson, Ella, 209
Johnson, James P., 38, 150
Johnson, Johnny, 101
Johnson, Lil, 35
Johnson, Lonnie
  Big Maybelle and, 102
  as blues crooner, 63
  blues revival and, 49
  career of, 132–133
  Jefferson, Blind Lemon, compared to, 27
  King, B. B., influenced by, 136
  recordings of, 213
  as stylist, 33
Johnson, Louise, 212
Johnson, Merline, 35
Johnson, Pete, 38, 65, 138, 155, 195
Johnson, Robert
  blues tourism and, 55
  career of, 133
  Clapton, Eric, influenced by, 114
  country blues and, 37–38
  Cream covers of, 171–172
  Deep South blues and, 71
  House, Son, and, 38, 126
  influence of, 44
  James, Elmore, and, 128, 212
  recordings of, 28, 184, 202–203
  songs of, 129
  as stylist, 36
  Williamson, Sonny Boy II, and, 163
Johnson, Steady Roll, 45
Johnson, Tommy, 71, 100, 183

Johnson, Willie, 179
Jones, Compton, 194
Jones, Curtis, 52
Jones, Floyd, 180, 181
Jones, Jo, 116
Jones, Quincy, 202
"Jordan for President," 134
Jordan, Louis, 36, 68, 76, 170
  career of, 133–134
Journal of American Folklore, 34
Jug bands, 25, 26, 66, 69, 74–75, 109,
  142, 143, 173, 187, 195. *See also*
  Cannon, Gus
"Juke," 139
Juke bands, 69, 75
Juke houses, 26
"Juke Joint Woman," 213
Jukeboxes, 33
Jump bands, 36, 40, 43, 63, 68, 100, 102,
  156, 172, 180, 184
Jump blues, 75–76, 80, 81. *See also* Blues
  shouters; Rhythm and blues; West
  Coast blues
Junior Parker, 100
"Just Worryin' Blues," 111

Kansas Joe, 142, 207
"K.C. Moan," 195
Keb Mo, 56, 61
"Keep It to Yourself," 164
"Keep On Chooglin'," 177
"Keep On Eatin'," 207
Kelly, Jo Ann, 65, 101
"Key to the Highway," 177
"Killing Floor," 127
Kimbrough, Junior, 56, 73, 100, 175–176
King, Albert, 54, 56, 120, 197, 208
  career of, 134–135
King, B. B.
  Bland, Bobby "Blue," and, 104
  career of, 135–137
  Clapton, Eric, and, 115, 203
  Cray, Robert, and, 214
  Guy, Buddy, influenced by, 119
  Hill, Z. Z., and, 122
  influence of, 44
  Johnson, Lonnie, influence on, 132

King, B. B. *(continued)*
  King, Albert, and, 134
  recordings of, 115, 166, 207–208, 208
  soul blues and, 48, 78
  as stylist, 41, 44
  white audiences and, 54, 56
King, Black Ivory, 46
King, Earl, 77
King, Freddie, 80, 100, 114
King of the Blues, 207–208
King of the Blues Guitar, 208
King, Willie, 100
Kirkland, Leroy, 180, 202
Knowling, Ransom, 197
"Kokomo Blues," 140
Korner, Alexis, 66, 101

Ladnier, Tommy, 115, 147, 189
Lane, Ernest, 210
Lang, Eddie, 132, 213
LaSalle, Denise, 100, 212–213
"Last Chance Blues," 110
"Last Minute Blues," 147
"Laundromat Blues," 135, 208
Lawhorn, Sammy, 200
Lawlars, Ernest, 143
"Layla," 114
Layton, Chris, 185
Lazy Lester, 48, 79
Leadbelly
  blues revival and, 52
  career of, 137–138
  as itinerant musician, 18
  the Lomaxes and, 34
  lyric themes of, 97
  recordings of, 214
  skiffle and, 52, 66
  Texas blues and, 80
"Leave My Woman Alone," 112
Ledbetter, Huddie. *See* Leadbelly
Lee, Julia, 63, 100, 209
Lenoir, J. B., 97, 100, 179, 184
Let's Dance, 156
"Let's Work Together," 109, 195
Lewis, Alfred, 178
Lewis, Furry, 49, 71, 100, 198
Lewis, Jerry Lee, 46, 143, 202

Lewis, Meade Lux, 38, 65, 155, 174
  career of, 138–139
Lewis, Noah, 187
Lewis, Smiley, 45, 77
"Life Is Suicide," 211
Liggins, Joe, 76
Lightnin' Slim, 48, 79, 149
"Lightnin's Boogie," 201
The Lionel Hampton Orchestra, 172
Lipscomb, Mance, 80, 100, 215
Little Milton, 78, 100
"Little Queen of Spades," 202
Little Richard
  blues and, ix
  blues-rock and, 62
  Hendrix, Jimi, and, 54, 120
  recordings of, 217
  rock and roll and, 46, 100
Little Son Joe, 143, 207
Little Walter, 44, 67, 117, 168, 176, 200
  British fans and, 53
  career of, 139–140
Live at the Regal, 136
Living Blues, 54
Living the Blues, 108
Lockwood, Robert, "Junior," 36, 163, 209
Lomax, Alan
  field trips by, 210
  House, Son, and, 126
  Leadbelly and, 34, 137
  McDowell, Fred, and, 140, 188
  Terry, Sonny, and, 154
  Waters, Muddy, and, 159
Lomax, John A., 34, 137, 141, 161
"Lonely Avenue," 112, 196
"Long Distance Call," 200
"Long Lonesome Blues," 131
"Lord I'm Discouraged," 145
Lornell, Kip, 35
Louis Jordan's Tympany Five, 68, 76,
  134, 170
"Louise," 140, 162
"Louisiana Blues," 200
"Love in Vain," 203
"Love Is So Good When You're Stealing
  It," 122
Love, Kid, 20

"Love Or Confusion," 121
Love, Willie, 173
Lovelle, Herbie, 202
Lovie Austin's Blues Serenaders, 115
The Lovin' Spoonful, 75
Lucas, Jane, 185
Lutcher, Nellie, 100
Lynchings, 11

"Ma Rainey," 147
MacLeod, Doug, 61
Magic Sam, 44, 46, 67, 100, 166–167, 201
   recordings of, 166–167
"Mama Let Me Lay It on You," 118
"Mama Mama Blues," 134
"Mama Tain't Long Fo' Day," 141
"Man, You Won't Give Me No Money," 207
Mandel, Harvey, 144
"Manic Depression," 121
"Mardi Gras in New Orleans," 145
Mardi Gras rhythms, 77
Marl Young's Orchestra, 157
Martin, Sara, 25, 81, 198
Martin Scorsese Presents the Blues: A Musical Journey, 208
"Matchbox Blues," 162
The Maxwell Davis Orchestra, 211
May, Butler "String Beans," 20
Mayall, John, 53, 66, 101, 114, 203
"Maybelline," 199
Mayfield, Percy, 63, 100, 112, 210–211, 213
McClennan, Tommy, 36
McCormick, Mack, 125
McCoy, Charlie, 33, 35
McCoy, Joe, 33, 35, 142
McCoy, Robert Lee, 33, 197
McCracklin, Jimmy, 100
McDaniels, Hattie, 32
McDonald, Earl, 75, 188
McDowell, Fred, 34, 71, 73, 177
   career of, 140–141
McGhee, Brownie
   Big Maybelle and, 202
   East Coast blues and, 72

   Fuller, Blind Boy, and, 119, 154
   Terry, Sonny, and, 38, 43, 154–155
McMurry, Lillian, 164
McNeely, Big Jay, 76, 100
McShann, Jay, 76
McTell, Blind Willie, 30–31, 34, 204
   career of, 141–142
"Me and My Chauffeur Blues," 143
"Me and My Gin," 151
"Me and the Devil Blues," 133
"Mean Mistreater Mama," 111
"Mean Old Bedbug Blues," 213
"Mean Old Frisco Blues," 116
"Mean Old World," 139, 157
Mean Old World: The Blues from 1940 to 1994, 209
Melrose, Lester, 33, 116
"The Memphis Blues," 20
Memphis Five, 35–36
The Memphis Horns, 135, 208, 214
The Memphis Jug Band, 75, 100, 195
Memphis Minnie, 33, 45, 147, 207
   career of, 142–143
Memphis Slim, 33, 36, 45, 52, 61, 100, 106, 118, 174, 209
Mendelsohn, Denny, 202
The Mercury Blues 'n' Rhythm Story, 1945-1955, 209
"Merry Christmas, Baby," 107
"Merry Christmas, Pretty Baby," 178
Microphone, invention of, 26
"Midnight Special," 214
"Mighty Long Time," 164
Migration, 12, 39, 40, 64, 66, 77, 115
Milburn, Amos, 100
Miller, Bob, 21
Miller, Jay, 48
Milton, Roy, 76, 100
Minstrelsy, vaudeville blues and, 24
"Mississippi County Farm Blues," 28
"Mississippi River Blues," 106
Mississippi Sarah, 217
The Mississippi Sheiks, 74, 100, 183
"Mississippi Swamp Moan," 178
"Mistake in Life," 152
"Mister Charlie," 125
Mitchell, George, 35

Mitchell, Mitch, 121, 175
Mitchell's Christian Singers, 38
"Moanin' at Midnight," 127, 178–179
"Moanin' Groanin' Blues," 115
Modern blues, 54–57. *See also*
    Contemporary blues
The Modern Downhome Blues Sessions:
    Arkansas & Mississippi 1951-1952,
    Volume 1, 210
"Mohair Sam," 206
"The Mojo," 179
"Mona," 199
Monroe, Bill, 9, 168
Montgomery, Little Brother, x–xi, 45, 61,
    71, 119, 133, 203
"Moonshine Blues," 147, 210
Moore, Gatemouth, 63
Moore, Johnny, 107, 167, 205
Moore, Scotty, 186
Morton, Jelly Roll, 24
Moss, Buddy, 31, 36, 51, 72
Mother of the Blues: 1923-1928, 210
Mr. Memphis Minnie, 45
Musselwhite, Charlie
    career of, 143–144
"My Babe," 118, 139
"My Baby Left Me," 211
"My Black Mama," 126
"My Butcher Man," 207
"My Country Man," 103, 179–180
"My Home Is in the Delta," 200
"My Kitchen Mechanic," 96
"My Mama Don't Allow Me," 116
Myers, Dave, 168
Myers, Hubert, 184
Myers, Louis, 168

"The Natchez Burnin' ," 200
"The Negro Blues," 21
"Never Been Touched Like This," 213
New Age music, 60, 145
The New Masses, 36
New Orleans Blues, 76–77, 80
"New York City," 214
Newborn, Calvin, 136
Newman, Floyd, 187
Nicknames, Blues, 45

Nighthawk, Robert, 163
"Niki Hoeky," 149
"96 Tears," 103
Nixon, Hammie, 187
"No Place to Go," 127
"No Shoes," 124
"Nobody's Dirty Business," 128

O'Bryant, Jimmy, 115
Odum, Howard, 34
"Oh Papa Blues," 210
"Oh, Pretty Woman," 135, 208
"Oh! Red," 101
Oliver, King, 24
"On the Road Again," 108, 180–181, 194
"One Monkey Don't Stop No Show,"
    149, 202
Orendorff, George, 184
Ory, Kid, 147, 210
Oster, Harry, 34–35, 162, 206
Otis, Johnny, 76, 100, 129, 209

Pace, Harry, 23
Page, Hot Lips, 102
"The Panama Limited," 161
Papa Lord God, 46
"Papa's on the Housetop," 110
Parker, Little Junior, 104
Parton, Dolly, 168
Patton, Charley
    career of, 144–145
    Deep South blues and, 71
    Hendrix, Jimi, influenced by, 121
    House, Son, and, 126
    Howlin' Wolf influenced by,
        126–127
    as itinerant musician, 18
    Johnson, Robert, influenced by, 133
    McDowell, Fred, and, 140
    recordings of, 211–212
Paul Butterfield Blues Band, 50, 53,
    62
Peabody, Charles, 34
Pentecostal sects, 12
Perkins, Carl, 46, 62
Perkins, Pinetop, 200
Pettiford, Oscar, 112

Petway, Robert, 216–217
Phillips, Dewey "Daddy-O," 143
Phillips, Sam, 104, 127, 179
"Phonograph Blues," 133, 202
Piano Red, 45, 61, 72
"Piccolo Rag," 118–119
"Pick a Bale of Cotton," 214
Piedmont blues, 71
"Pine Top's Boogie Woogie," 65, 208
"Playing with the Strings," 132, 213
"Please Come Home for Christmas," 107
"Please Set a Date," 143
Poet of the Blues, 210–211
"Poor Boy," 127
"Poor Boy Long Ways from Home,"
    109
"Poor Man's Blues," 181
Pork Chops, 45
Postwar blues, 77
"Praying on the Old Camp Ground," 128
"Preachin' the Blues," 126
"Preaching Blues," 133, 202
Presley, Elvis
    blues and, 100–101
    blues-rock v., 62
    Crudup, Arthur "Big Boy," influence
        on, 116, 211
    Musselwhite, Charlie, influenced by,
        143
    Phillips, Sam, and, 179
    recordings of, 186
    rock and roll and, 9, 46
Prewar blues, 77
Price, Sam, 116, 155
"Pride and Joy," 156
"Prison-Bound Blues," 110, 181–182
Producers, 33
Professor Longhair, 77, 167
    career of, 145–146
    recordings by, 186–187, 209
Psychedelic blues/rock, 54, 180. See also
    Clapton, Eric; Hendrix, Jimi
Pullum, Joe, 113
Punk rock, 7, 56

Queen Elizabeth, 158
? and the Mysterians, 103

Race music/records, xv, 23, 24, 32, 43,
    49, 225
    decline of, 31
Rachel, Yank, 36, 68, 197
Racism, 11, 52, 95, 97
Radio, 26, 42–43, 46, 122–123
the Raelettes, 112, 188
"Rag, Mama, Rag," 118
Ragtime, 5, 12, 17–18
Railroad Bill, 16
"Rain Down Rain," 202
Rainey, Ma
    blues, adoption of, 19
    career of, 146–147
    as itinerant musician, 18
    jug bands and, 25
    nickname of, 45
    recording repertoire, 20
    recordings of, 182, 210
    Tampa Red and, 152
    vaudeville blues and, 25, 81
Rainey, William "Pa," 146
"Raining in My Heart," 149, 206
Raitt, Bonnie, 61, 101, 107, 141
"Ramblin' on My Mind," 114, 133
Ramey, Ben, 195
Rankins, Leroy, 173
Rap music, 7–8
Reconstruction, 11
"Reconversion Blues," 134
Record collecting, 28–29
Record companies, the Great Depression
    and, 31–32
"Red House," 122
"The Red Rooster," 200
Redding, Noel, 121, 175
Redman, Don, 150
Reed, Jimmy
    British blues and, 66
    British fans and, 53
    career of, 147–148
    Chicago/South Side blues and, 67, 79
    Harpo, Slim, and, 150, 206
    Johnson, Robert, influence on, 36, 44,
        184
    Lenoir, J. B., and, 179
    recordings of, 198

Reinhardt, Django, 136
Religion, 12
Rent parties, 18
Rhythm and blues, 7, 23, 43, 76–77, 78,
    101, 104, 113, 135, 167, 187
"Rich Woman," 108
Riding with the King, 115
Riffs, 4, 13, 61, 64, 65, 70, 88–89, 105,
    108, 121, 122, 123, 125–126, 148, 225
"Right Next Door (Because of Me)", 214
Riley, Judge, 197
"The Road Song," 108
Robinson, Bobbie, 183
Robinson, Eli, 202
Rock and roll. *See also* Berry, Chuck;
    Charles, Ray; Clapton, Eric; Diddley,
    Bo; Hendrix, Jimi; Jordan, Louis;
    Presley, Elvis; Turner, Big Joe
    Berry, Chuck, and, 182
    blues revival and, 49, 50
    blues v., 47
    as blues/blues-based, 7, 46, 57, 100
    boogie-woogie and, 65
    British, 52–53
    British blues and, 66
    CD anthology of, 216–217
    Crudup, Arthur "Big Boy," and, 116,
        117
    heavy metal, 62
    New Orleans blues and, 77
    Presley, Elvis and, 186
    psychedelic, 54, 62
    rhythm and blues and, 78
"Rock Island Line," 214
Rock Me Mama, 211
"Rock Me, Mama," 117, 211
Rock music/groups, ix
"A Rockin' Good Way," 159
Rodgers, Jimmie, 9, 61–62, 168
Rogers, Jimmy, 67, 100, 160, 200
Roland, Walter, 61, 71
"Roll 'Em Pete," 155
"Roll Over Beethoven," 182
"Roll with Me, Henry," 129
"Rollin' and Tumblin' ," 160, 194
The Rolling Stones, ix, 53, 66, 75, 149
The Rooftop Singers, 110

Roosevelt, Franklin D., 32
"The Rooster Song," 216
"Rootin' Ground Hog," 96
Ross, Doctor, 100
"Run Joe," 134
"Running Wild Blues," 145
Rural blues, 69
Rush, Bobby, 56, 74
    career of, 148–149
    recordings of, 183–184, 212
Rush Hour, 149
Rush, Otis
    Chicago/West Side blues and, 67, 100
    Clapton, Eric, and, 114, 203
    Guy, Buddy, and, 119
    King, B. B., influence on, 44
    recordings of, 198, 201
Rushing, Jimmy, 38, 63

"Sad Hours," 139
"Saddle My Pony," 127
Saffire, 61
Sallie Martin Gospel Singers, 158
"Salty Papa Blues," 158
"Same All Over," 195
"Santa Fe Blues," 203
"Saturday Night Fish Fry," 134
"Say Man," 199
Scales, George, 176
"School Days," 134
Scott, Joe, 176, 194
"Screaming and Crying," 160
Seals, Baby, 20, 21
"See See Rider," 111
"See See Rider Blues," 182
"See That My Grave's Kept Clean,"
    131–132
Segregation, 6, 11
"Selling My Pork Chops," 142
"Send Me to the 'Lectric Chair," 150
"Seventh Son," 118
"Shade Tree Mechanic," 123
Shade, Will, 49, 143
"Shake 'Em On Down," 140, 161
"Shake, Rattle and Roll," 155, 195
"Shake Your Hips," 150, 206
Shakey Jake, 201

Shannon, Tommy, 185

Sharecropping, 12

"She Want to Sell My Monkey," 153

Sheet music, 21

"She's a Cool Operator," 153

Shines, Johnny, 44, 100

"Short-Haired Woman," 125

Sidney Bechet's New Orleans
    Feetwarmers, 38

"The Signifying Monkey," 117

Sims, Son, 159

"Sit and Cry (The Blues)", 119

"6/88 Glide," 213

"61 Highway," 140

Skiffle, 52, 53, 66, 75, 107, 226

"Skoodle Do Do," 106

The Sky Is Crying, 212

"The Sky Is Crying," 129, 182–183

Slack, Freddie, 155

Smith, Bessie
    career of, 150–151
    "From Spirituals to Swing" and,
        37–38
    Hammond, John, and, 50
    recordings of, 181, 205
    Smith, Bessie Mae, and, 45
    vaudeville blues and, 81
    Washington, Dinah, and, 159

Smith, Bessie Mae, 45

Smith, Clara, 25, 81, 100, 150

Smith, Clarence "Pine Top," 29, 65

Smith, Mamie, 22, 24, 81, 100, 208

Smith, Pine Top, 138, 208

Smith, Ruby, 45

Smith, Tab, 158

Smith, Thunder, 125, 201

Smith, Trixie, 23, 81

Smith, Willie, 200

"Smokestack Lightnin' ," 200

Smokin' in Bed, 212–213

Snow, Hank, 112

"So Glad You're Mine," 117

"Soft and Mellow," 152

"Someone Else Is Steppin' In," 123

"Something's Wrong with My Little
    Machine," 96

Songsters, 17–18

"Sonny Boy's Christmas Blues," 164

Soul blues, 48, 54, 56, 78, 80, 100, 122,
    126, 130

Soul music
    blues and, 48–49
    blues v., 47
    blues-rock and, 62
    Charles, Ray, and, 31, 112, 188
    gospel music and, 44
    Hendrix, Jimi, and, 54
    pioneers of, 104
    rhythm and blues and, 7, 78

Soul to Soul, 156

South Side blues, 67. *See also* Diddley,
    Bo; Howlin' Wolf; James, Elmore;
    Little Walter; Reed, Jimmy; Rogers,
    Jimmy; Waters, Muddy; Wells,
    Junior

Spann, Otis, 36, 61, 100, 140, 176, 200

Spasm bands, 75

Speckled Red, 61

Spivey, Victoria
    blues revival and, 32
    Johnson, Lonnie, and, 213
    recordings of, 174–175
    vaudeville blues and, 25, 81, 100

"Spoonful," 114

"St. Louis Blues," 20, 205, 217

St. Louis Blues, 150

St. Louis Jimmy, 209

Stafford, Mary, 22

Stagolee, 16

*Stand Back! Here Comes Charley
    Musselwhite's Southside Band*, 144

"Standing Around Crying," 160

"Standing at the Crossroads," 129

Staples, Roebuck, 145

Starr, Ringo, 53

"Statesboro Blues," 141

"Stealin' Stealin' ," 195

Steele, Willie, 179

Steinberg, Lewie, 187

Steppin' On the Blues, 213

Stevenson, Adlai E., 134

Stewart, Teddy, 158

"Still a Fool," 200

"Stone Crazy," 119

"Stones in My Passway," 133, 203

"Stop and Listen Blues," 183

"Stormy Monday Blues," 104

String bands, 69, 75, 183

Strong Persuader, 213–214

"Sue," 183–184

"Sugar Mama Blues," 162, 197

"Sugarbelle Blue," 198

"Suicide Blues," 111

Sullivan, Joe, 155

"Sunnyland," 129

Sunnyland Slim, 179, 201, 209

"Sunshine of Your Love," 114

Super Blues, 140

Surf music, 7, 47, 105

Swamp blues, 48, 79

"Sweet Home Chicago," 184

"Sweet Little Angel," 153

The Sweethearts of Rhythm, 102

Swing, 42, 63, 133, 169, 226

Sykes, Roosevelt, 33, 36, 61, 71, 174

   career of, 151–152

Taj Mahal, ix, 50, 61, 101, 142

   bio of, xii

"Take Me for a Buggy Ride," 151

Take This Hammer, 214

"Tales of Brave Ulysses," 114

Talking blues, 79

Tampa Red

   career of, 152–153

   city blues and, 68

   combos of, 35–36

   Georgia Tom and, 30, 74

   hokum blues and, 30, 74

   James, Elmore, influenced by, 128

   nickname of, 45

   recordings of, 198

   as stylist, 33

Tampa Red and the Chicago Five, 76

The Taskiana Four, 217

Taylor, Art, 112

Taylor, Eddie, 147, 148, 198

Taylor, Johnnie, 78

Taylor, Koko, 117, 204

   career of, 153–154

Taylor, Larry, 108, 180

Taylor, Sam, 202

"T-Bone Shuffle," 157, 184–185

Teagarden, Jack, 151

"Tell Mama," 130

Temple, Johnnie, 33, 133

"Te-Ni-Nee-Ni-Nu," 150

Tent shows, 81, 115, 146

"Terraplane Blues," 203

Terry, Sonny, 30, 38, 43, 72, 118

   career of, 154–155

Texas Blues, 79–80

Texas Flood, 156, 214–215

"Texas Flood," 185–186

Texas Songster, 215

Tharpe, Sister Rosetta, 38

"That Thing Called Love," 22

"That's All Right," 186, 211

Theater Owners' Booking Association

   (T.O.B.A.), 25

"Them's Graveyard Words," 151

They Call Me the Fat Man, 215–216

"They're Red Hot," 202

"Thirteen Question Method," 199

"This Is the End," 119

"This Little Girl of Mine," 112

Thomas, George W., 21

Thomas, Henry "Ragtime Texas," 18,

   80, 108, 170

Thomas, Rufus, 62, 63, 100, 187

Thomas, Tabby, 56

Thompson, Lucky, 158

Thornton, Big Mama, 43, 64

Thorogood, George, 62

"A Thousand Miles From Nowhere," 206

"3 O'Clock Blues," 136, 166

"Three Hundred Pounds of Joy," 200

"The Thrill Is Gone," 136, 208

"Thumbin' a Ride," 162

"Time Was," 195

"Tip On In," 150

"Tipitina," 145, 186–187

Titon, Jeff, 35, 69

"Tomorrow Night," 132

Too Tight Henry, 45

"Toothache Blues," 213

Toscano, Eli, 200

Toussaint, Allen, 145

Townsend, Henry, 197
Travis, Merle, 186
Triple Threat, 156
"Trouble Blues," 107, 205
"Trucking My Blues Away," 118
Tucker, Bessie, 217
"Tupelo," 124
Turner, Big Joe, 38, 40, 63, 195
    career of, 155–156
Turner, Ike, 100, 201, 210
Turner, Othar, 194
"29 Ways," 153
"The Twist," 54

The Ultimate Collection: 1948-1990, 216
Uncle Tom, 48
Unplugged, 114–115
Urban blues, 68, 80, 100
Urbanization, blues and, 39, 40

The Vandellas, 124
Vaudeville blues, 19–20, 24–26, 31, 61,
    62, 74, 80, 100, 142, 189. See also Cox,
    Ida; Rainey, Ma; Smith, Bessie;
    Spivey, Victoria
Vaughan, Jimmie, 156
Vaughan, Stevie Ray
    blues-rock and, 56, 62
    career of, 156–157
    King, Albert, influence on, 135
    recordings of, 185–186, 214–215
    Texas blues and, 80
Vestine, Henry, 28, 108
"Vicksburg Blues," 203
Vincent, Gene, 47
Vinson, Eddie "Cleanhead," 76, 100, 209
Vinson, Walter, 183
"Viola Lee Blues," 110, 187
"Violent Love," 118
"Voodoo Chile," 122

"Waiting for the Cards to Fall," 198
"Walk Right In," 110
Walker, Aaron "T-Bone"
    Berry, Chuck, influenced by, 101
    as blues shouter/crooner, 64
    career of, 157–158

    guitar style of, 41
    Jefferson, Blind Lemon, and, 41
    King, B. B., influenced by, 136
    recordings by, 184–185
    Texas blues and, 80
Walker, Ruby, 45
"Walkin' the Dog," 187
"Walking Blues," 202
"Walking Through the Park," 160
Wallace, Sippie, 32, 81, 209
"The Wallflower," 129
Wand, Hart, 21
"Wang Dang Doodle," 118, 127, 153,
    200
"Wants Cake When I'm Hungry,"
    142–143
Washboard bands, 75
Washboard Sam, 33, 45, 100, 106, 161,
    197, 217
Washington, Dinah, 43, 64, 78, 153
    career of, 158–159
    recordings of, 172–173, 209
"Wasted Dream," 211
Waters, Ethel, 23, 32, 81, 100
Waters, Muddy
    Berry, Chuck, and, 101
    blues revival and, 52
    British blues and, 66
    British fans/musicians and, 52, 53
    career of, 159–160
    Chicago/South Side blues and, 67, 143
    combos of, 42
    Dixon, Willie, and, 117, 153
    Guy, Buddy, and, 119
    Hendrix, Jimi, and, 120, 197
    influence of, 56
    Johnson, Robert, influence on, 36, 44
    Little Walter and, 139, 140
    the Lomaxes and, 34
    Musselwhite, Charlie, and, 144
    nickname of, 45
    record collectors and, 28
    recordings of, 176, 200
    Taylor, Koko, and, 204
Weaver, Curley, 56, 204
Webb, Chick, 134
Websites/films, 240–245

"Wee Wee Hours," 101

Weldon, Casey Bill, 134

Wells, Junior, 67, 119, 120

West Coast blues, 80, 81

West Side blues, 67. *See also* Guy, Buddy;
Magic Sam; Rush, Otis

Western swing, 6

"What Is That Tastes Like Gravy," 152

"What'd I Say," 112, 188, 196

Wheatstraw, Peetie, 33, 46, 61, 100, 133,
198

Wheels of Fire, 114

"When Do I Get to Be Called a Man,"
106

"When the Saints Go Marching In,"
216

"When the Sun Goes Down," 111

*When the Sun Goes Down: The Secret
History of Rock & Roll*, 216–217

"When You Get Home, Write Me a Few
Little Lines," 188

White blues, 81. *See also* Blues-rock;
British blues

White, Bukka, 49, 51, 73, 92, 136
career of, 160–161

White, Georgia, 33

White, Josh, 36, 51, 52, 72, 97, 100, 213

"Who Do You Love," 105

"Who Will the Next Fool Be," 104

"Whole Lotta Shakin' Goin' On," 202

"Whoopin' the Blues," 154

"Why I Sing the Blues," 136

"Wild Women Don't Have the Blues,"
189

Wilkins, Robert, 51

Williams, Big Joe, 36, 100, 143, 144, 163,
197, 198

Williams, Clarence, 20, 21, 23, 150

Williams, Cootie, 158

Williams, Eddie, 205

Williams, Hank, 159

Williams, Joe, 181

Williams, Robert Pete, 35, 71, 79, 92
career of, 161–162
recordings of, 206–207

Williams, Sonny Boy, 45

Williamson, John Lee "Sonny Boy"
British musicians and, 53
career of, 162–163
Deep South blues and, 71
Lewis, Noah, and, 187
Little Walter influenced by, 44, 139
namesakes of, 45
Rachel, Yank, and, 68
recordings of, 196–197
as stylist, 33, 36–37

Williamson, Sonny Boy II, 114, 127, 163,
173, 212

Willis, Chuck, 100

Willis, Ruth, 204

Wilson, Alan, 28, 108, 109, 180, 181

Wilson, Gerald, 158

Winter, Johnny, 53, 62, 80, 101

Winwood, Steve, 114

Witherspoon, Jimmy, 64, 100, 209

"Woke Up This Morning," 136

"W-O-M-A-N," 130

"Woman Woman Blues," 189

Word War II, blues and, 39

Wright, Bill, 63

"Write Me a Few Lines," 140

Yancey, Jimmy, 65, 100, 138

"Yancey Special," 138

The Yardbirds, 53, 66, 113–114, 203

"Yellow Dog Blues," 205

"You Can't Judge a Book By Its Cover,"
105

"You Don't Have to Go," 147

"You Don't Love Me," 199

"You Got Me Dizzy," 148

"You Shook Me," 200

"You Upset Me Baby," 136

Young, Dave, 158

Young, Marl, 157

"You're My Best Poker Hand," 157

Zydeco, 48, 81–82, 167, 226. *See also*
Chenier, Clifton

ZZ Top, 62, 101